ADVANCE PRAISE FOR

PAR EntreMundos

"*PAR EntreMundos: A Pedagogy of the Américas* powerfully engages the theory and practice of participatory action research in ways that revolutionize its potential for critically understanding the particularities and universalisms of the cultural traditions of the Américas. In so doing, the editors of this book bring together a striking collection of educational essays that illustrate the pedagogical and political force of a communal methodology for radically comprehending the beautifully diverse and complex hemisphere that informs our labor as educators and cultural citizens of the world."

—Antonia Darder, Leavey Presidential Endowed Chair in Ethics and Moral Leadership at Loyola Marymount University and Distinguished Visiting Professor of Education at the University of Johannesburg

"*PAR EntreMundos: A Pedagogy of the Américas* draws upon Freirean praxis, critical race and borderland theories, South American liberation psychologies, and social movement histories to propose pedagogical practices that disrupt and dismantle traditional academic binaries between the researcher/researched, expert/novice, and institution/community. Latin communities in the U.S. are looking for ways to use education to empower a new generation of student leaders. This volume provides several powerful examples of how this is being done right now in schools and communities throughout the U.S. For those who want to use education as a means to challenge discrimination and marginalization, this book will serve as an invaluable resource."

—Pedro Noguera, Distinguished Professor of Education at the Graduate School of Education and Information Studies at UCLA

PAR EntreMundos

Critical Studies of LATINOS/AS in the Americas

Yolanda Medina and Margarita Machado-Casas
General Editors

Vol. 15

The Critical Studies of Latinos/as in the Americas series
is part of the Peter Lang Trade Academic and Textbook list.
Every volume is peer reviewed and meets
the highest quality standards for content and production.

PETER LANG
New York • Bern • Berlin
Brussels • Vienna • Oxford • Warsaw

PAR EntreMundos

A Pedagogy of the Américas

Jennifer Ayala, Julio Cammarota,
Margarita I. Berta-Ávila, Melissa Rivera,
Louie F. Rodríguez, AND María Elena Torre,
EDITORS

PETER LANG
New York • Bern • Berlin
Brussels • Vienna • Oxford • Warsaw

Library of Congress Cataloging-in-Publication Data
Names: Ayala, Jennifer, editor.
Title: PAR EntreMundos: a pedagogy of the Américas / Jennifer Ayala, Julio Cammarota,
Margarita I. Berta-Ávila, Melissa Rivera, Louie F. Rodríguez, María Elena Torre.
Description: New York: Peter Lang, 2018.
Series: Critical studies of Latino/as in the Americas; vol. 15
ISSN 2372-6822 (print) | ISSN 2372-6830 (online)
Includes bibliographical references and index.
Identifiers: LCCN 2017018078 | ISBN 978-1-4331-4485-1 (paperback: alk. paper)
ISBN 978-1-4331-4475-2 (hardback: alk. paper) | ISBN 978-1-4331-4486-8 (ebook pdf)
ISBN 978-1-4331-4487-5 (epub) | ISBN 978-1-4331-4488-2 (mobi)
Subjects: LCSH: Hispanic Americans—Education—Social aspects.
Critical pedagogy. | Action research in education.
Classification: LCC LC2669 .A93 2018 | DDC 371.829/68—dc23
LC record available at https://lccn.loc.gov/2017038338
DOI 10.3726/b11303

Bibliographic information published by **Die Deutsche Nationalbibliothek.**
Die Deutsche Nationalbibliothek lists this publication in the "Deutsche
Nationalbibliografie"; detailed bibliographic data are available
on the Internet at http://dnb.d-nb.de/.

Front cover image: *Queen of the River* by Tanya Torres, Watercolor on Paper.
Approximately 5" x 7", 2008. www.tanyatorres.com

© 2018 Peter Lang Publishing, Inc., New York
29 Broadway, 18th floor, New York, NY 10006
www.peterlang.com

Dedication

In remembrance of our ancestors
With the joy, sorrow, and strength of nuestras familias
With the wholeness of our bodies minds and spirits
embracing the beauty, dolor, and messiness
in-between mundos
In recognition of the blood, sweat, and tears
of our community's struggle and sacrifices,
We dedicate this to the peoples of resistance
De ayer, hoy y mañana

TABLE OF CONTENTS

TABLES

FIGURES

ACKNOWLEDGEMENTS

With deep gratitude to our communities of scholars, educators, activists and artists (listed in alphabetical order):

All of those who participated in and shaped the work represented in this collective volume, the youth, educators, and community organizations *for your commitment and efforts. We especially want to acknowledge the young people who participated in the PAR projects represented in this book.*

Gloria Anzaldúa, *for embodying these principles and pioneering the path*

Jose Cintron, *for convening us and initiating this collective*

Michelle Fine, *for creating openings for critical possibilities*

Patricia Lopez, *for providing critical insights along the way*

Margarita Machado-Casas, Sarah Bode, and everyone at Peter Lang, *for believing in our work and guiding the publication process*

NLERAP board, advisory council members, madrinas y padrinos and Grow Your Own tribe, *for being the catalyst for our collective and providing us with invaluable wisdom*

Sonia Nieto, *for affirming our culture, language and lineages in education and writing a beautiful foreword*

Pedro Pedraza, *for imagining a space where PAR could root and grow*

The Public Science Project, *for developing an institute dedicated to critical participatory action research*

Tanya Torres, *for offering us your exquisite artistry for our cover*

Angela Valenzuela, *for continuing the work of NLERAP*

And the Spirits that bless and guide our existence
the earth we inhabit, the infinite cosmos
and the Mystery that holds us

FOREWORD

Sonia Nieto

Participatory Action Research (PAR) is not new, although its iteration as a methodology in social science research is relatively recent. Nevertheless, it's probably safe to say that groups and communities throughout the world have practiced PAR for hundreds of years, though it's likely they didn't call it PAR. An excellent example is the literacy work Paulo Freire did with Brazilian peasants in the 1960s. But wherever and whenever people come together, especially across generations and other differences, to identify, investigate, and come up with solutions to questions and concerns about their lives, we can say that they are engaged in participatory action research. It is in this sense that *PAR EntreMundos* is such a significant accomplishment. In this book, teachers, youths, community members, and university researchers demonstrate how Latinx communities seek to solve their own problems and create their own futures.

The newest addition to the scholarly and community-based research by, for, and about Latinx, the authors of *PAR EntreMundos* are continuing the important legacy initiated in 2000. It was then that Pedraza Pedraza, a researcher at the Centro de Estudios Puertorriqueños at Hunter College in New York invited a group of scholars, community activists, and others to come together in forums throughout the United States to dialogue about education in our communities. The result was the National Latinx Education, Research, and Policy Project (NLERAP). I was privileged to take part in this initiative from the beginning. Committed to a different vision of research, community outreach, and solidarity with Latinx communities around the country, NLER-AP was instrumental in bringing the voices and perspectives of Latinx to the attention of a broader range of people in subsequent years through a number of publications and national conferences. A critical approach to working with communities through solidarity and humility, NLERAP is significant because of its innovative use of research methodologies, something that is evident in the inspiring book you are about to read. Using Freirean and critical race theory as well as borderland, decolonizing, and other methodologies, the authors present actual examples of trailblazing research in the service of community empowerment.

PAR EntreMundos is also significant in how the authors and participants challenge what counts as research and who counts as researchers. Here, research begins as a bottom-up instead of as a top-down process, relying on those who know and can speak to the issues in their lives with most authenticity and passion. Rather than rely solely on university researchers as experts, as is generally the case, *PAR EntreMundos* also includes classroom teachers, students, and community members, among others, as experts in their own right, as intellectuals and as scholars-in-process, who deserve to have their voices heard. Consequently, probably the most powerful component of the work presented here are the models of PAR in practice. Several significant examples are included in this volume, from the well-known and much-maligned Tucson Mexican American Studies (MAS) program, to less well-known, though equally compelling projects. Using surveys, interviews, case studies, ethnographies, digital media, and many other research approaches, what the chapters have in common is a disruption of the view of research as belonging only in the ivory tower and reserved for just the tiny percentage of researchers in the Ivy League. In this book, the definition of researcher is expanded beyond anything that has come before; here, teenagers, community leaders, university-based scholars, and others are also researchers. Moreover, the examples of Grow-Your-Own (GYO) initiatives included in the volume provide a model for other universities interested in using the rich resources of our Latinx communities in their teacher preparation programs.

Another important contribution made by the talented group of authors of *PAR EntreMundos* is its depiction of those involved in the PAR projects described in these chapters. Youths are often presented in the media—and fixed in the popular consciousness—as apathetic, uncaring, and undeserving members of society. The examples in this book reveal a different, and far more realistic, portrait of young people as caring, engaged, and significant actors in their lives, their communities, and our nation. In addition, Latinx university scholars, especially those in education departments, often are frequently less valued than their majority-group counterparts. In this book, in contrast, they are depicted as scholars with a deep and abiding concern for the partners with whom they work, and as academics who are making important intellectual and practical contributions to the education of Latinx youths. Big projects or small, year-long or short-term, the examples featured in this book portray all researchers regardless of age or level of education with dignity and respect.

There is no denying that U.S. schools are changing dramatically, and we can see examples of this change every day in big cities, small towns, and rural areas. I recently attended the convocation of the public schools in the small town where I live. I was astonished to see that there are now four Puerto Rican women administrators in the schools (including my daughter), something I would never have imagined when we moved here from New York City 41 years ago. At the time, not even one Puerto Rican teacher could be found in the entire system. I was happy to see this change. But I am also reminded of the fact that numbers alone do not necessarily lead to substantive change. The long experience of Black South Africans under Apartheid, in spite of the fact that they far outnumbered White South Africans, is a sobering example. So, while our numbers are increasing in school-age populations, educators, and researchers, this alone will not guarantee that the educational experiences of our young people will become more socially just or fulfilling. It will take many more educators, youths, and community leaders committed to changing the situation, including engaging in PAR practices, before we will achieve our goal of a truly equitable education for Latinx. In the meantime, *PAR EntreMundos* is a persuasive example of what can happen when dedicated people come together to change their local realities.

Sonia Nieto,
Professor Emerita, Language, Literacy, and Culture
College of Education
University of Massachusetts, Amherst

INTRODUCTION

For a high school student, walking through the school hallways between class-es can be an uneventful experience, just a transition from one class to anoth-er. One day Zach Rubio, a 16-year-old Mexican American student thought his transition through the hallway was as innocuous as the many other times he has traversed his school, but a teacher overhearing a conversation he was having with a classmate thought differently. She heard Zach and his class-mate speak Spanish, which she believed was inappropriate and "abnormal". The teacher reported Zach to the principal who summarily suspended him for 1½ days. After learning that his son was suspended for speaking Spanish, Zach's father went to the principal to find out what policy had been violated. The school district did not have a policy preventing students from speaking non-English languages. In fact, the district superintendent rescinded the sus-pension after learning about the incident, stating that "the district does not prevent students from speaking foreign languages at school". Although his statement indicated that speaking Spanish is not grounds for suspension, it was very telling as to how Latinxs are perceived in the education system—as a foreign, uninvited presence.[1]

Zach's suspension happened in a high school located in Kansas City, one of the new areas with emerging Latinx communities. Punishment for speaking

non-English languages is a significant part of educational history throughout much of the U.S. Southwest, West Coast, and East Coast. The fact that
Zach's suspension occurred in America's heartland portends a new chapter
in the history of Latinx education. The border between the U.S. and Latin
America is no longer represented by a North/South divide; Latinxs have long
traversed this geopolitical and cultural division and now bring new life and
energy into the heart of the U.S. landscape. The Latinization of U.S. schools
is made apparent with Latinx students like Zach who move with their culture,
language, and identities into hallways and classrooms (Irizarry, 2011).

What may not be as obvious is how Latinization has influenced pedagogies throughout Las Américas, both North and South. The traditional perspective of how ideas and history move geographically assumes a North to
South orientation. In other words, the erroneous assumption is that modern development not only has occurred along a linear timeline, but also has
moved predominately from the North and into the South. Although certain
forms of militarism, imperialism, and corporatism have migrated from North
to South, the movement of history, culture, people, and ideas has flowed back
and forth in both directions. We would like to argue that the development
of critical, decolonizing pedagogies, especially those related to participatory
action research, has a clear South to North orientation. The flow of ideas
about critical, decolonizing pedagogies starts from the southern hemisphere
and has moved to spread throughout Las Américas. These pedagogies successfully facilitate learning, engagement, and social activism in Latinx and other
communities but within a limited scope. Small schools, such as El Puente
in Brooklyn, N.Y. (see Rivera et al., this volume), or small programs, such
as the Social Justice Education Project in Tucson, Arizona (see Cammarota,
this volume), utilize critical, decolonizing pedagogies inspired by thinkers and
movements located in the southern hemisphere. With the vast increase of
Latinx students and students of color in the U.S. education system, we must
expand the use of community action-based pedagogies informed by the work
and ideas of educators connected to the South. In view of this, we describe
and further develop a framework of Participatory Action Research (PAR)
that is EntreMundos/Among Worlds as one such pedagogy (Torre & Ayala, 2009). We view PAR EntreMundos as a research approach, epistemology
and creation-space that emerges from the inquiry, relationship, and organizing work of multi-generational collectives that are intimately tied to the
social justice issues in question, and who attend to power dynamics within
and outside the group. What makes this a PAR that is EntreMundos is its

assumptions/enactments of multiplicity and bridging, residing among the in-between spaces of self and other, and the psychological, social, cultural, sexual and structural boundaries we move between daily. In this book, we attempt to demonstrate how a PAR EntreMundos has successfully elevated the critical consciousness and intellectualism of teachers, collective members, Latinx students, and other students of color, while encouraging the expansion of these pedagogies to meet the growing diversity of many U.S. schools. Before delving further into discussion of PAR-EntreMundos, we unpack what and who we mean by Latinxs in the context of this work.

Latinidades in Context

We begin by centering this work on the lived experiences of Latinxs, with the understanding that this term can encompass a set of identities that differ according to national origin, immigration status, gender, generation, socio-economic status, phenotypic expression, and sexuality, among other dimensions. There are commonalities in terms of histories of colonization and resistance, as well as cultural and linguistic elements. What was at first a government-imposed grouping of a heterogeneous people became a political act of renaming, reclaiming and recreating a pan-ethnic identity and space from which to organize according to common strengths, needs, concerns, and injustices. The U.S. Census started using the term "Hispanic" in 1980 to classify and group together U.S. residents of Latin American origin (i.e. Mexican, Puerto Rican, Cuban, Dominican, Central and South American). The term "Hispanic" allowed for greater visibility and recognition of people who do not easily fit into either white or black categories. However, many, including the authors of this volume, who have direct lineage to Latin America, reject "Hispanic" precisely because the term connotes Spain or Europe as the primary origin of our identities. Latinx has become the preferred identification, as it refers to not only Europe as a cultural and historical source but also acknowledges indigenous and African heritage.

We would also like to note that, in this book, we use the term Latinx to also reflect gender inclusive, non-binary language. As a group, we the editors discussed this usage. Previously, we used "Latin@" since we felt that term encompassed a both/and gender inclusive symbol. Before that, "Latino/a" was the term popular for those of us who wanted to avoid using the masculine form (Latino) as representative of all genders. Since about 2014, people in online spheres began shifting from Latin@ to Latinx, to be more inclusive of multiple genders, and several blogs and online magazines have argued for and against this term (for examples, see Guerra & Orbea, 2015; Scharron-del Rio & Aja, 2016). Understanding some of the critiques scholars have about this usage, we felt we should change our manuscript to reflect this new expression of gender inclusivity. We think that Latinx is in line with Anzaldúa's theorizing, which we draw from in our PAR EntreMundos framework. She too emphasizes an approach of multiplicity, hybridity and disrupting binaries. She also wrote about how we use language, in particular the mix of English and Spanish, in what she described as her "pocha Spanish" rather than crisp Castellano or Standard English. Deliberate in her biliteracy in writing and speaking, she played with language to fit our hybrid realities. Thus, we feel that this term reflects this spirit, even though using it can feel messy at times.

Latinx identities have a hybrid nature; a recent study found that ⅓ of Latinxs see themselves as "mixed", specifically, "mestizo" or "mulatto" (Gonzalez-Barrera, 2015). As such, there are multiple spaces for connections with diverse communities. Connecting our roots as Latinxs to our indigenous and African ancestries, for example, can offer a shared ground of understanding among other racial and ethnic communities. Like Anzaldúa's concept of nos-otras, where the colonizer and colonized can reside, albeit uneasily, in one body, our multiplicities create spaces for mutual implications and multiple connections (Torre, 2009).

We the authors reflect these differences, commonalities, and complexities. We call ourselves African-American, Chicanx, Ecuadorian/Cuban, Euro-American, Latinx, mestiza, Nuyorican, Puerto Rican, Raza. We are U.S. born and 1.5 generation. We live in the Northeast, South, Midwest and West of the U.S. and have strong familial and ancestral links to the Caribbean and Latin America. We have walked along different paths in our educational journeys, yet reached similar academic milestones. We connect according to shared passions for social justice educational work with Latinx communities and other communities of color.

According to the Pew Research Center (Krogstad, 2014), the population of Latinxs in the U.S. has grown significantly; in the first decade of the millennium, over half of the country's growth in population was made up of Latinxs. Growth in the Latinx population occurs primarily through births instead of the popular misperception that immigration is responsible for the increase in numbers. By 2050, it is estimated that the numbers of Latinxs in the US will continue to grow, actually doubling in size (Krogstad, 2014).

In school contexts, Latinx student numbers are also increasing. Between 2002 and 2012, we have seen a 6% increase in the number of Latinx students enrolling in public school, which amounts to 3.5 million more students (National Center for Educational Statistics [NCES], 2015). In areas of the country, such as Southern and Midwestern states, where Latinxs represent emerging communities, this significant demographic shift in student population requires school districts to identify new curricula and pedagogical strategies to attend to the changing diversity in education. Given these trends, it is important that the needs and strengths of Latinxs are addressed in school and policy contexts. The National Latino/a Education Research and Policy Project (NLERAP) is one organization that was founded "to voice Latino/a perspectives on educational reforms and the knowledge base needed to sustain that vision" (NLERAP, 2003).

Our Origin Story

Over the past 15 years, NLERAP has gathered hundreds of educators, students, families, community and business leaders, policy-makers, and researchers, to develop a vision connected to an action plan for Latinx education (Nieto, Rivera, & Quiñones, 2012; NLERAP, 2003). From its inception, community-based approaches have been central to NLERAP's vision of transforming Latinx communities. Specifically, NLERAP affirms that "…research is more meaningful and inclusive when it is defined through a participatory action research approach" (Nieto et al., 2012).

Given NLERAP's embrace of participatory action research (PAR) as both an epistemology and methodology in which research participants are not only the focus of the inquiry but partners in it (by being part of the research process), PAR scholars were invited to design and guide NLERAP's research in Latinx education.[2] It was then that many of us began working together, weaving our individual and collective PAR experiences and implementing an emerging vision of PAR (what would eventually become PAR EntreMundos).

Our approach to PAR, building on what Torre and Ayala (2009) have termed PAR EntreMundos (described more fully in Chapter 1), is steeped in Freirean praxis, critical race and borderland theories, South American liberation psychologies and social movement histories. By "EntreMundos" (among worlds), we refer to a pedagogy that disrupts and dismantles traditional academic binaries such as researcher/researched, expert/novice, and institution/

community. In the context of schooling, part of the goal of this approach is to merge these and other binaries and co-create transformative spaces of education through democratic collectives of research, inquiry and social action.

Over the years, our PAR collective (with seven decades of experience between us all, across various contexts and geographies) gathered from across the U.S., charged with creating, articulating and ultimately guiding the implementation of a form of PAR that is distinctly relevant to the needs of Latinx communities within education. We wove our personal histories of PAR with parents, public school students and their families, under/graduate students, classroom teachers, teacher aids, and teaching artists, community artists, local activists and social entrepreneurs in public schools and universities, after school programs and community-based organizations in the United States, Puerto Rico and Latin America to imagine and develop an emerging model of PAR for diverse Latinx educational contexts. The PAR framework proposed in this book is inclusive of teacher education but also reaches into many areas of education and other disciplines concerned with working with Latinx communities.

In 2011, a subgroup of the national PAR committee participated in meetings in Dallas, Texas and Sacramento, California with members of various other NLERAP committees, organizations and community members to co-develop a framework for an emerging Grow Your Own (GYO) Teacher Education Initiative (see Mercado, 2016). Simply put, the GYO initiative involves recruiting young people from particular communities to become teachers and then placing them back to teach in the same communities from which they originate. At first, we imagined that the GYO framework could be articulated within a single handbook. At these meetings, we decided that we could more fully express the overall vision rooted in critical pedagogy, engaged policy, social justice, community partnerships, and participatory action research through multiple manuscripts. The idea of a book series evolved—beginning with two texts, a handbook (what is now Growing Critically Conscious Teachers: A Social Justice Curriculum for Educators of Latino/a Youth), and a book focusing on PAR in education contexts (this volume). *PAR EntreMundos: A Pedagogy of the Américas* is a result of the work started at the above meetings and continued through subsequent weekly discussions representing an exploration of the PAR root and its evolution. We offer this volume for teacher educators, educators, students, scholars, and activists alike to understand how PAR can transform education into both a practice of liberation and a vehicle for social justice. A liberatory social justice approach to education addresses the educational needs of marginalized communities by challenging the forms of oppression that prevent students, particularly students of color, from realizing their full potential to learn.

Why PAR EntreMundos?

Much of what we see of public education today is "an unsustainable reality based on a corporate agenda, one that sees education functionalism rather than on true learning, based on competition rather than collaboration, on rigid accountability rather than authentic growth" (Nieto, 2015, p. 253). The neo-liberal ideology driving this corporate agenda promotes a hyper-individualism in which students believe they must fend for themselves in school and society, instead of striving to cooperate and be accountable to others, while others become accountable to them. In addressing "why on earth teach now" in this era of individual accountability and standardization, Nieto (2015), concludes that we must renew the commitment to social justice in education. Incorporating a social justice perspective into pedagogical structures allows marginalized communities and students to understand and address the oppressive forces limiting their potential to seek and bring about necessary social, economic, and educational changes (Cammarota, 2011). Social justice pedagogies can take many forms, and we offer PAR EntreMundos as one approach that works toward this goal.

Anzaldúa and Keating used the term EntreMundos/Among Worlds as another way to name the borderlands (Keating, 2005), an alternate space between social worlds that traverses cultural and psychological boundaries of aqui and alla; of U.S. and Latin America, of gender, class, and sexualities. She names it a space of uncertainty and creativity, where people gather threads from different social worlds to make their own identity tapestries. A PAR that is among worlds suggests that it does not fit neatly into one conceptual category; it is research, method, a way of knowing, an approach to relationships, and an examination of power within and without. It is an engagement of collective spirit and movement. It is a hybrid form that is messy, ambiguous, and embodies conceptual/personal/social passions with little space for distance.

Forging linkages across different levels of power, PAR EntreMundos builds primarily from the ground up to ensure that the voices of the most marginalized are clearly heard in a collective of critical inquiry. Participatory action research consistently reminds us that any real, lasting positive change

in education must derive from ideas and voices of those living and learning on the ground, such as students, teachers, and parents. As we articulate
here an interpretation of a PAR EntreMundos, framed as a Pedagogy of Las
Americas, we consider the ways in which this approach, developed from a
southern hemispheric tradition, can have broad community impact in various contexts. Similar to how Latinxs identify in complex ways that link with
indigenous, African and European lineages, PAR EntreMundos is historically
rooted in the southern hemisphere, rendering its form and content relevant
to multiple racial and ethnic communities. Part of the goal of this approach is
to co-construct complex, transformative spaces of education through democratic collectives of research, inquiry and social action. These collectives can
include youth, educators and community members (for instance, parents or
neighborhood organizers) as collaborators in the research conceptualization,
process, analysis and outcomes. In most cases, PAR EntreMundos collectives
operate with an intergenerational structure that builds relationships among
youth and adults to promote and sustain social justice action within particular
communities. The most marginalized within these collectives are empowered
through an equity framework that shifts power from the top to the bottom
while placing leadership responsibilities in their hands. With leadership rising
up from the grassroots, transformation occurs on personal and collective levels, making the process an important outcome of the research.

   With YPAR (Youth Participatory Action Research) approaches, the experiences of young people, as the most marginalized within school settings, are at
the center. Much is written about their roles in the PAR process within collectives. Recognizing that youth voices, particularly when we study school experiences, tend to be in the background of research and reform efforts, YPAR offers
a way in which to privilege youth voice in this kind of context (Cammarota &
Fine, 2008; Connor, Ebby-Rosin, & Brown, 2015). At times, this means that
adults struggle with their roles in relation to youth in research collectives, interpreting youth-centered as adult absent, or conversely tokenize youth involvement, focusing on their participation in terms of benefits to youth development,
rather than on the benefit to the issue itself and the knowledge/action produced
(Fox, 2016; Jones, Stewart, Galletta, & Ayala, 2015). Though there are examples of youth-run collectives, particularly around organizing, we feel that much
of the PAR we see tends to be multigenerational (Fox, 2016); recognizing that
power is negotiated across generations within collectives. Both youth and adults
in collectives scaffold each other's efforts—influence and power is not unidirec-
tional, but moves across generational links. In classroom contexts, the teachers/

adults in collectives always manage an unequal power, even when engaging in processes that are meant to equalize power within the classroom. This intergenerational matrix is further complicated given our current, digital age. Technology has shifted power dynamics, regarding information and communication, and educational processes are profoundly informed by these changing relationships and dynamics. PAR EntreMundos offers a new role for adults in the learning process, moving from experts depositing knowledge into children and young people to curators and facilitators of knowledge and experience. Thinking of this as intergenerational focuses on the relationships and exchanges that occur within collectives as they work towards multi-level change. As Fox argues: "Through participation across generations, the recognition of multiple kinds of expertise, and a critical frame, we have the best chance of achieving the most positive development for youth, which is structural change" (2016, p. 56).

Participating in PAR EntreMundos often leaves a deep impact on the individuals undertaking it. Reclaiming and reimagining denied or suppressed indigenous knowledge; challenging oppression that limits personal transformation; analyzing and actively forging new spaces of opportunity in the cracks between constraining boundaries of racism, classism, heterosexism and patriarchy; being respected as legitimate knowledge producers, partners in inquiry, and change agents; becoming part of something larger; are all powerful experiences for those involved. Through collective inquiry, we reach for transformation; the very nature of the activity presumes movement towards becoming. It is not something that can be trapped within a single image or moment. We turn to a PAR EntreMundos because it begins from a place of fluidity and multiplicity, of identities, power relationships, perspectives and approaches—to change from without and within. The work presented in these chapters is grounded in the experiences and theorizing fluidity, multiplicity, and hybridity of Latinidades, and as such, it can connect to multiple communities and experiences.

Organization of the Book

This book is split into three parts. In Part I, we discuss the various lineages of PAR and highlight the PAR EntreMundos approach from which we developed a set of guiding principles. In this chapter on lineages, we briefly highlight some of the theoretical madrinas and padrinos, to offer grounding in this evolving approach. Our theoretical lineage starts with a nod to the southern tradition, with particular attention paid to Fals-Borda, Freire, and Martín-Baró but does not end there. It builds on the work of these scholars, as well as critical race and feminist theories, towards what Torre and Ayala (2009) term "PAR EntreMundos". This allows us to move our theory and practice through a variety of spaces, connect with multiple ideas, and embrace the borderlands to live in the intersection of new emergent perspectives and possibilities. We close this chapter with a set of eight guiding principles. These principles include unique components with more explicit mind-body-spirit connections, and that pay attention to indigenous cosmologies, power with(in), and creative praxes.

In Part II, we introduce a set of examples from across the country that embody the various principles of PAR EntreMundos, detailing the processes behind the projects, and describing the ways in which they expand critical consciousness while improving the education of Latinx communities and beyond. The first example describes Rodríguez's PRAXIS Project, Participatory Research Advocating for Excellence in Schools. This is a school-based, university-affiliated research collaborative aimed at recognizing and responding to the education crisis facing the U.S. The context is the Inland Empire, which includes San Bernardino and Riverside Counties in California and is home to nearly 5 million people. Nearly 80% of the school-age population is either African-American or Latinx, over 30% of the students are English Language Learners, and the community is faced with an over 50% dropout rate. In response to the dropout/pushout crisis, The PRAXIS Project engaged youth, educators, and leaders in a participatory action research initiative that centered on youth experiences to: (1) understand the realities facing students of color in struggling schools and communities, (2) create curricular and pedagogical approaches that engage youth, (3) use research to shape and transform educational policy and practice at the local level, and (4) transform outcomes and educational attainment outcomes for students in the community.

In Chapter 3, Cammarota documents the Social Justice Education Project (SJEP), which started at Cerro High School in the Tucson Unified School District (TUSD) of Arizona in the 2002/2003 school year. This specialized social science program was aligned with state-mandated history and U.S. government standards and involved students in participatory action research (PAR) projects. The SJEP was a year-long course in which students gained all their social science credits for graduation and learned graduate-level participatory action research techniques. Students conducted their own original qualitative research study and participated in every step of the research process. Based on their research findings, students proposed actions to solve problems in their particular social and economic contexts. This chapter follows one particular PAR project through each phase of the work.

Rivera and colleagues explore participatory action research in the context of a small, community-based high school in Brooklyn, New York, one dedicated to peace and justice. This PAR example briefly describes a decade-long collaborative research process between teacher-artists, a community-based organization, and university researchers. From this work emerged the Creative Justice Approach (CJA) theoretical framework, an approach to learning and human development rooted in creativity and social justice. The CJA learning systems includes three lenses: social ecology (via a cultural cartography), learning renaissance (via a creative learning cycle), and personal revolution (via transformative selves). The CJA offers a personal and collective transformative learning experience rooted in relational principles and global human rights and activated through critical, creative, and compassionate pedagogy.

Another example described in Chapter 5 features the work of the New Jersey Urban Youth Research Initiative, a short-term collective of education activists, community-based organizations, high school students and university researchers across three NJ cities. The NJUYRI worked together on a participatory project that centered on what was, at the time, a shift in the graduation requirements at the secondary level. This chapter describes the process and pedagogy associated with this outside-the-classroom project, from developing the collaborative, structuring the research process, analysis and critical dialogue within research camps, to deciding what actions to take, engaging in multiple forms of action, and assessing the work within a "school" context, as youth were offered college credit. Work samples and other artifacts are included in the appendix to offer readers more concrete examples of how the project took shape. Finally, the authors reflect on the process, considering relationships and balance points, and the challenges and opportunities in doing this work.

In Chapter 6, Mayorga describes the Education in our Barrios project, or #BarrioEdProj, which involves a digital, critical participatory action research (D+CPAR) project that examines the interconnected remaking of public education and U.S. urban Latinx core communities in the midst of the devastating trauma of racial neoliberal urbanism. This chapter highlights a description of the theoretical, personal and political commitments that frame the project as a braiding of participatory action research (PAR), cultural political economy, and digital social science. Chapter 7, the final chapter in Part II, documents the development of Jóvenes con Derechos (JcD), a collective of multilingual Latinx high school students, which started at Roosevelt High School in Minneapolis, Minnesota in the 2012/2013 school year. JcD was born out of the creation of a series of Spanish as a Heritage Language classes. Using a cohort model and a sociocultural approach to language and literacy development, students and their teacher spend two years together. In this time, youth use and develop their multiple varieties of both Spanish and English to study critical race theories, justice movements across Latinx, Chicanx, and Indigenous communities across the U.S. and the Americas, borderlands identities, and arts-based approaches to collective action and transformational voicing of selves and communities. In their second year together, students engage in PAR, developing critical and community-based research techniques and digital storytelling skills and utilizing arts-based methods for representation.

In Part III, we offer three chapters that describe how the PAR EntreMundos framework was put into direct action in the context of two different Grow Your Own (GYO) Teacher Education initiatives that support NLER-AP's goals. In Chapter 8, Irizarry describes Project FUERTE (Future Urban Educators conducting Research to Transform Teacher Education), a multi-generational participatory action research collaborative. He draws from data collected as part of a three-year ethnographic study of 14 high school students who participated in Project FUERTE to critically examine how African American and Latinx youth might more effectively be recruited into the teaching profession and prepared to transform schools so they work in the best interests of their communities. Using Critical Race Theory and Latinx Critical Race Theory as analytical tools, this chapter documents how a group of African-American and Latinx high school students who were apathetic about the teaching profession modified their professional aspirations to consider education-related careers, including teaching, after engaging in a systematic critical examination of the policies and practices that negatively impact the educational experiences and outcomes for urban youth of color. It highlights students' evolving perceptions of teaching as an act of resistance and challenges oversimplified notions of teacher diversity that seek proportionate representation without preparing all teachers to challenge the social reproductive function of schools.

Baker and Berta-Ávila's Chapter 9 focuses on NLERAP's GYO Teacher Education Initiative launch, subsequent progress and outcomes after two years of implementation, at Sacramento State University. The challenges and successes of the program are told through recounting the journeys of two teacher candidates who participated in the program. Taking part in this initiative, educators were exposed to a transformative pedagogy in PAR that put the academic and social needs of prospective classroom students at the forefront. They found that participating educators gained skills in connecting subject matter content to local and national social issues identified by the students in the classroom, and in implementing and refining strategies and methods, they learned through the single subject program. As a result of their participation, they also presented in academic conferences, authored and proposed English language development social justice courses integrating PAR in the districts where they teach, and in general, continue to integrate PAR with their content as first-year teachers in the field.

In Chapter 10, Gonzalez explores how high school students used Participatory Action Research (PAR) projects to make their campus more democratic, equitable, and socially just through critical civic engagement and activism over the course of two years. A first year teacher who participated in the GYO initiative as a student teacher described in the previous chapter, Gonzalez used ethnography of communication and events to explore several areas. One was how students have successfully demanded and obtained institutional change at the departmental and school-wide levels and how this process has transformed students both socially as well as academically. Another area of exploration involved stories of teacher support and resistance toward students undertaking this work.

The book ends with concluding thoughts about the potential of PAR EntreMundos, for education, research, social and personal transformation, both within Latinx communities and beyond. Our intention is that this book will inspire educators, students, practitioners, and community members to implement PAR projects that address pressing educational issues and social problems, while leading to the development of responsive pedagogies for Latinx students. We attempt to answer more than the general inquiry of "how to" implement PAR in the context of schools. This book provides a philosophical vision for understanding how education, through PAR EntreMundos, can develop critical consciousness and community engagement among marginalized youth in the interest of societal transformation and social justice.

Critical Consciousness Within PAR EntreMundos

Our belief is that marginalized youth and adults reach their full intellectual potential by developing a critical consciousness that facilitates an understanding of the social and economic structures preventing their well-being. This awareness extends beyond understanding the circumstances stifling healthy existence to cultivating the capacity to challenge those injustices that harm the spirit and shatter the hopes of achieving fulfilled lives. Young people must experience a sense of value and wholeness about who they are and what they are capable of as they embark upon generating positive contributions for themselves and the world. PAR EntreMundos allows for this deeper understanding of self through continuous reflection while recognizing one's efficacy to initiate social change through steadfast action. The praxis of PAR EntreMundos builds the critical consciousness to challenge and overcome the structural constraints suppressing young people's dreams and aspirations. PAR EntreMundos can lead to better academic outcomes for marginalized youth; however, these improvements often occur as by-products of personal and social transformations emerging from a critical, decolonizing pedagogy. Therefore, PAR-based pedagogies can be powerful tools to engage young people to become active participants in making healthier lives, free from oppressive circumstances, for themselves and for others within and beyond their communities.

Young people, particularly those marginalized by the conventional education system, become better students when their learning serves a higher purpose of liberation from the social and economic bondages denying their full humanity. The current neo-liberal practices of "accountability" within education, of high-stakes tests and Common Core standardization, attempt to produce efficient workers and consumers for the global economy. However, in the end, this strategy will not matter to students who feel they are denied the right to self-determination. PAR EntreMundos operates as a critical, decolonizing pedagogy that provides students with the opportunity to determine their identities and engage in actions for social justice. Latinxs and other communities of color must first heal from the social and economic toxins polluting their sense of hope and spirit before they strive for great accomplishments. PAR EntreMundos engages young people in healing through a social justice framework that challenges the oppressive structures limiting their potential for personal and social transformation. Moreover, PAR EntreMundos engages a praxis of hope—and hope should be the first and last word in an education meant to liberate and inspire those who desire a life of love, freedom and peace.

Notes

1. For more on Zach Rubio and his suspension for speaking Spanish see "Spanish at School Translates to Suspension" by T.R. Reid (http://www.washingtonpost.com/wp-dyn/content/article/2005/12/08/AR2005120802122.html)
2. Initially, committee members included the following participatory action researchers (in alphabetical order): Jennifer Ayala, Saint Peters University; Julio Cammarota, Iowa State University; Nilda Flores-González, University of Illinois, Chicago; Jason Irizarry, University of Connecticut; Pedro Pedraza, Hunter College, CUNY; Melissa Rivera, WE Scholarship; Louie F. Rodríguez, University of California Riverside; María Elena Torre, Public Science Project; and Mayida Zaal, Montclair State University.

References

Cammarota, J. (2011). From hopelessness to hope: Social justice pedagogy in urban education and youth development. *Urban Education*, 0042085911399931.

Cammarota, J., & Fine, M. (Eds.). (2008). *Revolutionizing education: Youth participatory action research in motion*. New York, NY: Routledge.

Connor, J. O., Ebby-Rosen, R., & Brown, A. S. (2015). *National society for the study of education yearbooks: Student voice in American educational policy, 114(1)*. Columbia, NY: Teachers College.

Fox, M. (2016). On research, art, and transformation: Multigenerational participatory research, critical positive youth development, and structural change. *Qualitative Psychology*, 3(1), 46–58.

Gonzalez-Barrera, A. (July 10, 2015). 'Mestizo' and 'mulatto:' Mixed race identities among U.S. Hispanics. Pew Research Center. Retrieved from http://www.pewresearch.org/fact-tank/2015/07/10/mestizo-and-mulatto-mixed-race-identities-unique-to-hispanics/

Guerra, G., & Orbea, G. (November 19, 2015). The argument against the use of the term "Latinx". The Phoenix: Swathmore's Independent Campus Newspaper. Retrieved from http://swarthmorephoenix.com/2015/11/19/the-argument-against-the-use-of-the-term-latinx/

Irizarry, J. G. (2011). *The Latinization of U.S. schools: Successful teaching and learning in shifting cultural contexts*. Boulder, CO: Paradigm Publishing.

Jones, V., Stewart, C., Galletta, A., & Ayala, J. (2015). Creative expressions of agency: Contemplating youth voice and adult roles in participatory action research. In Jerusha O. Connor, Rachel Ebby-Rosen, & Amanda S. Brown (Eds.), *National society for the study of education yearbooks: Student voice in American educational policy, 114(1)*. Columbia, NY: Teachers College.

Keating, A. (2005). *Entremundos/among worlds: New perspectives on Gloria E. Anzaldúa*. New York, NY: Palgrave Macmillan.

Krogstad, J. M. (December 16, 2014). With fewer new arrivals, Census lowers Hispanic projections. Pew Research Center. Retrieved from http://www.pewresearch.org/

fact-tank/2014/12/16/with-fewer-new-arrivals-census-lowers-hispanic-population-projections-2/

Mercado, C. I. (2016). Teacher capacities for Latino and Latina youth. In A. Valenzuela (Ed.), *Growing critically conscious teachers: A social justice curriculum for educators of Latino/a youth.* New York, NY: Teachers College Press.

National Center for Educational Statistics (NCES). (2015). Racial/ethnic enrollment in public schools. Retrieved from http://nces.ed.gov/programs/coe/indicator_cge.asp

Nieto, S. (2015). *Why we teach now.* New York, NY: Teachers College Press.

Nieto, S., Rivera, M., & Quiñones, S. (Guest Eds.). (2012). Charting a new course:

Understanding the sociocultural, political, economic and historical context of Latino/a education in the United States. [Special Issue] *AMAE: Association of Mexican American Educators, 6*(3).

NLERAP. (2003). *National Latino/a education research agenda project: Education research framework and agenda.* New York, NY: Center for Puerto Rican Studies, Hunter College, City University of New York.

Scharron-del Rio, M. R., & Aja, A. A. (April 8, 2016). The case for Latinx—And why this term matters for intersectionality. *Everyday Feminism Magazine.* Retrieved from http://everydayfeminism.com/2016/04/why-use-latinx/

Torre, M. E. (2009). Participatory action research and critical race theory: Fueling spaces for Nos-otras to research. *Urban Review, 41*(1), 106–120.

Torre, M. E., & Ayala, J. (2009). Envisioning participatory action research entremundos. *Feminism & Psychology, 19,* 387.

· PART I ·

ROOTS & PRINCIPLES OF PAR
ENTREMUNDOS

In Part I of this text, we present to the reader theoretical lineages we identify as informing a PAR EntreMundos approach in the context of education. The EntreMundos concept, drawn from the late Gloria Anzaldúa's
borderlands theorizing (1987), is linked to the approach of PAR (Torre &
Ayala, 2009) and elaborated upon in relation to formal and informal education spaces. We describe PAR's southern hemisphere ancestry, and draw
from literatures on critical race theory, feminist approaches, and spiritual
activisms/indigenous cosmologies to inform and contextualize the PAR
pedagogies we advocate for here. Building on these traditions, as well as a
growing literature on PAR, we articulate the ways in which this PAR approach addresses the social, economic, and political conditions of our lives
alongside the transformative work within the bodymindspirit (Lara, 2002)
space. From these literatures, we developed a set of principles that are meant
to be used as a guide for the development of PAR projects that fit an EntreMundos framework.

References

Anzaldúa, G. (1987/1999). *Borderlands la frontera: The new mestiza.* San Francisco, CA: Spinsters/Aunt Lute.

Lara, I. (2002). Healing suenos for academia. In G. Anzaldúa & A. Keating (Eds.), *This bridge we call home: Radical visions for transformation* (pp. 433–438). New York, NY: Routledge.

Torre, M. E., & Ayala, J. (2009). Envisioning participatory action research entremundos. *Feminism & Psychology, 19,* 387.

· 1 ·

THEORETICAL LINEAGES & GUIDING PRINCIPLES

Julio Cammarota, Jennifer Ayala, Melissa Rivera, Louie
F. Rodríguez, Margarita Ines Berta-Ávila, and María Elena Torre

> If you have come to help me, you are wasting your time. But if you come because your
> liberation is bound up in mine, then let us work together.
>
> Aboriginal Activist Group

Academic research has often been seen as a tool used against people of color, as a way to study and understand "others" to justify policies and practices that maintain subordination. Acknowledging this oppressive history, and as a counter to it, we as Latinx educators, scholars, and activists ascribe to participatory action approaches that use research as a collaborative tool to be used *with* communities towards liberatory and social justice goals. In the following paragraphs, we briefly highlight some of our theoretical madrinas and padrinos in this work, to offer grounding in this evolving tradition.

Participatory action research (PAR) is recognized generally as an approach or orientation in which research participants are not only the focus of the inquiry but partners in it, by being part of the research process. PAR researchers collaborate with "local participants to define the research questions, describe their experiences in their own terms, and use the research results to effect change" (Chataway, 1997, p. 750). This partnership between "outside-researchers" and "research subjects" renders PAR a democratic approach in which decision-making around the methods and results of the inquiry is a collaborative endeavor (Krumer-Nevo, 2009, pp. 280–281). The democratic characteristic of PAR provides for a more multidimensional and complete understanding of the patterns and possibilities for social change (Healy, 2001, p. 95). Democratization also represents a release of who controls the production and use of knowledge by allowing "the people" greater access to the scientific methods that produce and apply knowledge in society (Reason, 1994, p. 332).

The purpose of PAR, however, varies according to two major traditions—Southern and Northern (Fals-Borda, 1996; Hall, 1981; Reason, 1994). The work of Whyte (1991) and Lewin (1946) represent the northern tradition, with its emphasis on organizational change and efficient management systems (Fals-Borda, 1996). The southern tradition follows the ideas of Fals-Borda (1979) Martín-Baró (1994), and Freire (1993, 1994, 1998) and their efforts to create the conditions to liberate marginalized populations from oppression by combining critical inquiry and activism. The focus on "education, research and social action" renders the southern version of PAR a widely practiced approach throughout the globe (Hall, 1981) and in a variety of fields, including education, health, social work, and youth development (Cammarota & Fine, 2008; Healy, 2001; Khanlou & Peter, 2005; Nelson, Ochocka, Griffin, & Lord, 1998). With NLERAP's mission of educational justice and equity, the southern tradition inspires its program of PAR.

In the context of Latinx education initiatives, the researched communities are often our own. We draw from Latina feminist/womanist scholarship to inform our understandings and practices of the southern tradition in sites we may call home. Anzaldúa, Moraga (1987, 1999, 2002) and others have articulated "theories of the flesh" whereby we reflect on the embodied personal and political projects of living hybridity. Therefore, as Latinx scholars, we derive practices of the southern tradition not only from the geographical South but also from the multiple physical, mental and spiritual sites we inhabit, and the political, cultural and ideological borders we cross throughout all of the las Americas. In her borderlands scholarship, Anzaldúa (1987) describes how we hold multiple identities, cross the borders between different social worlds, and live EntreMundos: in between spaces of our own creation since we cannot fit neatly into categories made for us. Her concept of mestiza consciousness can involve interrupting hierarchical and dualistic thinking and embracing a multiplicity of perspectives that is not always comfortable. In a view of PAR that is informed by these ideas, we can imagine, at their best, that PAR collectives create alternate spaces whereby co-researchers enjoy new parts of themselves and new forms of relationships with each other, experiences that often run counter to traditional social hierarchies. Anzaldúa tells us these spaces, even if uncomfortable and unpredictable, can create passageways to new ideas and consciousness, *EntreMundos*—that "by crossing you invite a turning point, initiate a change" (Torre & Ayala, 2009, p. 389).

Ultimately, the work of PAR can lead to mutual transformation and liberatory change, not only as a result of the action efforts, but also from the process of research itself. Our version of the southern tradition, then, is best described as what Torre and Ayala (2009) call "PAR EntreMundos", allowing us to move through a variety of spaces, connect with multiple ideas, and embrace the borderlands to live in the intersection of new emergent perspectives and possibilities. Undoubtedly, architects of the southern tradition, including Martín-Baró, Fals-Borda, and Freire, inform our practice of PAR EntreMundos but inspirational and intellectual legacies do not end with these noted South American scholars. Because our personal lineages link us to diverse geographical locations throughout America Latina, our varied positionalities facilitate traversing borders in our daily lives, as we move back and forth from dominant spaces to the margins. Traversing involves more than crossing ideological and political borders but also moving through the quotidian landscapes of academia, community, family life, artistic creation, and camaraderie. Therefore, our intellectual travels transport us fluidly along and by multiple sites in the Américas to learn from the critical race theories of the U.S. civil rights movement, the indigenous cosmologies of native peoples, and the womanist pedagogies of feminist activist scholars.

Taking our cues from the resiliency and resistances of the Caciques and Cimarron's, we stand alongside those that have used innovation, flexibility and endurance to overcome the oppressive, annihilative force of colonization (Jose Lopez, May 28, 2011, personal communication). Our discussion of PAR EntreMundos may begin in the southern hemisphere, yet travels through the Américas to glean from the knowledge produced by organic intellectuals who work with marginalized communities to struggle against oppression. In the paragraphs below, we highlight four lineages that inform our vision of a PAR EntreMundos: the southern tradition, critical race theory, feminist theorizing, and indigenous cosmologies.

The Southern Tradition

Liberation is a praxis: the action and reflection of men and women upon their world
in order to transform it.

— Paulo Freire

Although Freire never applied the term PAR to his work, he is considered a major figure in the development of the southern tradition by combining education and research in his conceptualization of praxis (Gaventa, 1993; Hall, 1981; Selener, 1997). The nexus of critical reflection and action represents a praxis that intends to transform reality while fostering a liberation for those fettered by oppression. Praxis occurs in what Freire described as "culture circles" that consist of community-based literacy projects devoted to empowering people to generate changes in their life conditions (Ferreira & Gendron, 2011, p. 155). The goal of the culture circle is to engender the learners' concientizacion, or critical awareness of the conditions that lead to their oppression. Concientizacion moves the learner from the static position of an "object" created and molded by society to that of a dynamic "subject" who becomes empowered to transform his or her reality (Ozanne & Saatcioglu, 2008). Critical awareness encourages marginalized individuals to dig through past ideologies that prevent them from realizing their capabilities to affect changes in their lives (Guishard, 2009, p. 89). Praxis-oriented research or PAR assists with this process by producing the knowledge to demythologize or "de-ideologize" the causes that foment social and economic problems (Ibid, p. 91).

Research in Freirian praxis is understood as a process for investigating and identifying "generative themes" in the learners' lived context. These themes are words that have great emotional value and connect to the learners' social, political and cultural realities. Learners use these words to generate other words relevant to their lives. These new words compose a vocabulary that facilitates an analysis of the learners' everyday experiences and of the oppressive forces that impede their progress. The amalgamation of generative words illuminates "the situation in which people exist and the goals toward which they move in transforming their world in the direction of human liberation" (Wingeier, 1980, p. 564). Once concientizacion is attained through thematic research, the next and most important step of praxis is to take action in order transform reality and seek liberation from oppression.

Fals-Borda (1979) also realized the significance of praxis as a research and liberatory process in which reality is investigated in order to transform it. He further elaborated the idea of praxis as a blending of theory and practice to facilitate an intellectual development focused on understanding the conditions that lead to social and economic injustice. Praxis also involves a commitment, or what Fals-Borda called "Vivencia", in which the researcher identifies deeply with the struggles facing the oppressed community participating in the research while becoming committed to improving life conditions (Fals-Borda, 1996, p. 159). Praxis, according to Fals-Borda, is achieved through participatory action research, which he claims has a justice-based southern tradition emerging from the turbulent, "earthquake" type crises common in developing countries (1996, p. 156).

Fals-Borda is perhaps the foremost spokesperson for the PAR southern tradition, basing much of his academic work on defining this tradition. He describes the southern approach as including the following elements: that PAR is interdisciplinary, focused on local settings, useful for liberation from oppression, a collective effort, a reclamation of indigenous history and culture, popular in the sense that knowledge is accessible for all, an amalgamation of knowledge that emerges from academia, general wisdom, and common experience, transformative for the researchers by orientating their personal perspective and commitments toward the liberation of the researched community.

Critical Race Praxis

…when the ideology of racism is examined and racist injuries are named, victims of racism can find their voice. Furthermore, those injured by racism and other forms of oppression discover they are not alone in their marginality. They become empowered participants, hearing their own stories and the stories of others, listening to how the arguments against them are framed, and learning to make the arguments to defend themselves (Solórzano & Yosso, 2002, p. 27).

The second framework that guides our view of PAR EntreMundos is Critical Race Praxis (Lynn & Parker, 2006). That is, in addition to drawing from the theories and frameworks from the southern tradition, PAR is vigorously committed to engaging in practical and policy changes that are driven by an analysis of race and racism, sexism, classism, and homophobia and its intersections. It challenges the dominant ideologies that guide how education and its role in communities of color are understood and analyzed, commits to social justice and transformation, and includes historically marginalized groups as definers and creators of knowledge through interdisciplinary consideration of racism and other forms of oppression (Yosso, 2005). In addition, LatCrit , a term used to describe Latinx critical race theory, is also particularly applicable to the PAR EntreMundos approach, as it includes conditions and realities that are specifically associated with salient issues in the Latinx community, including immigration, language and language politics, and issues of culture, identity, and sexuality (Solórzano & Delgado Bernal, 2001).

PAR EntreMundos also aims to provide a counter-narrative to historical and contemporary struggles facing Latinxs and other marginalized groups in the U.S. In doing so, Critical Race Praxis not only privileges the voices, experiences, and knowledge bases of our communities, but also positions our praxis to be deliberately aimed at social justice in our classrooms, schools, and communities (Garza-Falcón, 1998; Parker & Villalpando, 2007; Yosso, 2005). The tenets of CRT are particularly informative to the work of the PAR EntreMundos (Solórzano & Yosso, 2002; Torre, 2009).

Scholars within the CRT tradition typically outline five core tenets that inform how researchers and practitioners engage in their work, particularly in the field of education (Yosso, 2005). The five core tenets of CRT include the following:

1. an examination of the intersectionality of race and racism with other forms of oppression such as sexism, classism, and discrimination by language;
2. an examination of the need to challenge dominant ideology, particularly those used to explain the experiences of historically marginalized groups;
3. a commitment to social justice and transformation;
4. a commitment to examining the experiential knowledge bases of marginalized groups;
5. a commitment to engaging in an interdisciplinary analysis of race in the U.S. (Yosso, 2005).

These tenets allow us to centralize issues of racism, sexism, and classism in our research methodology, curriculum, pedagogical approach, and evaluation of our work. These principles also provide a language of critique by challenging long-held deficit perspectives of Latinxs in general but immigrants and English Learner students specifically. For instance, Delgado Bernal's (2002) application of CRT to the experiences of Chicanas/Latinas in the academy provides an example of the use and application of theory to praxis. We aim to engage in similar analyses and applications of CRT to the realities facing primarily K–12 education and how Latinxs are served.

Similarly, Delgado Bernal and Villapando's (2002) work on knowledge apartheid and Yosso's (2005) work on Community Cultural Wealth in the Latinx community provides us with solid examples that illuminate the historically narrow and negligent perspectives of knowledge; who defines knowledge, and who creates knowledge have typically excluded people of color, immigrants, English Learners, and Latinxs specifically. PAR EntreMundos aims to extend this line of work by using these frames to inform our research, activism, and outcomes.

Finally, the interdisciplinary and intersectional nature of CRT allows us to connect the PAR EntreMundos approach with the other lineages that drive our work. For example, recognizing the contributions of multiple disciplinary perspectives such as Feminist and Indigenous epistemologies is a direct guiding principle of CRT—its commitment to interdisciplinary engagement. We believe that developing educators who serve the Latinx community need to be driven by multiple disciplines and epistemological foundations, and CRT helps inform this approach.

The Critical Race Praxis lineage is rooted in the application of these theories to the lives and conditions that face the Latinx community, making it a relevant paradigm to inform our PAR EntreMundos framework. Because we are committed to praxis, CRT not only gives us a language to engage our work, but also a framework to guide our actions for social justice and educational equity. As noted earlier, challenges to dominant ideologies, such as patriarchy, and critical examinations of the intersections between racism, classism, sexism and homophobia, are also characteristics found in feminist/womanist scholarship. We explore this lineage in more depth in the following section.

Feminist Lineages

You say my name is ambivalence? Think of me as Shiva, a many armed and many legged body with one foot in brown soil, one on white, one in straight society, one in the gay world, the man's world, the women's, one limb in the literary world, another in the working class, the socialist, and the occult worlds. A sort of spider woman hanging by one thin strand of web. Who me, confused? Ambivalent? No, only your labels split me. (Gloria Anzaldúa, 1987)

In tracing the feminist lineages of this work, we turn to ideas related to standpoint, intersectionalities and embodiment. We honor those women before us who walked along the sharp edges of geography and discipline, of sexual, classed and cultural boundaries, who roughed out bridge spaces and traveled new avenues that we now follow as we continue to build. Intellectual madrinas and standpoint theorists, such as Anzaldúa (1987), Hill Collins (1991), hooks (1994), Matsuda (1995), and Harding (1993) bring to light the importance of positioning ourselves in our teaching, research, and writing. Ourselves, our histories, they ways we are situated in relation to power and privilege, are part of the web of work in which we engage and provide the lenses through which we view and understand our experiences and the worlds before us. Our positionality situates the knowledge we create and influences the angles we see and the connections we make; therefore, it becomes important to acknowledge who we are in relation to the work we do. It encourages us to "theorize from the flesh" as Anzaldúa and Moraga (1981) viscerally write—to build understandings, theory, and knowledge from the pain, exploitation, resistance, and joy we have lived through body and spirit. It reminds us that there are multiple perspectives that inform our truths. Excavating and making these perspectives explicit in our work provides us with what Harding (1993) would call "strong objectivity", that while at moments it can reveal our vulnerability, it roots our work deeply in the rich knowledge beds of our communities, histories, and experience.

As standpoint theory reminds us, our identities and lived experiences are not separate from the work we do; intersectionality tells us that these identities are multiple and interacting. We are not simply representative of one identity, but of a constellation of identities in motion that includes ethnicity, race, social class, gender, and sexuality. Our identities are in constant conversation, performing a dialectical dance of our multiplicity. In other words, our struggles as women cannot be separated from our struggles as Latinas—we are always "both/and", even as we are too often asked to sort and separate ourselves into different pockets of expression and experience (Hurtado, 2003). As the opening quote to this section illustrates, Anzaldúa writes powerfully about this pressure for fragmenting our multiple, nuanced selves into clearly labeled pieces that fit others' interpretations and expectations. Part of this pressure towards fragmentation involves the imposed splits between the needs and expressions of our bodies, minds, and spirits (Lara, 2002), legitimizing only our "neck up" experiences and knowledges. Other theorists call attention to this false division, and ask us to remember our embodied knowledges. Jungian psychologist, social activist, poet and cantadora, Clarissa Pinkola Estés (2010) encourages us to "show who you really are, the legends that are written on you". Estés and other feminists of color (Delgado-Bernal, 2002; Lara, 2002; Moraga & Anzaldúa, 1981) are reclaiming the body in our scholarship, spirituality, and social activism, rooting our theories in an embodied lived experience, embracing the sacred wisdom of our bodies—the multiple ways of knowing that are written in and on us. This weaving of spirituality, sexuality, science, and solidarity opens us to a living dialectic, where the ways of knowing are expanded, where emotional, sensory and intuitive understandings can co-exist with scientific research, where imagination, art, and dreams live with data and empirical evidence. Lara (2002) invites us to "suture the ruptures of binary thinking and attempt to embody what [we are] theorizing", to theorize from the flesh (Moraga & Anzaldúa, 1981). To help us think further about how we can heal these ruptures, we burrow more deeply into the grounded wisdom of our ancestries, as they invoke notions of collective and spirit knowledge.

Indigenous Cosmologies

Those who have gotten away from the traditions may act as if they don't remember but all of us know inside. Our memories are long, as long as the line of the genera-tions. (Anonymous Native American Woman, 2005 in Schaefer, 2006)

In order to begin the process of understanding our "self" in the context of a collective, "speak[ing] to an inherent belief system that we are all spirit-ually connected so that a transgression against another human being is a transgression against the self", (Borunda, 2011) we first must be open to transcend and acknowledge what has been systematically lost—Our Sacred Spirit. To define what our "Sacred Spirit" is to each other is not the charge here. However, the call from our elders, from both the Northern and South-ern indigenous nations, (Fitzgerald & Fitzgerald, 2005; Paiva, 1992; Perez, 2010; Council of Thirteen Indigenous Grandmothers/Schaefer, 2006) is to re/collect our memories—our ways of knowing—as part of a process that can assist in naming for ourselves our "sacred spirit", which in turn merges with a collective "soul". Our elders state (Fitzgerald & Fitzgerald, 2005; Wall, 1993) that the time has come to unlearn in order to understand, desapren-der para conocer (Paiva, 1992; Perez, 2010). The question, then, is how do we reclaim a spirit that is complete in us individually but also universally (our collective extension)? Indigenous Peruvian teachings (Paiva, 1992) proffer that one manner is through a cyclical process of self-reflection. Self-reflection begins with three core questions:

Quien soy yo/who am I?
Que es la vida/what is life?
Que pretendo de ella/what do I seek from life?

In answering these questions, loving and healing is a first step to seeking justice. However, "justice" cannot stay within us; it must expand to the collective. Thus, it is necessary for the process of reflection to transcend and embody "activismo, investigacion/investigation, y desarollo personal" (Paiva, 1992, p. 135). In this embodiment of "activismo, investigation, desarollo personal" we begin to interface between our body, spirit, and mind. Anzaldúa understood this interface (Keating, 2008) and named it a process of "spiritual activism" that looks to find balance and engagement between the body and the spirit. Starhawk (2003) reflects on the concept of spiritual activism by understanding that the spiritual and political are inseparable, signifying that our "sacred spirit" is informed by our activismo and the real life issues addressed (inequities/injustice). Perez (2010) further explores this by expressing that our work is to co-exist—the spiritual and the activismo politico. This paralleled interface has to be with intention/intentional—meaning that we cannot evoke our spirits without confronting the injustices that exist and reflecting on "?Quien soy yo, Que es la vida, Que pretendo de la vida?" One way Perez believes the latter can transcend is through creativity and the arts.

These works [art] ultimately remind us that we are inescapably, in visible and invisible ways, each other's other selves, an idea expressed in the Mayan *In Lak'ech* which means "tu eres mi otro yo/You are my other me". It is my hope that Chicana art may contribute to a greater and more healing understanding of ourselves and each other, and that we may be spurred along on the great spiritual, social, political, and artistic adventure of more fully realizing our best selves, societies, and globe as a part of the interconnected web of life into a future that will succeed us, and for which we too are responsible.

The path of art can support us to truly embrace a living dialectic, residing in and integrating the multiple names we call ourselves and multiple identities we live rather than rejecting, silencing, or alternating between them. As anthropologist Arrien (1993) writes,

> ...every culture has ways of maintaining health and well-being. Healers throughout the world recognize the importance of maintaining or retrieving the four universal healing salves: storytelling, singing, dancing and silence. Shamanic societies believe

that when we stop singing, stop dancing, are no longer enchanted by stories, or become uncomfortable with silence, we experience soul loss, which opens the door to
discomfort and disease. The gifted healer restores the soul through use of the healing
salves.

The arts have been medicine for communities of color in the United States,
a way to shake off the insidiousness of oppression, to voice both pain and
suffering, beauty and ecstasy, to share our embodied stories, and to truth-tell
(Jenoure, 2000; Kelley, 2002; Rivera, 2003). Ensler (2011) communicates
these ideas in the language of poetry:

> I dance to the drums of the forest and rivers
> I dance to the beat of the cicadas
> I dance to the traffic
> to the crowds
> to the silence
> I dance to the end of unkindness
> I dance past the killing fields
> I dance past Wounded Knee
> I dance past the skeletons and bones
> I dance past slave branding
> And Holocaust tattoos
> I dance past inflicted identities
> and demeaning looks
> I dance past the limited determinations of my
> abilities and worth
> I dance past your lustful eyes
> Your dirty interpretations of my teenage body
> I shake off the burqas and bindings
> and corsets and diets
> I shake off restrictions and illegitimate rules
> I shake off your suffocating warnings
> I dance to the heartbeat of life
> I dance because girls are the ultimate survivors

In this way, if we are to unravel injustice and co-create a more conscious, just,
and compassionate world, then we have to harvest these ancient archetypes
and ways of knowing buried in our hearts and release them through our imaginations by connecting with our bodies. As Carl Jung affirmed, "the symbols of
the self arise in the depths of the body (1981, para 291.)". With our individual
and collective selves and through the personal and communal body, we can
heal and whole.

Moving Toward a PAR EntreMundos

We build on Torre and Ayala's (2009) notion of a PAR EntreMundos by following the rounded contours of several linked and linking lineages: the southern tradition, critical race theory, indigenous and feminist knowledges. By advocating for a praxis that is reflexive and interdisciplinary in nature, it is inclusive of theories and methods from the physical sciences, social sciences, arts, and humanities. The site for research is the local community, acknowledging the expertise of community members, identifying the indigenous counter-narratives to the dominant versions of history and culture, and challenging the oppressive conditions that surround us. The methods for collecting and presenting data are embedded in the cultural and creative productions of the local community, and often include poetry, music, dance, theater, and other forms of cultural and artistic expressions (Fox, 2015; Rivera & Pedraza, 2000). Knowledge production is understood as a collective process that involves community members as researchers and becomes an accessible mixture of scholarly theory and everyday experience. The intersectionality of race and racism with other forms of oppression, including sexism, classism, homophobia and xenophobia, is a central approach to analysis. Because of its collaborative nature, it is also deeply reflexive and takes seriously the relational aspects of the research collective. At its best, the local site of the research is not only transformed but the researchers are "awakened" to a critical sense of social injustice and inspired as activists.

A PAR EntreMundos seeks personal and collective transformation, engages the richness of our multiplicities, and works from a position of integration, amidst, or perhaps because of, choques or conflict (Anzaldúa, 1987; Torre & Ayala, 2009). From a position of integration or wholeness, our individual lives, bodies, and emotions can be validated along with our intellectual work. As the collective work challenges knowledge hierarchies, other binaries can be more easily be questioned, interrupted or dismantled. The work of a PAR EntreMundos then, can in part be a way to heal communities and ourselves by "wholing" the fragmentations imposed upon us. We stress the *search* part of research: a search for silenced knowledges and actions of reclaiming, re-collection and re-creation. Re-creation, because our flowing in, blending with, and traversing between multiple ways of knowing, is an act of creation/ creativity, though not necessarily a harmonious one. As bell hooks describes teaching to transgress (1994), we see PAR EntreMundos as a methodology and epistemology that transgresses, edge-walks, and bridge-builds. Perhaps this "transgression" is a step towards the transformation we seek in teacher education.

Informed by these lineages and the work of other PAR collectives, we developed a set of eight guiding principles for a PAR EntreMundos. We offer these as a guide rather than a formula, which presupposes a "standard" way of conducting PAR. These principles are as follows:

Participation. Practitioners and stakeholders should be involved in all steps of research (design, data collection, analysis, dissemination).

Critical inquiry. The work needs to be grounded in critical-race and decolonizing theories that examine the socio-historical, socio-political and material contexts and conditions of our lives.

Knowledge co-construction. Knowledge that informs action is produced in collaboration with communities, where researchers and researched become a collective of knowledge-producers/actors.

*Power with(in)** The collective critically reflects on its own process, fosters trusting relationships of mutuality between members, examines power within the group, and engages in deep self-inquiry.

Indigenous cosmologies. In the spirit of an approach to PAR that is EntreMundos and that grows from the southern tradition, we see it as a way to reclaim and reimagine indigenous ways of knowing and engaging in this work as a healing process for the individual and community.

Creative praxes. The methods for collecting and presenting data are embedded in the cultural and creative productions of the local community, which may include poetry, music, dance, theater, and other forms of cultural and artistic expressions.

Transformational action. There is a commitment to conscious action and social change using creative praxes and engaged policy.

Concientizacion para la colectiva. This work is part of a movement, not simply separate sets of isolated actions, whose goals include critical consciousness, social justice, and mutual liberation/emancipation from oppression.

These principles have common elements with other articulations of PAR, particularly that, within projects, participation is key, knowledge is co-constructed, reflective actions are taken, relationships within collectives are attended to, and issues of power are critically examined. We add to these formulations ideas that stem from the lineages discussed earlier in the chapter, including vocabularies of mestizaje, concientizacion, and creative praxes. In Part II, we explain the workings of a set of projects that illustrate the various principles described above.

References

Anzaldúa, G. (1987/1999). *Borderlands la frontera: The new mestiza*. San Francisco, CA: Spinsters/Aunt Lute.

Arrien, A. (1993). *The four-fold way: Walking the paths of the warrior, teacher, healer and Visionary*. New York, NY: HarperOne.

Borunda, R. (2011). *What is the color of your heart: A humanist approach to diversity*. Des Moines, IA: Kendall Hunt Publishing.

Cammarota, J., & Fine, M. (Eds.). (2008). *Revolutionizing education: Youth participatory action research in motion*. New York, NY: Routledge.

Chataway, C. J. (1997). An examination of the constraints on mutual inquiry in a participatory action research project. *Journal of Social Issues, 53*(4), 747–765.

Delgado Bernal, D. (2002). Critical race theory, Latino critical theory, and critical raced-gendered epistemologies: Recognizing students of color as holders and creators of knowledge. *Qualitative Inquiry, 8*(1), 105–126.

Delgado Bernal, D., & Villalpando, O. (2002). An apartheid of knowledge in academia: The struggle over the "legitimate" knowledge of faculty of color. *Equity & Excellence in Education, 35*(2), 169–180.

Ensler, E. (2011). *I am an emotional creature: The secret life of girls around the world*. New York, NY: Villard.

Estés, C.P. (2010). *The dangerous old woman: Myths and stories of the wise woman archetype*. Boulder, CO: Soundstrue.

Fals-Borda, O. (1979). Investigating the reality in order to transform it: The Colombian experience. *Dialectical Anthropology, 4*, 33–55.

Fals-Borda, O. (1996). A north-south convergence on the quest for meaning. *Qualitative Inquiry, 2*(1), 76–87.

Ferreira, M. P., & Gendron, F. (2011). Community-based participatory research with traditional and indigenous communities of the Americas: Historical context and future directions. *The International Journal of Critical Pedagogy, 3*(3), 153–168.

Fitzgerald, J., & Fitzgerald, M.O. (Eds.). (2005). *The spirit of Indian women*. Bloomington, IN: World Wisdom, Inc.

Fox, M. (2015). Embodied methodologies, participation and the art of research. *Social and Personality Psychology Compass, 9*(7), 321–332.

Freire, P. (1993). *Pedagogy of the oppressed.* New York, NY: Continuum Press.

Freire, P. (1994). *Education for critical consciousness.* New York, NY: Continuum.

Freire, P. (1998). *The Paulo Freire reader* (M. A Freire & D. Macedo, Eds.). New York, NY: Continuum Press.

Garza-Falcón, L. (1998). Maria Cristina Mena's Elite, Fermina Guerra's "Folk": The struggles of their distinct and converging worlds. In *Gente Decente: A Borderlands Response to the Rhetoric of Dominance.* Austin: University of Texas Press,133–155.

Gaventa, J. (1993). The powerful, the powerless, and the experts: Knowledge struggles in an information age. In P. Park, M. Brydon Miller, B. Hall & T. Jackson (Eds.) *Voices of change: Participatory research in the United States and Canada.* Ontario: OISE Press, 21–40.

Guishard, M. (2009). The false paths, the endless labors, the turns now this way and now that: Participatory action research, mutual vulnerability, and the politics of inquiry. *Urban Review, 41*(1), 85–105.

Hall, B. L. (1981). Participatory research, popular knowledge and power: A personal reflection. *Convergence, 14*(3), 6.

Harding, S. (1993). Rethinking standpoint epistemology: What is "strong objectivity?" In L. Alcoff & E. Potter (Eds.), *Feminist epistemologies.* New York, NY: Routledge.

Healy, K. (2001). Participatory action research and social work: A critical appraisal. *International Social Work, 44*(1), 93–105.

Hill Collins, P. (1991). *Black feminist thought: Knowledge, consciousness, and the politics of empowerment.* New York, NY: Routledge.

hooks, b. (1994). *Teaching to transgress: Education as the practice of freedom.* New York, NY: Routledge.

Hurtado, A. (2003). *Voicing Chicana feminisms: Young women speak out on sexuality and identity.* New York, NY: New York University Press.

Jenoure, T. (2000) *Navigators: African American musicians, dancers and visual artists in academe.* New York, NY: SUNY Press.

Jung, C.G. (1981). *The archetypes and the collective unconscious* (Collected Works of C.G. Jung Vol. 9, Part 1, 2nd ed.). Princeton, NJ: Princeton University Press.

Keating, A. L. (2008). Working toward wholeness: Gloria Anzaldúa's struggles to live with diabetes and chronic illness. In A. Chabram-Dernersesian & A. De La Torre (Eds.), *Speaking from the body: Latinas on health and culture* (pp. 133–143). Tucson, AZ: The University of Arizona Press.

Kelley, R. D. G. (2002). *Freedom dreams: The black radical imagination.* Boston, MA: Beacon Press.

Khanlou, N., & Peter, E. (2005). Participatory action research: Considerations for ethical review. *Social Science & Medicine, 60*(10), 2333–2340.

Krumer-Nevo, M. (2009). From voice to knowledge: Participatory action research, inclusive debate and feminism. *International Journal of Qualitative Studies in Education, 22*(3), 279–295.

Lara, I. (2002). Healing suenos for academia. In G. Anzaldúa & A. Keating (Eds.), *This bridge we call home: Radical visions for transformation* (pp. 433–438). New York, NY: Routledge.

Lewin, K. (1946). Action research and minority problems. *Journal of Social Issues, 2*(4), 34–46.

Lynn, M., & Parker, L. (2006). Critical race studies in education: Examining a decade of research in U.S. schools. *The Urban Review, 38,* 257–334.

Martín-Baró, I. (1994). *Writings for a liberation psychology.* Cambridge, MA: Harvard University Press.

Matsuda, M. (1995). Looking to the bottom: Critical legal studies and reparations. In K. Crenshaw, N. Gotanda, G. Peller, & K. Thomas (Eds.), *Critical race theory: The key writings that formed the movement* (pp. 63–79). New York, NY: New Press.

Moraga, C., & Anzaldúa, G. (1981). *This bridge called my back: Writings by radical women of color.* Watertown, MA: Persephone Press.

Nelson, G., Ochocka, J., Griffin, K., & Lord, J. (1998). "Nothing about me, without me": Participatory action research with self-help/mutual aid organizations for psychiatric consumer/survivors. *American Journal of Community Psychology, 26*(6), 881–912.

Ozanne, J. L., & Saatcioglu, B. (2008). Participatory action research. *Journal of Consumer Research, 35*(3), 423–439.

Paiva, A. P. (1992). *Y...El anciano hablo [And...The elder spoke].* Cusco, Peru: J.C. editors.

Parker, L., & Villalpando, O. (2007). A racial(ized) perspective on educational leadership: Critical race theory in educational administration. *Educational Administration Quarterly, 43*(5), 519–524.

Perez, L. (2010). Decolonizing sexuality and spirituality in Chicana feminist and queer art. Tikkun Magazine Queer Spirituality and Politics Online Exclusive, 24(4) http://www.tikkun.org/article.php/july2010perez.

Reason, P. (1994). Three approaches to participatory inquiry. In N. K. Denzin & Y. S. Lincoln (Eds.), *Handbook of qualitative research.* Thousand Oaks: Sage, 324–339.

Rivera, R. (2003). *New York Ricans from the Hip Hop Zone.* New York, NY: Palgrave Macmillan.

Rivera, M., & Pedraza, P. (2000). The spirit of transformation: An education reform movement in a New York City Latino/a community. In S. Nieto (Ed.), *Puerto Rican Students in U.S. Schools.* Mahwah, NJ: Lawrence Erlbaum Publishers.

Schaefer, C. (2006). Grandmothers counsel the world: Women elders offer their vision for our planet. South Africa: Trumpeter.

Selener, D. (1997). *Participatory action research and social change* (No. Ed. 2). The Cornell Participatory Action Research Network, Cornell University.

Solórzano, D. G., & Bernal, D. D. (2001). Examining transformational resistance through a critical race and LatCrit theory framework Chicana and Chicano students in an urban context. *Urban Education, 36*(3), 308–342.

Solórzano, D., & Yosso, T. J. (2002). Critical race methodology: Counter-storytelling as an analytical framework for education research. *Qualitative Inquiry, 8,* 23–44.

Starhawk. (2003). Toward an activist spirituality. *Reclaiming Quarterly. Tikkun Magazine,* July/August On-line Exclusive.

Torre, M. E. (2009). Participatory action research and critical race theory: Fueling spaces for nos-otras to research. *Urban Review*, *41*(1), 106–120.

Torre, M. E., & Ayala, J. (2009). Envisioning participatory action research entremundos. *Feminism & Psychology*, *19*, 387.

Wall, S. (1993). *Wisdom's daughters: Conversations with women elders of Native America*. New York, NY: Harper Collins Publishers.

Whyte, W. F. E. (1991). *Participatory action research*. London: Sage Publications.

Wingeier, D. E. (1980). Generative words in six cultures. *Religious Education*, *75*(5), 563–576.

Yosso, T. J. (2005). Whose culture has capital? A critical race discussion of community cultural wealth. *Race Ethnicity and Education*, *8*(1), 69–81.

· P A R T I I ·

PAR ENTREMUNDOS IN ACTION

From tracing our theoretical roots, to summarizing our understandings of PAR within a set of principles that guide our work, we move next to a set of PAR examples in action. These are projects that various members of the NLERAP PAR committee have engaged in over the years. With these projects, we attempt to illustrate different ways that guiding principles have been expressed within particular projects. Though they may address many of the principles to varying degrees, each case will highlight only a few, documenting the challenges and opportunities related to participatory work in education contexts. Rodríguez's PRAXIS Project focuses on the themes of critical inquiry and knowledge co-construction; Cammarota's SJEP project delves into participation, concientizacion de la colectiva and creative praxes; Rivera and colleagues' work highlights creative praxes, power with(in), and indigenous cosmologies; the NJUYRI discusses transformative action and participation; Mayorga's piece emphasizes concientizacion para la colectiva; and Cushing-Leubner & Eik's linguistic right article describes participation, critical inquiry and describes transformational action. Across the projects, authors describe the goals and outcomes of the work, couched in terms of self-knowledge, community expertise and action, and humanistic engagement alongside academic skill work. We include some detail in these chapters about the process and pedagogy of PAR, revealing behind-the-scenes glimpses of PAR in action across sites in the US.

· 2 ·

THE PRAXIS PROJECT

Participatory Research Advocating for Excellence in Schools

Louie F. Rodríguez

Context

The PRAXIS Project, Participatory Research Advocating for Excellence in Schools, is a school based, university-affiliated research collaborative aimed at recognizing and responding to the education crisis facing the Inland Empire. The Inland Empire, including San Bernardino and Riverside Counties in Southern California, is home to nearly 5 million people. Nearly 80% of the school-age population is either African-American or Latino, over 30% of the students are English Language Learners, and the community is faced with a 50%+ dropout rate. Educational attainment figures are dismal, especially among communities of color. Less than 10% of adults between 25 and 29 years of age have a bachelor's degree, and year after year less than 10% of high school graduates are eligible for the state university system. Beyond education, the region faces one of the highest crime rates in the country (Institute of Applied Research, 2016), a significantly high unemployment rate (The Inland Empire Center, 2011), and had one of the highest foreclosure rates in the country during the nation-wide economic recession (Swanstrom, Chapple, & Immergluck, 2009).

It is within this social and educational context that a response was needed. The objectives would need to be complex and multifaceted including transforming the institutional conditions that facilitate counterproductive outcomes, engaging students in the research and action process itself, and community-focused by engaging as many stakeholders as possible. These objectives would facilitate a series of outcomes that would be focused on equity, social justice, and creating opportunities for students, teachers, and other stakeholders develop an individual and collective community consciousness.

Therefore, The PRAXIS Project was born at Community Regional High School (CRHS)[1]. CRHS serves over 3,300 students with a majority-minority student population. Latinxs comprise of over 80% of the student population with a remainder of African-Americans, Asian-Americans, and Whites making up the other 20%. Two-thirds of the student body qualifies for free-reduced lunch and nearly 1/3 of the students are English Language Learners. Given the demographic transformation of the region, Latinx immigrant students have maintained a slow but steady increase over the last decade. A vast majority of the teaching corps is White and middle class, although there has been a steady increase in Latinx teachers over the last several years. Despite the diversity of the school, there are at least two worlds within the school. A walk through the school would show that the high level academic courses (i.e., Honors, AP) are filled by mostly White and Asian students whereas Latinx students are either relegated to the low-level courses or placed in the AVID program. The AVID program serves low-middle achievers interested in college. There are currently 500 students in the AVID program and the program leaders would like to see the program expanded but there are at least two barriers. The first is that certain faculty members are not interested in adopting the model, which has demonstrated to be very successful at CRHS. The second challenge is the economic restraint on the school. Because the AVID program requires an "elective" assignment for many students, the school has to choose between providing required courses for graduation or electives such as AVID. According to several conversations with the principal, this dilemma is attributable to the financial situation affecting the school (and the entire state for that matter).

Once a California Distinguished School in 1986, the school has recently faced many academic, financial, and cultural challenges. While there are always a small group of successful students that matriculate into four-year colleges, a majority of graduating seniors either enter the dismal workforce, attend private for-profit 2-year schools, or don't have a plan at all. Aside from the graduating classes that pass through CRHS, for decades, only half of all entering freshman actually graduate four years later. Each year about 1,100 students enter as freshman but only 500 students walk across the stage four years later, according to the information that was shared with me by one of the counselors. While the situation is on the radar for school administrators and counselors, there is not much recognition of this crisis beyond these educators. The community is largely unaware of the school's graduation rate as are many of the teachers. It is as if the 500+ students that disappear over this four-year span is something that is expected. In other words, there is a degree of complacency in expectations or altogether unawareness of the challenges facing the school. When I asked one of the administrators what happens to those 500+ students, he simply said, "we don't know".

Origins of the PRAXIS Project

In recognition of this complacency and knowledge that schools do indeed matter, The PRAXIS Project was born. The Principal Investigator and a majority of the research team are not only affiliated with California State University, San Bernardino, but we are also alumni of Community Regional High School. Many of us still live in the community, have family that attend the school, and are committed to developing equitable opportunities for students, particularly those that have historically been left behind.

Recognizing the significance of rigorous, empirical research, The PRAXIS Project aims to serve as a partner with schools and community stakeholders to effectively respond to the education crisis facing the region. The PRAXIS Project institutes a series of pedagogical and curricular experiences for youth to engage with research, share their experiences and voices, and create a public platform to affect research, policy and practice. In addition to the research, The PRAXIS Project aims to institute a series of advocacy efforts that are rooted in collaboration, community-building, and an expectation of excellence for all children across the Inland Empire.

Project Description

In December 2009, the principal of CRHS contacted Dr. Louie F. Rodríguez from California State University, San Bernardino. The principal was interested in collaborative efforts to help improve the overall quality of education for all students at CRHS. As an educator and researcher in urban education, Dr. Rodríguez responded by focusing on his area of expertise—helping to recognize and respond to the dropout/graduation rate crisis in the Inland Empire by focusing on an initiative at CRHS.

Prior to work at CRHS, the Dr. Rodríguez directed several school-based, university affiliated research projects related to issues of student engagement, school culture, school dropout, and school policy analysis as it related to student achievement and experiences in school (see Conchas & Rodríguez, 2007; Rodríguez, 2004, 2008a, 2008b, 2010; Rodríguez & Brown, 2009; Rodríguez & Wasserberg, 2010). These projects took place in Boston, Miami, and now the Inland Empire. This work has focused on the voices and experiences of low-income youth of color. It is well documented in educational research that students are one of the most neglected and voiceless groups when it comes to educational reform and change. This reality is counterintuitive when the people most directly affected by the theories, policies, and practices in education—the students—are the least likely to be consulted to evaluate their effectiveness. Thus, The PRAXIS Project aims to fill this void, not just as a contribution to research, but in school, district, and state policy-formation, pedagogical decision making, evaluation, and school and classroom practice.

The PRAXIS Project is comprised of Louie F. Rodríguez as its principal investigator and a research team of 6 researchers and student assistants currently in college (CSU, San Bernardino, UC Riverside, Riverside Community College, and San Bernardino Valley College), or graduate school across the Inland Empire. Among the members of the team include 4 CRHS alumni from the 1980s, 1990s, and 2000s (during the 2011–2012 school year, we added two CRHS graduates from the Class of 2010. The research team also included the teacher-on-record and the entire group of student researchers (see below).

In agreement with school administration and a teacher-on-record, The PRAXIS Project entered on the classroom twice per week during the Spring 2010 semester and concentrated research efforts with two Multicultural Issues courses involving a total of 76 students. The classes were selected based on the curricular flexibility associated with the course, which was a social science elective for 11th and 12th grade students. After engaging students in several pedagogical activities, a contest was held and students creatively named themselves *Students Encouraging Change through Our Research* (SECTOR 45, periods 4 and 5). During the second year, we partnered with a new group of students (34) and concentrated efforts with just one class due to scheduling and accessibility.

Methods

Upon entry into the school, students were made aware of the two primary objectives of the research project: 1) to engage high school students in an action project that gives them a voice to address student engagement issues in school, and 2) to allow researchers to understand how participation in these processes will impact student engagement and achievement in large city high schools such as those in the Inland Empire. Parent consent and student assent were acquired. The objective of the project is to expand understanding of the role of meaningful student engagement to mediate against student failure and produce critical, high-performing, college-bound students. Through qualitative methods, this research plan aims to identify specific practices that alienate children from school and offer insights into how high school students meaningfully engage with school (Maxwell, 1996). This proposed project is driven by the following three overarching research questions.

1. What are the root causes of student (dis)engagement across two classrooms of high school students in two similarly structured urban public high schools in the Inland Empire?
2. In what ways can these students be re(engaged) to mediate dropout and promote student success (i.e., boost graduate and college-going rates)?
3. To what degree can the lessons learned from this project be utilized to guide our understanding and prevention of student dropout at the school, district, and national level?

In this research, The PRAXIS Project aims to establish a model that can be used to reduce dropouts among the students who have been historically marginalized. By utilizing the voices and experiences of students, we hoped that the research process itself will promote the process of school engagement for students, particularly low-income students of color in struggling schools. It should be noted that the three overarching research questions are different from the questions that are co-constructed with students in the PAR process (see Appendix A for matrix).

Theoretical Perspectives

Lessons from Freire's Liberatory Pedagogy. Freire contends that education either serves to domesticate or liberate the masses (Shor, 1993). Domesticating education reduces the educational endeavor to a prescribed method of instruction where knowledge transfer and fact memorization is the goal. Known as the "banking" method, teachers are responsible for depositing knowledge into students. In such classrooms, education is "something done to them [students]" (Shor, 1993, p. 26).

In liberatory education, on the other hand, teachers utilize problem-posing methods that encourage students to capitalize on knowledge from their own lives by connecting real-life issues with academic content and in some cases, such experiences and knowledge-bases become the academic content. As such, liberatory classrooms encourage students to ask critical questions, create and own knowledge, and work to realize democratic processes in classrooms and in society. The goal is to create spaces where students learn by "recreat[ing] the way we see ourselves, our education and our society" (Shor, 1993, p. 26). To work toward creating a liberatory education, there are several theoretical foundations drawn from the ideas of Paulo Freire: *desocialization*, *dialogic*, and *activist*.

Desocialization processes were employed to democratically engage students in the production of knowledge and social change. Because students, particularly in today's high-stakes standardized testing environment are often exposed to Test-Prep Pedagogies (Rodríguez, 2009) whereby passivity and domestication is expected, they are by and large taught to be silent listeners who regurgitate facts. Very little meaning is made and students are rarely incited to personally, politically, or intellectually connect with the "official" academic content. According to Freire, liberatory pedagogies must desocialize students against this anti-intellectual and authority-dependence culture that is often fostered in schools (Freire, 1970). Unfortunately, desocialization is necessary for high school students because they have been subjected to this form of domesticating education for much of their lives in school.

The second idea that informed this initiative is that of dialogical pedagogy. As proposed by Freire, dialogical practices privilege problem-posing processes between students and teachers. Learning is scaffolded and students are encouraged to create knowledge. Within this principle, education is not an endeavor that is "done" to students but rather they are active participants in the production and utilization of knowledge. Again, such practices are particularly significant in the Test-Prep Pedagogy era—pedagogies by which students and teachers are, because of pressure to perform on a test, subjected to teaching and learning activity that revolves around test preparation and reinforced by school cultures that perpetuate a test-taking ethos. Teaching and learning opportunities that privilege dialogue, for instance, are often absent in these environments. Dialogical practices aim to challenge this counterproductive culture by creating spaces to engage in dialogue and encourage students to be active participants by "doing" education.

Finally, this initiative was driven by the idea of activist engagement: the process and outcome of the educational endeavor is driven by transformation. In other words, the classroom culture and the intellectual work should prioritize a quest for social change. Students and teachers should be given the opportunity to practice and experience change in the classroom, as both a practice of freedom and as they work toward a larger goal for social change. These efforts and intentions should be fluid, dynamic, and democratic.

In The PRAXIS Project, our pedagogical approaches are directly informed by the core tenets of Critical Race Theory/Praxis. In our engagement with students, we are conscious of the representative voices in the room by race, generational status, language, gender, class, and sexual orientation. We are aware that voices of immigrant and English Learners can easily be drowned out by their U.S. born counterparts, even those that are of Mexican origin. Similarly, we are also conscious of class differences and gender dynamics so much so that we are conscious of male dominance during our dialogues. We also challenge dominant ideology, particularly through the curriculum, by introducing more culturally, contextually, and historically relevant material to students at Community Regional High School. Our curriculum not only disrupts traditional constructions of history and knowledge, but we also engage in pedagogical activities that are committed to social justice. We discuss the transformative role of teachers (hooks, 1994; Solórzano & Delgado Bernal, 2001), the significance of student-teacher relationships (Valenzuela, 1999), and give credence to the lived experiences of marginalized groups within the U.S. context (see Yosso's Community Cultural Wealth description, 2005).

Pedagogical Approach

Because of the action-oriented nature of Participatory Action Research (PAR), the research team strategically selected several core elements of a pedagogical and curricular experience. We arranged our approach around four key experiences we find to be crucial to the development of critical, reflective, and action-oriented student-researchers. The four elements are: (1) Educational Journeys, (2) the History of Educational Inequality, (3) Powerful Ideas in Education, and (4) the Group Research Project. Such efforts position student-researchers to gain consciousness about critical issues salient to the condition of education in the U.S. and the Inland Empire and acquire a series of practical skills such as developing and understanding research, identifying research questions, data collection strategies, data analysis, and dissemination. Below is a synopsis of the key areas covered in the course.

Educational Journeys

The Educational Journeys exercise is a pedagogical and curricular tool that reflects the values, beliefs, and principles that drive the PRAXIS Project. Freire stated, "…the starting point for a political-pedagogical process must be precisely at the level of the people's aspirations and dreams, their understanding of reality and their forms of action and struggle". In recognition of this, the Educational Journeys aim to provide students with the opportunity to reflect and represent key moments in their personal educational journeys that were most significant. Students are encouraged to identify both positive and negative experiences and capture those experiences on a large piece of chart paper. Some students elect to write poems, construct PowerPoint presentations, or create musical lyrics. To initiate the process, members of the research team share their journeys as a gesture to open-up, build community, and position ourselves in a vulnerable role of presenting to complete strangers about very personal educational experiences. Often times, the educational scars that students have endured within the school system are shared as well as moments of triumph and success. It's not uncommon to find tears of pain and joy shared during the student presentations.

The purpose of the Educational Journeys is to set the groundwork of the role of critical reflection and analysis as a way to theorize and find commonalities across our lives. We begin to see patterns of empowerment and disempowerment that is caused, perpetuated, or challenged by students' experiences in schools. We then dialogue about root causes and follow this with a series of questions based on their experiences (problem-posing pedagogy).

History of Educational Inequality

By and large, the history of people of color and their role as builders of knowledge are largely excluded from the curriculum and pedagogical practices in the K–12 school system. Thus, we aim to provide opportunities for students to explore relevant moments, court cases, and key figures and movements that have helped shape the path to educational equality and equity in U.S. schools and society. We cover history that privileges the experiences of African-Americans, Latinxs, Native Americans, Asian-Americans, and women. Below is a list of topics covered: Plessy v. Ferguson, The Great Debate between Booker T. Washington and WEB Dubois, Native American Education, Women in Education, Lopez v. Secommbe (1943), Mendez v. Westminster (1948), Brown v. Board of Education (1954), Plyler v. Doe (1981), Chicano Walkouts, and the Boston desegregation efforts in the early 1970s.

In addition to reading and discussing the cases, students are assembled into groups and "act out" their specific case. They are given creative license to communicate the core elements of the case in a 3-minute skit, mini-play, or other method of choice. This effort aims at acquiring a deeper understanding of the case and uses their creative energy to communicate the case to the entire class.

Powerful Ideas in Education

Another pedagogical approach to our work is to engage students in perspectives about education, schools, and society of which they are likely to have been deprived in their K–12 experience. In many ways, we share what critical scholars may teach university students, particularly those in certain teacher education and graduate programs across the country. The primary purpose is to expose students to the language and ideas that help guide the purpose of The PRAXIS Project. These key texts and authors include: Critical Race Theory by Daniel Solórzano, Pedagogy of the Oppressed by Paulo Freire, Teaching to Transgress by bell hooks, The Culture of Power by Lisa Delpit, The Hidden Curriculum by Jean Anyon, Subtractive Schooling by Angela Valenzuela.

By engaging with these key texts, students are encouraged to discuss, analyze, and connect these ideas with their own schooling experiences. These theoretical foundations serve as the basis by which they begin to engage in critical reflection of their own schooling experiences and shape a research topic for the group project.

Group Research Projects

The group research project is a core feature of the PAR project at Community Regional High School. Before assembling themselves into groups, students identify critical issues at their particular school and community. Then, based on topics, students select a group and commit to engaging in a two to three month research effort around that topic. Students create the research questions, identify participants, data collection methods, data analysis techniques, and shape the implications for their work. All students are required to present their findings to the class and are given the option to present their work to the school, school board, and community stakeholders. See Appendix A for a matrix that identifies the various topics, methodologies, and findings that have come out of these student-led projects.

Collaboration

The entire PAR process with the students is based on collaborative and dialogical decision-making. In recognition of the traditional power dynamics in classrooms, we aim to create a culture that values shared decision-making and shared power. Students have a direct say in every step of the process including the selection of research topics, identifying venues to share the research, and directions for advocacy and policy development.

Challenges and Opportunities

The most significant challenge we face is the resistance from the internal school culture. Because we aim to be very public about our work, it is not uncommon for us to share our findings in a public setting with a mixed crowd of both supportive and critical educators. At the end of year one, the student-researchers presented their findings to the entire CRHS staff (N=120) including administrators, teachers, staff, and specialists (i.e., instructional coaches, teachers on assignment, etc.). With an invitation from the school principal, we anticipated a warm reception. The reality was far from that.

Four student-research groups were scheduled to present on topics including dropouts, teaching quality, teacher quality, and the impact of the budget cuts on student engagement. When the students spoke about teacher quality and the important role teachers play in the lives of students, a subset of mostly teachers reacted quite surprisingly from the perspective of the research team. After the student-researchers shared their survey findings from a question about to what students attribute their motivation in school, not one respondent (out of 120 surveys) stated "teachers". In response to this finding, a small group of teachers responded with side chatter, laughter, and heard, albeit in a low tone a set of choice words in response to these findings. The student-researchers, the research team, and likely the other observers, were shocked. The student-researchers still in front of the room looked shocked and members of the research team gestured for them to continue on with their presentation.

The student-researchers finished their presentation and the principal proceeded to make an announcement. Because the contract day ended at 3:30 p.m. and there is no obligation for teachers to stay after that time, a significant number of teachers left, even when the principal urged teachers to stay and hear the last presentation, which focused on stellar teachers and excellence in teaching. Aware of the mass exodus out of the room, one student-researcher from the last presentation group said, "I appreciate those of you that stayed to hear our presentation. I'm offended that many teachers left and the disrespect is unacceptable. Teachers are supposed to be setting an example for us". We later learned that the teachers who actually stayed for the duration were the teachers who were already known to be supportive by the students and administrators.

Shortly after the presentation, we heard mixed reviews. However, the most enlightening responses were those expressing a "change of heart". Some of the audience members said something like, "after further thought, it was quite impressive to hear the students share their findings. While my initial response was defensive, we do indeed need to hear the voices and experiences of the people we serve—our students". A few days later, we received letters of support and encouragement by various stakeholders. Many stated, "we need to take advantage of this opportunity and listen to students".

This experience proved to be a pivotal point in the project. We came to realize that the work was not only important, but relevant given the responses we received. We realized that the wisdom associated with the students' voices can and will continue to face resistance depending on the context. We also discussed the meaning behind the reality of this very political act—the fact that young, mostly student-researchers of color can provide a structured and research-based critique of the school system and that the mostly middle-class educators can be largely resistant. We also realized that we needed to quickly build a network of community and parent support, so that we would not receive this response again.

Exactly one year later, we mobilized a cadre of powerful community members which included elected officials, regional and district school board members and administrators, parents, students, foundation leaders, non-profit presidents, and other professionals who were mostly Latinx alumni from CRHS. Students gave testimonies about their experiences with the project, parents in tears shared how proud they were of their children, and community members affirmed the work as critical to the advancement of the community. When the student-researchers presented at a community forum in April 2011, the once questionable reception we experienced was transformed into a space of love, recognition, and hope.

Impact

The need to be "public" about what is happening in public schools through the voices and experiences of Latinx youth is vital to the PAR-process. Because we were driven by dialogical pedagogy, Critical Race Praxis, and education for equity and social justice, the nature of our work is inherently political and shaped around advocacy and action. Thus, efforts to impact practice and policy was an intended goal of the project and evaluative metric for the PRAXIS Project. There have been at least three significant outcomes of our work so far.

1. After 8 years of implementation, the school's late policy has been eliminated as of August 2011. Our research, and the student-researchers' work specifically, designed, researched, and critiqued the negative impact of the school's tardy policy. We learned that because of the bureaucracy associated with the enforcement of the tardy policy, many students would miss most of their first class, even if they were one minute late. We also found that many students were tardy because of transportation issues associated with complicated family work schedules. As a result of our research, teachers are responsible for noting late students and they can immediately begin class without missing a significant amount of class time. During a meeting with the school principal in late August 2011, he noted that our research helped trigger a much needed conversation about the impact of the policy and a redirection which was supported by the district's highest levels of leadership.

2. The second significant impact of the PRAXIS Project is recognition of the dropout/graduation rate crisis facing the school. Because 50% of the students fail to graduate each year, one goal of The PRAXIS Project was to raise awareness of this problem and begin a conversation in and beyond the school. After being in the school for nearly two years, the school reported the highest graduation rate in the school's history as of June 2011. Although we cannot take sole credit for this increase

in graduation rates, we can say that putting emphasis on dropouts and raising issue with the graduation rate may have encouraged and incited action by the school's emphasis on promoting and pushing school staff to get students to graduate on time from high school. We learned that accountability comes in many forms and our goal to put this issue on the radar may have been just enough to get people to respond.

3. The third outcome is our ability to mobilize community members around key issues impacting the school and community. As of April 2011, we have begun to amass mostly CRHS alumni who are committed to creating opportunities, transforming outcomes, and promoting excellence at CRHS. Most of the interested alumni are Latinx professionals, living and not living in the immediate community and committed to engaging in meaningful work with the school. The PRAXIS Project is in the process of creating at least three work groups including students, alumni, and school staff.

Final Thoughts

The implications of The PRAXIS Project's work are multifaceted. Directly engaging with schools and districts suggests that shifts in institutional culture are possible when the local and district leadership are committed to change, and in this case, listening to and learning from the voices and experiences of students. Our work demonstrated both practical and policy changes are indeed possible at the local level. In some instances, policies across the district were positively impacted, such as the creation of mandatory student voice forums across the district high schools. This work also stimulated and implicated the significance that strong community-based support networks play when engaging in this work. We learned that there is an entire community of people ready and willing to support this kind of work. For many people like school alumni, there is interest and passion to "give back" yet many people do not see opportunities to do so. Our project facilitates community/alumni engagement. Finally, and perhaps most importantly, our work demonstrates the role that Participatory Action Research approaches play in transforming the consciousness of students. We believe that these kinds of experiences help create a dimension to students' identities that not only gives them an experience, but positions them as powerful and capable voices in the school and community. These experiences transform individuals that in turn help liberate entire communities.

Epilogue: The PRAXIS Project Update

At the time of this writing, the PRAXIS Project was essentially in "Phase II". While the majority of the story in this chapter revolved around key findings associated with the direct PAR work with youth and the larger school community, there were several elements of our action work that were referenced. In fact, over the last six years, we have been actively engaged in several partnership activities with local schools and community centralizing praxis. For instance, the Excellence Campaigns that were launched at one of the core sites continues to this day. In fact, in our region, Excellence Campaigns spread to three districts and several different sites including an elementary, middle, and high school. One district embraced the excellence work and launched a series of efforts that touches every school in its district in some way. One Excellence Campaign led to a series of school-based projects aimed to improve the schooling conditions and opportunities for students.

In addition to these tangible changes, several of the principles that evolved from the "10-Point Plan" have had important implications at the local level. Prior to this work, student voice was nowhere on the local or regional radar. Since our work, there has been more attention toward and inclusion of students' voices in the practical and policymaking processes of schools and districts. While there remains much work to be done, we are hopeful that a spark has been ignited. Finally, our work has contributed to the knowledge base that highlights the power and significance of bridging institutions across the community. For example, in one case, the district typically functioned without any significant connection to the community. As a result of our work, there are more conversations and more concrete examples that provides more opportunities for students (i.e., internships, jobs, skill development) and the community. Our hope is that the work continues led by the youth and the community.

References

Conchas, G. Q., & Rodríguez, L. F. (2007). *Small schools and urban youth: Using the power of school culture to engage students*. Thousand Oaks, CA: Corwin Press.

Freire, P. (1970). *Pedagogy of the oppressed*. New York, NY: Herder and Herder.

hooks, b. (1994). *Teaching to transgress: Education as the practice of freedom*. New York, NY: Routledge.

Institute of Applied Research. (2016). 2016 Inland Empire Annual Survey. San Bernardino, CA. Retrieved from http://iar.csusb.edu/reports/documents/AnnualReport2016FINAL.pdf

Maxwell, J. A. (1996). *Qualitative research design: An interactive approach.* Thousand Oaks, CA: Sage.

Rodríguez, L. F. (2004). Latinos and school reform: Voice, action and agency. *Revista: The Harvard Review of Latin America*, 3 (2), 38–39.

Rodríguez, L. F. (2008a). "Teachers Know You Can Do More": Manufacturing deliberate cultures of success for urban high school students. *Educational Policy*, 22(5), 758–780.

Rodríguez, L. F. (2008b). Struggling to recognize their existence: Student-adult relationships in the urban high school context. *The Urban Review*, 40(5), 436–453.

Rodríguez, L. F. (2009). Over-coming test prep pedagogy: Getting urban high school students to educate pre-service teachers using liberatory pedagogy. *The Sophist's Bane: The Journal of the Society of Professors of Education*, 5 (1/2), 30–36.

Rodríguez, L. F. (2010). What schools can do about the dropout crisis. *Leadership*, 40(1), 18–22.

Rodríguez, L. F., & Brown, T. M. (2009). Engaging youth in participatory action research for education and social transformation. *New Directions for Youth Development*, 123, 19–34.

Rodríguez, L. F., & Wasserberg, M. (2010). From the classroom to the country: Project POWER engages Miami's youth in action research initiatives for educational rights. *The Journal of Urban Education: Focus on Enrichment*, 7(30), 103–107.

Shor, I. (1993). Education is politics: Paulo Freire's critical pedagogy. In P. McLaren & P. Leonard (Eds.), *Paulo Freire: A critical encounter* (pp. 25–35). London: Routledge.

Solórzano, D. G., & Delgado Bernal, D. (2001). Examining transformational resistance through a critical race and LatCrit theory framework: Chicana and Chicano students in urban context. *Urban Education*, 36, 208–342.

Swanstrom, T., Chapple, K., & Immergluck, D. (2009). Regional resilience in the face of foreclosures: Evidence from six metropolitan areas (Working Paper 2009–05). Building Resilient Regions, Institute of Governmental Studies. Retrieved from http://brr.berkeley.edu/brr_workingpapers/2009-05-swanstrom_chapple_immergluck.pdf

The Inland Empire Center. (2011). Waiting for recovery. *Inland Empire Outlook: Economic and Political Analysis*, 2(2), 1–31. Retrieved from http://roseinstitute.org/wp-content/uploads/2015/02/Fall2011IEO.pdf

Valenzuela, A. (1999). *Subtractive schooling: U.S.-Mexican youth and the politics of caring.* Albany, NY: State University of New York Press.

Yosso, T. J. (2005). Whose culture has capital? A critical race theory discussion of community cultural wealth. *Race, Ethnicity, and Education*, 8(1), 69–91.

· 3 ·

THE SOCIAL JUSTICE EDUCATION PROJECT IN TUCSON, ARIZONA

Julio Cammarota

In the 2002/03 school year, the Social Justice Education Project (SJEP) started at Cerro High School in the Tucson Unified School District (TUSD) of Arizona. This specialized social science program has expanded (in only a few years) to three schools including Campo, Pima, and Mountain High Schools. There are a total of seven SJEP courses offered every year in TUSD. Students who tend to enroll in the SJEP are working-class Latinxs from the southwest area of Tucson. This high concentration of Latinx students results from the schools' locations, primarily in Latinx neighborhoods. White, African-American and Native American students are also enrolled in the SJEP.

Most importantly, the social science program is aligned with state-mandated history and U.S. government standards and involves students in youth participatory action research (YPAR) projects. The SJEP is a year-long course in which students gain all their social science credits for graduation and learn graduate-level participatory action research techniques. YPAR, in short, requires students to conduct their own original qualitative research and participate in every step of the research process. Furthermore, based on their research findings, students propose actions to solve problems in their particular social and economic contexts.

Their YPAR projects focus on critical analyses of social justice problems and include presentations to parents and members of their community to initiate change. Students learn qualitative research methods, most notably participant observation, for assessing and addressing the everyday injustices limiting their own and their peers' potential. Observations focus on different sites in the students' social context, which may include school, neighborhoods, and family. Students write up observations in weekly field notes. Students sometimes conduct interviews with peers or teachers at school. In addition, they may utilize other qualitative, visual or creative methods such as photo and video documentation or theater. These creative praxes usually involve presenting (through innovative modes) the evidence that supports the key patterns identified in field notes.

The objective of engaging young people in research is two-fold. First, when students delve into critical analysis of their own social and economic contexts, they begin to develop their critical consciousness. That is, they become aware of the forces of oppression limiting their potential for self-determination—the ability to define existence with a positive, healthy perception of Self. In addition, critical consciousness involves an awareness of the capability to challenge oppressive forces limiting self-determination. Second, the emergence of awareness of how to address oppression leads to a blossoming of a critical intellectualism in which students recognize they have the intelligence to transform themselves, education, and their communities. This transformation is based on redefining learning, or the attainment of knowledge as a process of action that intends to improve living conditions within the students' own social and economic contexts.

Meeting the objective of developing critical consciousness and critical intellectualism produces the outcomes of higher levels of engagement in education and community and improved academic performance. These outcomes occur when students realize that education is more than self-edification but also a way to take action to improve lives within and beyond their communities. This expansion of the meaning and purpose of education explains why SJEP students are the strongest activists for ethnic studies in Tucson, Arizona and outperform their Non-SJEP peers at school in standardized tests, graduation rates and college enrollment. A natural by-product of expressing critical consciousness and intellectualism is the establishment of a robust academic identity.

The Selection of Research Themes

Students choose to investigate problems and issues that affect them personally. For example, they select research themes from words in their own poetry that express various problems they face in their social worlds. " 'Words' are both part of the 'world' and the means through which it is shaped and transformed" (Roberts, 1998, p. 110). The following Poem, "Big Colorful Place" by Zulem Sonoqui is an example of a student poem that expresses words employed to generate themes for investigation.

> —I can't help but watch all these people interacting with each other. Some just talk, other people fight with an anger so deep that it fills their heads with rage.
> —They seem unhappy. The people living unhappy lives know what's going on, they know how it is to live in an unjust place.
> —But I also notice one thing. I notice how some human beings seem to think in their pinche cabezas that they are higher than another human being, that they are of big value and I notice how they spit in the face of these people whose skin is red and burnt from the flames of the sun and step on the hands that don't stop working, the ones that have blisters and their skin so rough and peely.
> —I hear the yells, I hear the altercations and the sayings.
> —They talk about society and illegal aliens coming in left and right to a whites only place.
> —We all know who they call illegal aliens, but would they call a person from Europe an alien?
> —I listen to all this bullshit and I just think to myself, "Why?"
> —They express it in the way of whoever doesn't have their color, falls beneath their shoes.
> —I think of just knocking the s*** out of them with the power that has been building up more and more and asking how does it feel to be down there.
> —They imagine that people like me are trouble and we evolved just to serve them.
> —But I try to believe and think positive.
> —We know there's a lot of people out there, with this attitude, so what do I do?
> —There's only the way to think outside the premises and say something!

Students collectively identify the poignant "generative themes" throughout their poems. From the above poem, students listed the themes of racism, discrimination, immigration, and political movements. Identifying "generative themes" or words from poetry derives from Freire's (1993, 1994, 1998) critical literacy approach. A critical literacy facilitates students' production of new meanings and ideas that counter dominant hegemonic messages, myths, and beliefs designed to perpetuate subordination (Renner, Brown, Steins, & Burton, 2010). "A 'generative theme' is a theme that elicits interest from the participants because it is drawn from their lives" (Peckham, 2003, p. 231). Themes are therefore relevant and moreover speak to the social, political, and economic conditions of students. Educators have employed generative themes for critical and transformative learning processes in a variety of educational areas/subjects, including special needs, bilingual education, math, and service learning (Gent, 2009; Goldstein, 1995; Gutstein, 2006).

Although SJEP students select generative themes from poetry, they conduct research observations prior to the creation of poetry and selection of themes. Observation of the student's lived context, according to the Freirean literacy approach, is a preliminary step for developing generative themes (Barndt, 1998). Freire recommends that "researchers" or "investigators" apart from the students should conduct the observations (Roberts, 1994). However, in the SJEP, students are the researchers who identify poignant words in their own lived context. Students who conduct systematic and structured observation ensure the selection of themes with the greatest relevance. For instance, in the above poetic example, a group of five students identified the topic of "discrimination" because they agree with the poem's author that some people treat Latinxs unfairly. This topic may lead to other themes, such as language oppression, anti-immigration laws, educational tracking, or suspensions, which may suggest how institutional policies instigate the problem of mistreatment.

Problematization of Themes

Once a generative theme is selected, the process moves to problematization in order to ensure that symptoms of problems noted in generative themes are not mistaken for root causes. Instead, students focus on the root causes and realize that a deviation toward symptoms will only lead to a superficial and ineffective understanding of the problem. For instance, if the students select the generative theme of racial tracking for investigation, they need to understand that dropping out and segregation are symptoms of the problem and not the root cause.

With the example of "discrimination" as a generative theme, the five students moved through a process in which they listed symptoms prior to understanding the root causes. Symptoms of discrimination may include disengagement, absenteeism, low achievement, or failure. After identifying symptoms, students began to discuss and identify root causes to the problem of discrimination. Students discussing the term's root causes noticed how power, colonization, or racism represented the foundation or "roots" for problems related to discriminatory or unfair treatment. Once the roots have been identified, students look for solutions by discussing how specific processes and practices influence or contribute to maintaining root causes in their own social environments. In regards to "discrimination", students pointed to educational policies and practices, such as English-only strategies or ability grouping programs (tracking) that continue to sustain the roots of power, colonization, and racism.

After students completed the problematization of discrimination, they determined the focus of their YPAR projects. Because several students in our thematic case of discrimination had direct experience with discriminatory treatment in ELD (English Language Development) programs, they selected the topic of ELD for a research focus. The five students from Mountain High formed a project group and focused their research on cultural/language discrimination at school. In the ELD programs, students' greater understanding of Spanish, more so than English, would instigate conflicts with their teachers. When students could not adequately articulate their thoughts or comments in English and resorted to Spanish to communicate, teachers would frequently castigate them. This castigation would include punishment in the form of extra assignments, afterschool detention, or verbal humiliation. The language/cultural discrimination group documented these interactions to demonstrate the colonizing approach to the teaching practices of ELD programs.

Data Collection

The primary method for documenting school experiences is participant observation and the writing up of field notes. We ask students to conduct observations of their day-to-day school life through the Freirian lens of "reading the world". This approach to observation requires students to understand Freire's critical literacy, with an emphasis on capturing the social practices and processes that influence their interactions with teachers and other students. In other words, students learn to pay attention to and document the external forces bearing down on their social relationships.

This orientation of capturing the social influences to one's existence requires what Freire calls conscientization. A student who attains conscientization no longer views obdurate social and economic obstacles (i.e. lack of resources or opportunities) as an internal problem with the Self but rather deriving from external factors (policies and practices) initiated by others. Conscientization allows one to stop blaming the Self for negative experiences and outcomes while realizing the actions of others, or lack thereof, present barriers to certain accomplishments and goals. Thus, changing one's existence involves addressing the conflicts in social relationships and attuning oneself to internal capabilities to bring about transformation.

The attainment of conscientization requires a deep commitment to observe the surrounding circumstances to understand how social practices and processes either facilitate or diminish human potential. Conducting observations with conscientization will lead to two important discoveries. First, students will notice how daily external pressures impede any forward progress and thus attainment of success. Second, students will become empowered and realize that they have the potential to excel regardless of other people's deleterious judgments. These discoveries are concomitant and manifest only when the student focuses observations on the social practices and processes that impede progress and therefore must be changed to improve educational experiences. By focusing on social impediments, students recognize that they have advanced cognitive capabilities because they inevitably intellectualize and theorize the moves necessary to bring about changes.

Conducting participant observation that leads to discoveries of social impediments along with personal capabilities is what Freire might define as praxis—critical reflection and action. Praxis involves reflecting or "observing" a situation and then understanding the changes necessary to improve conditions within this situation. The only way to properly identify the required change is to initiate actions that manifest improved circumstances. From these actions, new knowledge illuminates how the structure and content of situations are contingent upon human exigencies. Thus, the inevitable epiphany emerging from this new knowledge is that alternative and just human contributions will produce better and more equitable conditions.

Because students must provide a detailed reflection on a situation and write down thoughts on how to initiate improvements, observations and field notes constitute praxis. Subsequently, the participant observation method generates new knowledge on how to take action to ameliorate conditions. Praxis embedded in the students' participant observation provides details of the site in question and a strong commitment to write about an approach that engenders greater justice. Action occurs through this commitment to put down in writing the words that theorize new possibilities and practices of learning. The following represents the praxis of students' field notes in which they demonstrate their conscientization and their drive for social justice. I have taken the language/cultural discrimination group's raw observational data and created narratives to better understand meaning and context of the situation under discussion.

Student Observational Data

One student, Zury Gonzalez, writes in her notes about a teacher who misinterprets policies around language and education and tells her that she should not speak Spanish. In her freshman year, she was incapable of communicating or writing in English and would often rely on Spanish to communicate with peers to understand course material. The teacher decided to punish her for speaking Spanish by assigning Zury a paper with the topic of "Why We Shouldn't Talk Spanish in Class". She attempted to write the paper but had difficulty with the English language. Her limited English ability prevented her from completing the assignment, so the teacher decided to punish her with afterschool detention. She writes that she was not a special case and that many of her fellow ELL students received detention for speaking Spanish. These students started to make the erroneous connection between speaking Spanish and having disciplinary problems. Zury mentions that many of her ELL classmates started to internalize the belief that because they spoke Spanish, they were a "problem" or delinquent students. The unintended consequence of punishing students for speaking Spanish is that these students adopt the belief that there is something wrong with them, that they are not well-adapted, normal students. Students with this mindset will disengage, become marginalized, and feel incapable of learning.

Being reprimanded for speaking Spanish is a common occurrence. Similar to Zury's situation, Amanda Lopez writes about a friend, Leticia, who is told by a teacher to not speak Spanish in Algebra class. The teacher incorrectly cites language policy and demands that students speak only English. Amanda states that Leticia does not speak English, and when she attempts to communicate with Amanda in Spanish, the teacher publicly scolds Leticia in front of her classmates. This public humiliation thwarts Leticia's language development by making her feel uncomfortable communicating in any language.

Humberto Cardenas writes about how his teacher punished him and other students for speaking Spanish in an ELD class. He explains how his teacher would write on the board the names of students who spoke Spanish during class. Names would then have check marks next to them, which represented a day in detention. Students "caught" speaking Spanish more than one time might have several check marks next to their names. He also mentions how the teacher would become angry with these individuals and yell at them for speaking Spanish.

The English-only discourse translates into a hierarchy among students in which certain students believe they are superior and thus more entitled than others. SJEP student, Lisette Montoya, writes in her field notes about a language conflict between students in her English class. The conflict indicates how certain English–dominant students perceive that they are superior and the school therefore should cater to their cultural and language orientation. The incident happened after the school announcements over the PA system had completed. The announcements were given in both English and Spanish—English first and then Spanish immediately after. When the Spanish announcements were completed, one student shouted, "How Ghetto!" Lisette states that one girl yelled, "Speak English", while another added, "We're in America". A Latina student angrily stated, "Well, look around, the majority at this school are Hispanics". A white student responded by saying, "I speak English so everyone else should too, we're in America". The anti-Latinx students were obviously attempting to maintain their dominance over the majority at the school. Although the school's demographics were rapidly changing, white students wanted to sustain the English dominance at the school and thus keep their advantage. Becoming a white minority does not mean that these students would lose their power and status. An apartheid structure is a present and unfortunate reality. By maintaining English as the dominant language, these students continue to hold onto and argue for cultural superiority, even though they represent the minority.

At this same school, Martin Portugal reports on how many students make remarks like "shut up and go back to your country mojado" or how they call people "illegal aliens" even though they are the same race (Hispanic/Mexican/Latinx). Latinxs adopt and internalize racist discourses because they permeate and saturate their socio-cultural context. They hear these kinds of racist remarks every day, which then enter their heads to filter their own perspectives and communication. Martin also writes about the conversation he had heard from other students saying, "Students that were born here have to share their school with students from all over the world". The students continue, "It was not fair that these students get opportunities that they were not allowed to get". The idea of privilege derives from the belief that certain students, in this case Anglo students, experience the disadvantage of not receiving "special" treatment. Because they do not receive special treatment, they are supposedly missing out on vital opportunities. These Anglo students fail to recognize their privilege of having the entire school and curriculum adjusted for their success. Arguing against opportunities for students of color allows Anglo students to rationalize and maintain their own privileges by invoking the notion of "fairness". If students of color have advantages, then Anglo students can argue and feel justified to hold onto their own privileges.

Students who speak Spanish are also put at a disadvantage with language policy at schools. ELL students must spend most of their time at school learning English, even forgoing other course work necessary for graduation. Zury Gonzalez comments that ELL students often have scheduling problems in which they are scheduled primarily for English classes and do not have time for math, science or history. By the time they reach their senior year, many ELL students are missing credits for graduation. The only option at this point is to take weekend academy or summer courses. English requirements for ELL students impose serious obstacles to timely graduation.

Analysis and Presentation

After they conduct observations and write up field notes, SJEP students initiate an analysis process that involves identifying the relevant patterns in the data. Excerpts from field notes that reflect the relevant patterns are organized and placed within an analytical category called a "code". A code is a new term that the students create to reference the general meaning behind the pattern(s). For instance, the students organized the field note data presented above into a code that they termed, "The Spanish Disadvantage". The relative high frequency in which students were reprimanded for speaking Spanish led to the interpretation that the students' use of Spanish made them feel disadvantaged at school. Spanish had no other purpose other than allowing certain teachers and students to label Spanish speakers as delinquent or deficient. Thus, Spanish had the unfortunate consequence of placing ELL students in a disadvantaged position in regards to their education and ability to become literate in any language.

The coding analysis of the YPAR process draws from the students' creativity and imagination. They must reflect on the data and then create new and original terms that relate to the experiences documented in field notes. In many cases, students collect enough data to generate several codes or new terms. For instance, students not only created the "Spanish Disadvantage" but also invented a code called "English Submersion" to indicate how English requirements hold students down by taking away the time needed to meet other requirements (Math, Science, History) for graduation. "English Submersion" is also an imaginative play on words since the actual name for the teaching approach for ELD classes is called Structured English Immersion (SEI). By switching "submersion" for "immersion", students suggest that the SEI approach actually submerges students as opposed to uplifting them.

Students not only create codes or new terms, such as the "Spanish Disadvantage", from the data but also look to creative praxes to present them. After students create codes, they delve deep within their imagination to innovate an original representation of the new term. With "The Spanish Disadvantage", students created a role-playing skit from the supporting field note data, which re-told the racist incident with the bilingual P.A. announcements mentioned above. They wrote out the dialogue from the incident, including roles for the announcer, Latina students, and Anglo students. Every time they presented their research, the students would define the "Spanish Disadvantage" and then hand out cards with the different roles and dialogue. The skit would reenact the bilingual announcement incident, drawing dialogue straight from the field note data. The audience experienced a physical representation of the research in the form of drama. This creative presentation allowed some audience members to adopt roles and participate in the reenactment while others witnessed the embodiment of the incident through live human action and expression. The skit connects people physically to the meaning and experience of the "Spanish Disadvantage;" they acquire a sense in a dramatic way of how disadvantaged students may feel.

After students conduct the skit, they lead the audience in a dialogue about the "Spanish Disadvantage". The students initiate dialogue by eliciting the audience's general thoughts about the skit, and how this racist incident could be used for a "teachable moment" in the classroom. They also ask direct questions to those involved in the role playing, asking them how they felt reenacting the incident. The intention of the dialogue is to foster a praxis in which reflection on the situation is coupled with the action of drama. The creative expressions of theater allow people to not only think about discrimination but also act out the situation that provokes discriminatory practices. Therefore, knowledge produced through reflection and action or praxis evinces the causes to problems. Through this understanding of the production of problems, knowledge emerges to demonstrate how changes may occur.

Encuentros: The Final Production of Praxis

The students present their research at a parent/student meeting organized by the SJEP. This meeting is called an "Encuentro" and represents the final production of the students' work. Throughout the year, students collect data, conduct analyses, and craft presentations. When they complete this full cycle of YPAR, they present to family and community members at the end of the year Encuentro. We based this idea, the *Encuentro*, on theories of learning situated in processes of dialogue and the formative potential of tightening social bonds. At the beginning of the year, the students read Freire (1993), and now at the end of the year it is time to put into practice the building of knowledge through a dialogue based on the students' and the community's social experiences of marginalization and injustice.

In the SJEP, families are not perceived to exist in deficit. Rather, they are regarded as possessing valuable cultural resources, knowledge, and experiences that can enrich the education of students. The SJEP follows a "funds of knowledge" (Gonzalez, 1995; Gonzalez, Moll, & Amanti, 2005; Moll, Gonzalez, Amanti, & Neff, 1992) approach in which families cultivate cultural practices that become necessary for their survival and advancement. These cultural practices bear sophisticated intellectual content that is applied to negotiate the various exigencies of penurious existence. The SJEP program introduces families' "funds of knowledge" or "community cultural wealth" (Yosso, 2005) through *Encuentros* to dialogue about the injustices facing Latinxs in education. The SJEP holds several *Encuentros* throughout the year in which families' funds of knowledge or inherent cultural wealth mediates their children's learning.

Encuentros represent true funds of knowledge such that transformation occurs with students as well as their families. Students, through their actualizations as public intellectuals, see themselves as knowledgeable and thus solidify academic identities. Family members, including parents and siblings, realize that SJEP students act on their behalf by producing new funds of knowledge that could potentially create better opportunities for them and their communities. Buy-in and support for the SJEP has grown considerably over the past few years because of the prevalent belief among families that the experience provided by the program (in and of itself) will improve academic and social outcomes for Tucson's Latinxs.

At the Encuentro, the language/cultural discrimination group presented their PAR work. They conducted their drama/skit on "The Spanish Disadvantage" and then facilitated a dialogue with parents and community members. The students mentioned that school officials might tell a student that he or she is not allowed to speak in any language other than English. They added that the anti-bilingual law restricts teachers (NOT students) from speaking languages other than English for instruction. Thus, the law does not prohibit students from speaking Spanish or other non-English languages. Such legislation would violate the student's first amendment right to freedom of speech.

Students skillfully presented evidence of teachers and security monitors who forbid them to speak Spanish. The students also presented on language and speech rights to demonstrate how teachers and other school personnel violate their rights on a daily basis. After hearing the students' follow-up to their Spanish Disadvantage skit, one parent stood up and said that this unjust practice was happening at his workplace in which his boss would often tell him and co-workers they could not speak Spanish. However, after hearing his son explain about language rights, he said that he would tell his boss that such prohibitions violated his right to freedom of speech.

Encuentros represent the opportunity to participate in critical reading and engagement. This opportunity allows students to generate funds of knowledge that not only solidify academic identities among themselves but influence new possibilities of change for families and communities. The students' adoption of intellectual status promotes epiphanies among those who engage and listen to them. Their knowledge reveals the sense that they are acting in the best interest of others and could potentially lead to improved conditions in schools and communities. Trust is also a key element of success of the SJEP *Encuentros*. Families want their children to participate in the program not only for the academic benefits but also for the trust they initiate by producing funds of knowledge to help others engage in praxis by "reading the world" and "transforming it".

Conclusion

The language/cultural discrimination group evinces how learning a language through punishment, humiliation, and repetition is not how Freire theorized an effective literacy approach. His approach involves grounding words and language in the learner's socio-political context. Research indicates how involving students in real life discussions and analysis of race, gender, class, culture and power is an effective pedagogical strategy for language development (Goldstein, 1995). An effective literacy for ELL students, therefore, should include an examination of language policies and how current ELD programs are designed to prevent students from acquiring proficiency in any language. Looking at and discussing the labels, including English as Second Language (ESL), ELD, and ELL, would be appropriate generative themes that would encourage students to focus more closely on language policies that negatively influence their learning, thereby overcoming these barriers. Austin and Hickey (2008, p. 135) assert that

> transformative education requires authentic knowledge of and connection with the experiences, histories, and hopes of those who inhabit the margins. By this, we suggest that educators must give voice to those whose stories are typically unheard while at the same time opening for critique the dominant hegemonic narratives that would continue the silencing process.

An education that focuses on the role of power in learning is an empowering and transformative process for marginalized students. The examination of generative themes for education policy is the praxis strategy for the SJEP. Students analyze their own educational experiences, noticing how school policies, either formal or informal, have determined the form and content of the learning process. By noticing how some policies can be detrimental, students understand that failure is no fault of their own but rather manufactured by other people who hope to, by design, generate advantages for some and disadvantages for others. Recognizing how policies artificially construct barriers involves grasping the "limit situation" of the institutional structure. Limit situations are "limits that—once recognised as constructed rather than natural or determined—can be acted upon and deconstructed or transformed" (Klein, 2007, p. 191). These actions include recognizing the social impediments to success, ignoring the deficit discourses applied to rationalize explicit disadvantages, and embracing the funds of knowledge to initiate change. Once SJEP students assume these actions, they attain a fair amount of self-confidence that moves them beyond feelings of inadequacy to those of competence. They realize they can learn, and learn in ways that not only better themselves but also improve circumstances in education so others may succeed.

Epilogue

The PAR project described above was completed in 2010. By this time (2016), the SJEP and Ethnic Studies in Tucson schools were under attack by the State Superintendent of Public Instruction, Tom Horne. He lobbied the Arizona legislature to pass HB 2281, which effectively banned the SJEP and Ethnic Studies. It was not until January 2012 that the school district decided to adhere to the ban and suspend all SJEP and Ethnic Studies courses. Students were locked out of their classes, and books were stored away in boxes.

In 2014, the federal judge administering Tucson's desegregation order required the implementation of courses designed specifically to provide cultural and historical relevance for African-American and Latinx students. Academic disparities between white students and students of color were evident enough that something needed to be done to address this "gap". The district response was to create courses under the name of "Culturally Responsive Curriculum". These courses were modeled after the formerly banned SJEP and Ethnic Studies program, except for a greater adherence to state standards.

There is at least one teacher in one school who has revived the PAR component of the SJEP in her Culturally Responsive Curriculum courses. In name, the SJEP no longer exists, but the heart of PAR is still beating in Tucson.

References

Austin, J., & Hickey, A. (2008). Critical pedagogical practice through cultural studies. *The International Journal of the Humanities*, 6(1), 133–139.

Barndt, D. (1998). The world in a tomato: Revisiting the use of "Codes" in Freire's problem-posing education. *Convergence*, 31(1/2), 62–74.

Freire, P. (1993). *Pedagogy of the oppressed*. New York, NY: Continuum Press.

Freire, P. (1994). *Education for critical consciousness*. New York, NY: Continuum.

Freire, P. (1998). *The Paulo Freire reader* (M. A. Freire & D. Macedo, Eds.). New York, NY: Continuum Press.

Gent, M. J. (2009). On-campus service projects: An experiment in education for liberation. *Organization Management Journal*, 6, 166–177.

Goldstein, B. S. C. (1995). Critical pedagogy in bilingual special education classroom. *Journal of Learning Disabilities*, 28(8), 463–475.

Gonzalez, N. (1995). The funds of knowledge for teaching project. *Practicing Anthropology*, 17(3), 3–6.

Gonzalez, N., Moll, L. C., & Amanti, C. (2005). Theorizing practices. In N. Gonzalez, L. C. Moll & C. Amanti (Eds.), *Funds of knowledge: Theorizing practices in households, communities, and classrooms* (pp. 1–27). Mahwah, NJ: Lawrence Erlbaum.

Gutstein, R. (2006). "The real world as we have seen it": Latino/a Parents' voices on teaching mathematics for social justice. *Mathematical Thinking and Learning*, 8(3), 331–358.

Klein, M. (2007). Peace education and Paulo Freire's method: Towards the democratisation of teaching and learning. *Convergence*, 40(2), 187–203.

Moll, L. C., Gonzalez, N., Amanti, C., & Neff, D. (1992). Funds of knowledge for teaching: Using a qualitative approach to connect homes and classrooms. *Theory into Practice, 31*(2), 132–141.

Peckham, I. (2003). Freirian codifications: Changing walls into windows. *Pedagogy, 3*(2), 227–244.

Renner, A., Brown M., Steins G., & Burton, S. (2010). A reciprocal global education? Working towards a more humanizing pedagogy through critical literacy. *Intercultural Education, 21*(1), 41–54.

Roberts, P. (1994). Education, dialogue and intervention: Revisiting the Freirean project. *Educational Studies, 20*(3), 307–328.

Roberts, P. (1998). Extending literate horizons: Paulo Freire and the multidimensional word. *Educational Review, 50*(2), 105–114.

Yosso, T. J. (2005). Whose culture has capital? A critical race discussion of community cultural wealth. *Race Ethnicity and Education, 8*(1), 69–81.

· 4 ·

A CREATIVE JUSTICE APPROACH TO LEARNING

Melissa Rivera, Cristina Medellin-Paz, and Pedro Pedraza

In this chapter we introduce a framework for learning grounded in the arts and social justice, a pathway into personal transformation and collective development for Latinx. Research shows that Latinx students have historically been underserved by U.S. public school systems, and today by most conventional measures of educational success continue on this trajectory (Nieto, Rivera, & Quiñones, 2012; Pedraza & Rivera, 2005). El Puente Academy for Peace and Justice chose to responded to this educational crisis two decades ago by developing and sustaining a loving and caring community, where mastery in learning is realized via peace and justice and the arts. This case example provides a summary of our collaborative findings from a four-year research process, highlighting an approach to learning rooted in creativity and social justice as well as recommendations for its integration into classroom practice and educational policy.

Our research speaks to current and long-standing educational issues such as how we create sustainable and meaningful learning environments for diverse students and how we define educational success beyond traditional indices of achievement. We propose that principles such as PAR EntreMundos' knowledge co-construction, creative praxes and indigenous cosmologies are visionary and practical educational principles that encourage young people to imagine and create the world they want to see by connecting with others in authentic and caring relationships, rooting in ancient cultural wisdom, engaging in and transforming current realities, and becoming activated global citizens and leaders.

Project Context: El Puente

This story begins in Williamsburg, Brooklyn in New York City, where El Puente was founded as a community-based organization in 1982 by former Young Lord, Luis Garden Acosta with co-founder Frances Lucerna and other leaders (artists, activists, educators, and medical professionals). El Puente became a healing sanctuary from the systemic challenges and personal traumas that plagued residents in the neighborhood, providing an after-school program that addressed health and well-being issues through community surveys and vaccination clinics, education in the form of Spanish and English literacy classes, the arts via public mural painting, dance and theater classes and in-house repertory companies, and environmental justice through neighborhood tree planting, community gardens, campaigns against both lead pollution and garbage transfer stations for nuclear/chemical waste.

Figure 4.1: Creating a World Without Violence by Los Muralistas de El Puente

Source: Photograph taken by Joe Matunis

After a decade of community-building and bonding, in 1992 El Puente founded a public high school. El Puente Academy for Peace and Justice was one of the first innovative, small high schools from the New Visions school reform initiative in New York City (Pedraza et al., 2002; Rivera & Pedraza, 2000). Today, the school, grounded in the principles of El Puente (including love and caring, collective self-help, peace and justice and mastery), continues to serve its neighborhood families, most of whom are Latinx and African-American (98%). Over the past 20+ years, El Puente Academy has graduated hundreds of students, the majority of whom continue post-high school education.

Table 4.1: School Demographics

	2005–2006	2006–2007	2007–2008
Total N =	151	176	181
Gender			
Male	41%	42%	48%
Female	59%	58%	52%
Ethnicity			
African American	15%	15%	15%
Hispanic/Latino	83%	83%	83%
White/Other	2%	2%	2%
Free/Reduced Lunch	70%	79%	70%
Special Education (N =)	4	18	29
English Language Learners (ELL) (N =)	22	22	22
Graduation Rates (5 year)	100%	100%	100%
Data from El Puente Academy for Peace and Justice (2005–2008).			

Source: Melissa Rivera, Cristina Medellin-Paz, and Pedro Pedraza

Theoretical Framework

Our research was inspired by El Puente's history and community work and grounded in three intersecting literatures: participatory action research (PAR); sociocultural theory, and creativity in learning. These three literatures became influential in the co-development of our theoretical model, Creative Justice Approach, which emerged from an in-depth, recursive PAR process. As described earlier in this volume, PAR is a philosophy about knowledge creation, a radical social movement, and a practice of collective questioning, looking, doing, being, knowing (Fine et al., 2001; NLERAP, 2003; Pedraza & Rivera, 2005; Torre & Ayala, 2009). Sociocultural theory is an approach to human development that embraces the interrelations between an individual and her/his cultural environments. In our research we used Rogoff's (1995, 2003) three planes of analysis: apprenticeship, guided participation, and participatory appropriation, three inseparable lenses of sociocultural activity (community/institutional, interpersonal, and personal). Csikzentmihalyi's (1990, 1996) theory of flow and his systems approach to creativity (which approximates Rogoff's three planes) also informed our work. Our work aimed to address the conceptual gap within the literature, integrating theories of learning into a holistic theory of human development through creativity and social justice.

Methodology: How We Learned Together

Consistent with the principles of El Puente, we used a participatory action research (PAR) approach (Cammarota & Fine, 2008; Fine et al., 2001; Torre & Ayala, 2009), creating a research collective (with El Puente and El Puente Academy administrators, academic facilitators, teaching artists and Center for Puerto Rican Studies researchers) to co-construct research questions, collect and analyze data, and take action. Data were collected using ethnographic methods to provide a comprehensive snapshot of El Puente Academy's practice, including archival documents (handbook, previous documents, newspaper articles and research reports), oral histories and reflective essays with founding/veteran facilitators, participant observation notes (from annual research retreats and design, arts and youth meetings), classroom observations (in academic and arts classes), rehearsal and performance videotapes, and semi-structured interviews with students and facilitators. Three forms of analyses were employed to organize, analyze, and interpret the data: a relational, voice-centered method (Brown & Gilligan, 1992; Gilligan, Brown & Rogers, 1988; Rogers, 1994; Rogers et al., 1999), cross case analysis (Miles & Huberman, 1994), and a reflective writing process (Bean, 1996), allowing us to embrace the layered complexities within the narrative data. In the end, we discovered that the Creative Justice Approach emerged not only as a research finding, but also a research process and method for us.

Below we describe two essential elements of our research process in more detail: collaboration (how we worked with educators and scholars) and creative praxes (how we integrated a creative exercise into the data collection methods), illuminating how two principles of PAR EntreMundos lived in our collective inquiry.

Collaboration

Collaboration is an important principle of PAR EntreMundos and was central to our research process. Throughout the four years of our collaborative inquiry (following one high school cohort), we grounded ourselves in PAR principles (resonant with the ones described in this volume), which were co-developed by El Puente and El Puente Academy facilitators, NLERAP board members, Public Science Project co-founders and Centro de Estudios Puertorriqueños scholars. Principles such as collaboration, critical inquiry and creative praxes informed and shaped our evolving research.

It is important to note that our research wholeheartedly embraced these principles of participation and action, though the real-time practice of PAR was inevitably more gray and nuanced than our clearly articulated principles. We embraced a strong, collective conviction that guiding and supporting practitioner-researchers could offer the school community methods and resources for critical self-reflection and knowledge-producing processes, ones that could be sustained for years beyond any specific research project. We also believed the collaborative inquiry process provided a deeper level of validity and authenticity for our research work, examining the connection of our research questions and data collection strategies to practitioner/classroom-based, and student/community-level utility. Thus, the researchers and practitioners together embarked on this crooked, bumpy journey to investigate El Puente Academy's educational principles and practices as a way to understand and develop new frameworks for conceptualizing learning and human development.

Grounded in participatory action research (PAR), sociocultural theories of human development and a systems approach to creativity, we explored and inquired together, using a cultural, relational approach. In order to formulate research questions and gather meaningful data for the school community, our research collective with El Puente and El Puente Academy faculty and staff (administrators, academic and arts facilitators, and teaching artists) and Centro scholars gathered regularly to imagine, discuss, reflect, and create. We held annual research retreats as well as weekly meetings to engage in discussions about our evolving theoretical framework, the anchoring research questions, data collection strategies (co-construction of observation and interview protocols), lessons learned, and writing and presentation development. In these regular gatherings we shared current realities and new dreams and ultimately crafted a research process that integrated both. Overall, the retreats and meetings were a venue for including more voices in the research design process, creating a space for authentic feedback from those deeply engaged in the practice, determining questions that are important to the school community, and gathering information that would be useful in classroom facilitators' work with students (such as in developing curriculum, pedagogy and assessment). El Puente and El Puente Academy faculty and staff participation ensured that the research was grounded in truths from life at the school.

Creative Praxes in Action

In addition to archival documents, observation notes, personal reflective essays, and interview transcripts, we also infused the data collection process with a creative exercise. Given that art was central to the research project, as part of the interview process, research collective members decided to use an artistic prompt to help facilitate conversations with students, teachers and administrators. Prior to most interviews, students and educators were asked to draw, write, and/or create something that represents their most meaningful learning experience at El Puente Academy. Students and educators had a choice of colored construction paper and a variety of drawing/crafting materials to use. They were given approximately 15 minutes to complete a map, after which the researcher asked them to elaborate in words about their creation, weaving this exercise into the interview process. Below is an example of a map by an El Puente administrator in response to the prompt, "What is your most meaningful experience at El Puente?"

Figure 4.2: Facilitator's Map

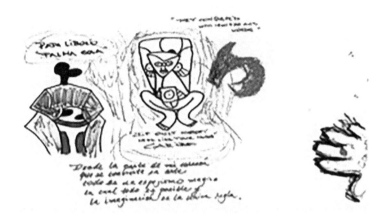

Source: Hector Calderon

Data Collection: What We Studied

Since its inception, El Puente Academy has utilized the arts and creative processes as an integral part of its pedagogical approach in both practice and theory, and the soul of the El Puente Academy's arts-soaked curricula has been its annual Integrated Arts Project (IAP). The IAP is an arts-based program that engages students in a dynamic, in-depth learning process by bringing together different academic and artistic disciplines, plus academic facilitators, teaching artists, and community and cultural organizations around a central theme. This process culminates in a final performance and/or series of presentations where students have an opportunity to demonstrate what they have learned through creative expression and exhibition.

For instance, El Puente Academy's inaugural Integrated Arts Project focused on the theme of sugar. Inspired by a local landmark, the Domino Sugar Factory, young people, facilitators, local artists, and community educators and organizers collaborated on an interdisciplinary, multi-arts study of sugar (Rivera & Pedraza, 2000). The history of sugar and its effects (including slavery dependent cultivation in the Caribbean and Latin America) as well as patterns of consumption in the United States were studied in global studies classes.

Students in biology conducted a school-wide survey of the amount of sugar and sugar based products consumed daily by young people in their neighborhood. An English class investigated the histories of people who worked on sugar plantations and studied the cultures of resistance, which grew out of their struggles. Video, dance and visual arts classes explored the cultural and spiritual expressions that emerged in Africa, Latin America and the Caribbean from oppression related to sugar.

The culmination of the sugar project was Sweet Freedom Sugar Feast, a parade and performance with stilt walking, Afro-Caribbean dance, spiritual songs, a student-written play and a presentation of a video by young people. This celebration took place outdoors in El Puente's community garden, *Espíritu Tierra*, with student-created murals as the backdrop. Combining elements of fantasy, political satire, and traditional cultural arts, Sweet Freedom was an example of the kind of deep, experiential learning that is possible with transformative arts projects, those activated through critical, creative and compassionate pedagogy and rooted in social justice.

Figure 4.3: Espíritu Tierra Community Garden by Los Muralistas de El Puente

Source: Photograph by Joe Matunis

What We Learned

As we explored the learning process at El Puente Academy, we uncovered layers of lessons about relationships, environments, creativity, collaboration, transformation and social change. In this chapter we will present two findings that map directly onto PAR EntreMundos principles: Power With(in), how relationships formed the foundation for all of learning and knowledge co-construction, and Creative Praxes, the Creative Justice Approach theory of learning that emerged from our collective inquiry (Rivera et al., 2010).

Power With(in): Relationships

Over the years, educational research has demonstrated that the art of teaching has been severely compromised by inhumane policies and structures, so severely that authentic relationships have become virtually non-existent in many schools and classrooms. Unfortunately, teachers in many classrooms are discouraged from cultivating and nourishing these relationships and often become primarily responsible for and accountable to drill and prep, that is, preparing children for required standardized exams and other pre-determined outcomes. This constricts the robust opportunities made possible only with deep, enduring relationships. We have found through our collective research that true fundamentals of learning are rooted in relationships. There are diverse relationships that are created, nurtured and sustained at El Puente Academy that invite the awakening of the power with(in), creative praxes and indigenous cosmologies principles. For instance, when power is examined and shared (Eisler, 2002), imaginations are released (Greene, 1995), spirits are embodied, and learning is robust, integrated and transformative.

This idea of shared power is visible in the relationship between students and facilitators at El Puente Academy. As Rogoff (2003) stated, "The most powerful way to help people learn is to be engaged with them in activities in which they are interested. Teachers act as guides, rather than bosses". According to Webster's dictionary, the word, facilitate, means "to make easier, to help bring about, to make possible". At El Puente Academy, adult educators are called facilitators, rather than teachers. This is not merely semantics. It denotes a shift in power and authority and crafts an openness in the learning space. It invites young people into their own learning, insists on self-directed exploration, and enhances the collective experience, encouraging a collaborative learning process. Adults' roles become ones of creating safety in the environment, introducing new ideas, curating and sharing resources (written, oral, visual, tactile, kinesthetic), inviting conversation, navigating the emotional terrain of adolescence (Siegel, 2014), holding co-developed boundaries, surrendering to the unfurling moment, and ultimately, standing witness to the revelatory journey. They affirm and inquire: "I see you. I hear you. What do you see, hear, notice, feel, and appreciate? What scares you, inspires you?" The sacred work of facilitators is to *make possible*. This philosophy and practice of teaching and learning insists on a participatory process, one grounded in playful wonder, expansive creativity, intense exploration, rigorous inquiry, and embodied expression. Adults yield exclusive authority so young people can author their own learning and lives.

As Parker Palmer (1999) reflects,

> authority is granted to people who are perceived as authoring their own words, their own actions, their own lives, rather than playing a scripted role at the great remove from their own hearts…Authority comes as I [the facilitator] reclaim my identity and integrity, remembering my selfhood and my sense of vocation. Then teaching [and learning] can come from the depths of my own truth—and the truth that is within my students has a chance to respond in kind.

El Puente Academy's Integrated Arts Project encouraged a reflection on and reorganization of power in the classroom, a new way of inviting everyone in the space to be a teacher, learner and creator.

Knowledge Co-construction and Creative Praxes: The Creative Justice Approach

The founders and leaders at El Puente have experienced and know the transformative power of the arts and have thus made them a sacred tenet in their organization. The arts via creative praxes have been essential in El Puente's human rights and social justice efforts, especially in their education programs. After deep collaboration over years, a theory emerged from the embodied, lived experiences of the El Puente community, an approach to healing, learning and human development grounded in creativity and social justice.

As we analyzed our data, listening for the patterns and truths in the stories and experiences of El Puente Academy educators and students, we realized an approach to learning was emerging. As we wove threads from the data together, a gestalt perspective on learning revealed itself, one based on knowledge co-construction and creative praxes. We called it the Creative Justice Approach (CJA), an approach to human development that examines learning through the lenses of creativity and social justice and offers a holistic perspective for understanding the developing self within community. The CJA learning system includes three lenses: social ecology (via a cultural cartography), learning renaissance (via a creative learning cycle), and personal revolution (via transformative selves).

Table 4.2: Creative Justice Approach

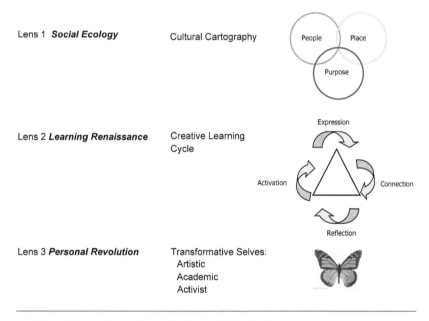

Lens 1 *Social Ecology*	Cultural Cartography
Lens 2 *Learning Renaissance*	Creative Learning Cycle
Lens 3 *Personal Revolution*	Transformative Selves: Artistic Academic Activist

Source: Melissa Rivera, Cristina Medellin-Paz, and Pedro Pedraza

Lens 1: Social Ecology

The first lens of the Creative Justice Approach is *social ecology*. At El Puente Academy for Peace and Justice, the social ecology represents the overall school culture, including the relationships created, nurtured and sustained among young people and adults, the physical environment, and the educational philosophy. This cultural cartography embraces three essential elements: people, place and purpose. People represents the many layered, dynamic, caring relationships that are developed and nourished (for instance, student to facilitator, facilitator to facilitator, and community-based organization to school). Place represents geography, the use of environment and space (physical, psychological, and sociocultural). Purpose represents the articulated and living philosophy and principles of the entire organization in the learning organism of El Puente.

Lens 2: Learning Renaissance

The Creative Justice Approach's second lens, *learning renaissance*, is best described via a creative learning cycle (CLC), a model that developed organically from El Puente Academy's educational practice. Throughout our research journey, we discovered that it naturally mapped onto the learning cycles described by Wallas (1926), Kolb (1984) and Zull (2002) and, more recently, Kotler (2014). We believe this creative learning cycle describes the experiences of young people and facilitators as they participate in the CJA's learning renaissance. The creative learning cycle begins with *connection* (connection with self, others, community, culture and artful processes), strolls into *reflection* (an incubation period, a time to play, experiment and explore), flows in *activation* (where freedom finds form, a time for synthesis), and is shared through *expression* (exhibition of embodied knowledge, a time of sharing together).

Lens 3: Personal Transformation

The Creative Justice Approach's third lens is *personal revolution* via transformative selves. By listening to the young people's voices and narratives, where they articulated and illustrated their learning experiences and affirmed the creative process as a major catalyst in their personal development into young adulthood, we learned about three transformative selves: the activist self, academic self, and artistic self. They expanded possibilities of who they could be/come and deepened their sense of self through the IAP experience.

Our participatory action research process illuminated for us that unleashing the creative powers within each student and her/his community dramatically transformed schools and learning spaces, creating fertile soil for social change. The CJA's first lens of *social ecology* invited a process that honored relationships among students and within families and communities, weaving intergenerational cultures and sociohistorical knowledges. The second lens of *learning renaissance* opened possibilities for holistic activities in classrooms (integrating mind, body and spirit), engagement with socioculturally-rich curricula and collaboration among educators, and finally, the third lens of *personal transformation* supported identity development among young people, providing expansive practices that freed the human spirit and supporting imaginations to dream a more hopeful world.

Challenge: Displacement

As we journeyed together through this collaborative research process, we encountered a major and unexpected challenge in the third year. The school was evicted from its home site of more than 10 years and relocated to two temporary locations for the duration of our research. Thus, given the experience of unexpected displacement or root shock (Fullilove, 2004), our entire research design was reshaped and tailored to their immediate experiences.

This first year of our research focused on reflecting upon, more deeply understanding, and clearly documenting both the history and current life of the Integrated Arts Project at El Puente Academy for Peace and Justice. In order to gain this clarity, veteran facilitators gathered for a series of conversations about the genesis and arc of the IAP to discuss how it was birthed and nurtured, how it evolved, and how it was being implemented (at the time in its then 10th year). The outcome of our first year was what would become the first lens of the Creative Justice Approach (social ecology via cultural cartography). In our second year we focused on exploring in-depth learning in the IAP program, specifically in three areas: environment (place and space), professional development (the relationship between academic facilitators and teaching artists), and student experiences. These three areas of inquiry ultimately informed the three lenses of the Creative Justice Approach. The research collective also articulated the desire to explore the transformation process among students and educators.

The original goal for year three of our research was to explore how the young people and facilitators experienced the IAP program, specifically looking at student and faculty development and transformation. That question emerged from previous discussions with veteran staff and was co-constructed with them during the previous year's annual retreat. Due to the unforeseen circumstance of eviction, the original question was revised to address El Puente Academy's experience of displacement and root shock (Fullilove, 2004), deeply integrating the young people's voices and leadership in the process. What started as root shock (filled with its tsunami of emotions) was transmuted into strength, resilience, courage, connection and growth in the face of challenge (McGonigal, 2015; Rankin, 2015). The stress and intense emotions were transformed into fuel for addressing this traumatic situation with grace together. In the end we focused on the community response to the displacement challenge in year three, specifically on the themes of courage and connection. Once settled into the temporary locations (and dedicated still to finding a permanent home), in year four we documented student and faculty experiences and learning within the IAP context, exploring possible areas of transformation. When discussing transformation, we viewed this process beyond merely higher academic achievement and included any changes in the students' lives, which would indicate an overall change in awareness about how they positioned themselves within society as global citizens and leaders. What emerged from this four-year exploration was the Creative Justice Approach, an approach to learning and human development that, like PAR EntreMundos, embraces shadows, traumas and challenges as well as wonder, delight and possibility within the collective educational experience.

Conclusion

In this chapter we have attempted to briefly describe a collaborative research process that culminated in a comprehensive approach to learning. We hope that the Creative Justice Approach will continue to provide a useful perspective for El Puente Academy to understand its practice and also be embraced and utilized in a variety of learning contexts (see Epilogue). We propose the following three policy recommendations for all learning communities interested in embracing CJA's principles:

- Social Ecology Recommendation: Schools and learning spaces are part of an ecosystem nested in a local neighborhood and are institutions that need to be considered vital for community development.
- Learning Renaissance Recommendation: We intend to integrate the Creative Justice Approach into a Grow Your Own initiative, developing curriculum for teachers and students as well as encouraging pre- and in-service teacher education programs to include the study of human development, creative processes, and social justice.
- Personal Revolution Recommendation: We advocate for a more holistic model of learning and assessment, one that moves towards embracing the whole person and moves away from mere numbers, providing a continuum of student growth and development.

We encourage you to reimagine and reorganize principles and pedagogies in your educational spaces (by interrogating power dynamics, dismantling hierarchies, coming together in crisis, imagining new worlds and collaborating for change) to invite more robust learning experiences, deepen the integration of disciplines and meaning-making, nurture caring relationships, and cultivate transformative leadership. We hope this peek into our process, this research snapshot, will inspire you and your learning communities to embrace a spirit of self-discovery, collective growth, and social change.

Epilogue by Melissa Rivera and María Elena Torre

After our five-year journey with El Puente Academy for Peace and Justice (2005–2010), exploring their Integrated Arts Project curriculum and identifying an emergent theoretical framework for learning through the arts and social justice (Creative Justice Approach), we embarked on new collaborative inquiry together. For three years (2011–2013) the Public Science Project (with Drs. María Elena Torre and Melissa Rivera, volume editors) evaluated El Puente's youth leadership development initiative (Torre & Rivera, 2013).

Using participatory action research, we collaborated with a leadership team from El Puente, the community-based organization that founded El Puente Academy. El Puente sought to formalize its practices and develop an institute for global leaders. We chronicled its development over three years, and one major finding was that El Puente utilized the Creative Justice Approach (CJA) in their professional development program. The CJA became an integral and integrated part of their internal leadership training program as well as of their Global Leadership Institute. In this second research project, there were some faculty and staff members that had been involved in the CJA project, and those leaders were instrumental in translating, codifying and weaving CJA principles and practices into the entire initiative.

The most powerful finding from the research was the breakthrough emergence of El Puente's framework of *Transformative Leadership Development*. Synthesizing and building upon 30 years of practice and 15 years of research, the formalization of the Global Justice Institute created a process that clarified the essential elements of the overarching leadership framework El Puente has been operating under. The three-year journey integrated personal and collective reflection as well as individual and organizational commitments to growth, knowledge and culture-building, community and social change. The process enabled leadership, staff and participants to fully articulate and name the approach that has long informed El Puente's holistic leadership work with youth and communities (Torre & Rivera, 2013). The Transformative Leadership Development (TLD) framework is a holistic, multifaceted teaching and learning approach for leaders, which includes three essential elements:

Mindset: psychoemotional inquiry, exploration and development of one's internal landscape

Skillset: functional, teachable, actionable skills (such as curriculum design and creation, facilitation and public speaking, art making)

Creative Action: meaningful, community offerings (such as internal staff trainings as well as external groups trainings, of which CJA is an integral component)

The TLD framework also integrates three central processes (across all elements listed above):

- *Ritual and Ceremony* (via guided meditation and sacred circle)
- *Conversation Circles* (via storytelling and "Kitchen Table Talks" among elders, veterans and new members)
- *Artful Reflection* (via participatory action research and creative processes)

The Creative Justice Approach provided a theoretical foundation on which El Puente leaders built, deepened and expanded to create the Transformative Leadership Development framework and program design for its Global Justice Institute (a place to train and nurture global leaders within El Puente and across other communities and contexts).

What we would love to highlight here is the developmental nature of this collaborative work. The nature of PAR and the CJA is that it iterates, grows and evolves over time as the people, issues and contexts shift, maintaining a continuous thread of certain principles and practices (such as creativity, collaboration and social change). The Creative Justice Approach continues its evolution through the Transformative Leadership Development programs at El Puente's Global Justice Institute, and PAR EntreMundos continues its journey to evolving our world through principled practices of knowledge co-construction, creative praxes and indigenous cosmologies. May you feel invited onto this path of collective inquiry and conscious social change.

References

Bean, J. (1996). *Engaging ideas: The professor's guide to integrating writing, critical thinking, and active learning in the classroom*. San Francisco, CA: Jossey-Bass, Inc.

Brown, L. M., & Gilligan, C. (1992). *Meeting at the crossroads. Women's psychology and girls' development*. Boston, MA: Harvard University Press.

Cammarota, J., & Fine, M. (Eds.). (2008). *Revolutionizing education: Youth participatory action research in motion*. New York, NY: Routledge.

Csikzentmihalyi, M. (1990). *Flow. The psychology of optimal experience*. New York, NY: Harper Perennial.

Csikzentmihalyi, M. (1996). *Creativity. Flow and the psychology of discovery and invention*. New York, NY: Harper Collins Publishers.

Eisler, R. (2002). *The power of partnership: Seven relationships that will change your life*. Novato, CA: New World Library.

Fine, M., Torre, M. E., Boudin, K., Bowen, I., Clark, J., Hylton, D., Martinez, M., "Missy", Roberts, R. A., Smart, P., & Upegui, D. (2001). *Changing minds. The impact of college in a maximum-security prison*. New York, NY: The Graduate Center of the City University of New York and Bedford Hills Correctional Facility.

Fullilove, M. (2004). *Root shock: How tearing up city neighborhoods hurts America, and what we can do about it*. New York, NY: One World/Ballantine.

Gilligan, C., Brown, L. M., & Rogers, A. (1988) *Psyche-embedded: A place for body, relationships, and culture in personality theory*. Boston, MA: Harvard Project on Women's Psychology and Girls' Development.

Greene, M. (1995). *Releasing the imagination: Essays on education, the arts, and social change*. San Francisco, CA: Jossey-Bass.

Kolb, D. (1984). *Experiential learning. Experience as the source of learning and development*. Englewood Cliffs, NJ: Prentice Hall.

Kotler, S. (2014). *The rise of superman: Decoding the science of ultimate human performance*. New York: New Harvest.

McGonigal, K. (2015). *The upside of stress: Why stress is good for you, and how to get good at it*. New York, NY: Avery.

Miles, M., & Huberman, A. M. (1994). *An expanded sourcebook: Qualitative data analysis*. Thousand Oaks, CA: Sage Publications.

Nieto, S., Rivera, M., & Quiñones, S. (Guest Eds.). (2012). Charting a new course: Understanding the sociocultural, political, economic and historical context of Latino/a education in the United States. [Special Issue] AMAE: Association of Mexican American Educators 6(3).

NLERAP. (2003). *National Latino/a education research agenda project: Education research framework and agenda*. New York, NY: Center for Puerto Rican Studies, Hunter College, City University of New York.

Palmer, P. (1999). *The courage to teach: Exploring the inner landscape of a teacher's life*. Hoboken, NJ: Wiley.

Pedraza, P., Matos, R., Rivera, M., Calderón, H., Thomases, J., De Jesús, A., & Mercado, C. (2002). *Final report on the participatory ethnographic research project at El Puente academy for peace and justice.* New York, NY: New York City Annenberg Challenge.

Pedraza, P., & Rivera, M. (2005). *Latino education. An agenda for community action research.* Mahwah, NJ: Lawrence Erlbaum Publishers.

Rankin, L. (2015). *The fear cure: Cultivating courage as medicine for the body, mind and soul.* Carlsbad, CA: Hay House.

Rivera, M., Medellin-Paz, C., Pedraza, P., & El Puente and El Puente Academy for Peace and Justice. (2010). *Imagination for an imagined nation: A creative justice approach to human development.* Final Report for Ford Foundation.

Rivera, M., & Pedraza, P. (2000). The spirit of transformation: An education reform movement in a New York City Latino/a community. In S. Nieto (Ed.), *Puerto Rican students in U.S. Schools.* Mahwah, NJ: Lawrence Erlbaum Publishers.

Rogers, A. (1994). Dissociation and repression in women's narratives of trauma. MA: Harvard Project on Women's Psychology and Girls' Relationships.

Rogers, A., Casey, M., Ekert, J., Holland, J., Nakkula, V., & Sheinberg, N. (1999). An interpretive poetics of languages of the unsayable. In R. Josselson & A. Lieblich (Eds.), *Making meaning of narratives.* Thousand Oaks, CA: Sage Publications.

Rogoff, B. (1995). Observing sociocultural activity on three planes: Participatory appropriation, guided participation, and apprenticeship. In J.V. Wertsch, P. Del Rio, & A. Alvarez (Eds.), *Sociocultural studies of mind.* Cambridge: Cambridge University Press.

Rogoff, B. (2003). *The cultural nature of human development.* New York, NY: Oxford University Press.

Siegel, D. (2014). *Brainstorm: The power and purpose of the teenage brain.* London: Scribe.

Torre, M. E., & Ayala, J. (2009). Envisioning participatory action research Entremundos. *Feminism & Psychology, 19,* 387.

Torre, M. E., & Rivera, M. (2013). *El Puente's global justice institute and transformational leadership development framework.* Final Report for Ford Foundation. New York, NY: Public Science Project.

Wallas, G. (1926). *Art of thought.* New York, NY: Harcourt Brace.

Zull, J. (2002). *The art of changing the brain. Enriching the practice of teaching by exploring the biology of learning.* Sterling, VA: Stylus.

· 5 ·

THE NEW JERSEY URBAN YOUTH RESEARCH INITIATIVE

Jennifer Ayala, Mayida Zaal, Francisco De Jesus, and Stan Karp

In 2008, a New Jersey coalition of education activists, community-based organizations, and university researchers met to design a participatory project that would engage adults and youth across three large cities in New Jersey—Jersey City, Newark, and Paterson—in the debate on secondary education reform and high school graduation requirements. From this advisory meeting, the *New Jersey Urban Youth Research Initiative* (NJUYRI) was launched. It was a collaborative effort between a civil rights organization (Education Law Center), two universities (Saint Peter's University and the Graduate Center City University of New York), one high school (Henry Snyder), and four youth-serving community based organizations (Abbott Leadership Institute, ASPIRA, New Jersey Community Development Corporation, and Project GRAD—Graduation Really Achieves Dreams). The overarching goal of this project was to establish an intergenerational collective of educators, community organizers, high school students, and university faculty that would research the potential impact of the changing graduation requirements and develop a plan of action that would stem from the findings. As a corollary to this larger goal, the youth involved would also gain research skills through the camps offered and the data collected, exercise critical thinking when they would analyze data, apply concepts toward the creation of artistic products, and practice public speaking across audiences (Zaal & Ayala, 2013).

The following narrative describes the development of our collaborative, the process of our participatory action research, and the decisions that were made along the way. We provide a chronology of the group's activities and discuss the ways in which this example illustrates some of the guiding principles related to transformative action, participation, and knowledge co-construction.

The Policy Context

With funding from the Schumann Fund for New Jersey, the purpose of the NJUYRI was to investigate and report on "opportunity to learn" issues raised by the new graduation recommendations of the NJ High School Redesign Steering Committee (http://www.state.nj.us/education/ser/). Included was an examination of districts' feasibility to prepare their students for these proposed policy changes. First released in early 2008 and ultimately adopted by the State Department of Education in June of 2009, the new graduation requirements included phasing in a series of college preparatory course requirements emphasizing advanced math and science and a new category of state assessments called "competency assessments". These new assessments were envisioned as a series of up to six end-of-course exams to replace the High School Proficiency Assessment (HSPA) administered to 11th graders. In the process, the Department of Education planned on eliminating the one alternative mechanism to the high stakes assessment high school juniors took in New Jersey at the time. In essence, instead of one high stakes exam, up to six were being proposed in order for high school students to graduate, while eliminating alternative paths to graduation.

Establishing the Collective

NJUYRI was conceived strategically as a cross-city, multi-generational and cross constituency research and policy group. Unlike participatory action research projects that decide as a group the issue they want to explore, NJUYRI was created in response to the lack of public awareness that existed regarding the new graduation requirements. As a result, the issue that would be investigated was determined and defined by the advisory group that met before youth members were recruited.

Recognizing that logistics would make our work across sites more difficult and that each community would be facing its own set of challenges as they related to the implementation of the new graduation requirements, the advisory group decided that in order to create research teams that were both deeply embedded within their communities and collaborative across, youth would be recruited from within local community-based organizations and one high school. This allowed each city to form their locally based research team that would be facilitated by the youth workers in the CBOs, and in the case of Jersey City, a high school guidance counselor. Nineteen youth involved in the project were primarily African-American with a few who identified as Latinx. The public high schools they attended included small schools, large comprehensive schools, and alternative programs.

Decision-making

To build the cohesiveness of our group, develop shared understandings, and share knowledge and expertise across sites, we held what some PAR scholars (Fine, Roberts, & Torre, 2004) have called "research camps". Three day-long or overnight research camps were held in Saint Peter's campus in Jersey City. The advisory group met prior to the first camp to decide the content and the structure of the day. The lead university facilitators provided the group with a draft plan. The group discussed the requirements for youth researchers, the needs of the CBOs, and the contributions that each group would make in terms of the expertise they could offer the collective. As part of the grant, each CBO would receive funding for facilitating local research teams and providing transportation to the research camps.

There were two possibilities of what youth researchers could receive for their participation, a stipend or college credits. The group was unanimously in favor of offering students college credit for their participation in the collective. Zaal and Ayala developed a draft syllabus and the advisory group made the final determination in terms of the expectations outlined in the course (see Appendix B). One of the collective's members, David Surrey, was able to leverage his relationships at Saint Peter's and created a Sociology course that granted students three college credits for completing the required coursework. Collective members Stan Karp and Michelle Fine also brought to bear their considerable resources in terms of contacts with both community organizations and high level education officials.

The group decided that to help us build community at the research camps one of the youth workers representing the CBOs would lead us in a team building activity. Then each local team would share their expertise with the group before engaging in an initial exploration of the issue. Prior to our first camp, the university facilitators met with youth researchers recruited at local sites to explain the broad goals of the group, the course requirements and discuss what each group would present at the first camp. This gave youth in local sites an opportunity to describe the work they do in their communities, ask questions about the project, and share their hopes and desires for the project. For instance, several students shared their desire to engage with college-age students while on campus.

Research Camps

The first research camp consisted of community building and issue framing activities. The Newark team presented a video they created as part of their organization's work. The Jersey City team presented a logo they created for the NJUYRI to help establish a visual identity for the project. The Paterson team discussed a recent campaign they were involved in against an unfair policy in their city. To frame and contextualize the issues, Stan Karp, of the Education Law Center, presented the history of the landmark finance equity decision, Abbott vs. Burke, statistics about the educational opportunity/achievement gaps in schools, and the proposed changes in high school graduation requirements made by the state. We worked in small intergenerational groups to examine data from the NJ School Report Cards and other sources made available by the Education Law Center, making comparisons across districts, and documenting questions and observations. From this work, three data gathering tools were developed: a draft survey based on the issues and questions youth raised, an equipment inventory form, and an inventory of courses offered. Youth researchers used the inventory tools to document the capacity of their particular school to offer the math and science courses proposed in the new policy. Between camps, youth researchers met with community partner facilitators and collected data from their respective high schools to determine students', teachers' and community views of the new graduation requirements. This included equipment inventories of their school's math and science facilities.

The second research camp centered on research methods—focusing on interviews and surveys. Youth constructed interview protocols for parents, peers, administrators, graduates and teachers and practiced their research skills by interviewing the day's speaker, the then President of the State Board of Education, and other guests at the camp that included members of each of their target demographic. Another youth research group from New York City, *Students Supporting Action Awareness*, presented the process and findings of their project. Finally, youth researchers and adult allies worked on revising the Graduation Requirements in Public Education Survey, a survey constructed based on their work from the first camp. The survey was subsequently posted on Survey Monkey for wide distribution. In addition to circulating it via the Internet, this statewide survey was distributed at educational meetings to determine perceptions of the new graduation requirements.

The third research camp was held overnight and focused on data analysis and creating initial products. Given the limited time we had available to work across cities, facilitators decided to conduct preliminary analysis of survey data, as a way of scaffolding a framework for understanding data analysis. A colleague analyzed the numeric survey data and shared the results and the process of quantitative data analysis with youth and adult allies as part of a statistics workshop. We also generated some initial themes for the open-ended data, compiled and made copies of the transcripts organized according to the open-ended questions that had appeared in the survey. We introduced this general framework, and then worked in smaller intergenerational groups to rearrange, revise and eliminate codes used to categorize the data.

After discussing themes across the groups, the youth moved to creating products, finishing up and presenting their first drafts the second day. Using the data as a reference point, one group worked on spoken word/poetry, another group wrote and video-taped a skit, and a third created post cards and graphics as part of an awareness campaign. Upon completing this work, youth researchers had a Salsa dance lesson facilitated by a faculty colleague, followed by a barbecue at the university's Social Justice House. At the barbecue, youth researchers were joined by college student mentors, who hosted them for a pool party and an overnight stay in the dormitories. The following day, youth researchers continued working on their collective projects. They also devised slogans summarizing their thoughts. Finally, the projects were presented and performed for the whole group.

Outcomes, Products, and Transformative Actions

Research findings, including our collective analysis of the survey data, were reported in the paper entitled: The New Jersey Urban Youth Research Initiative: Report on The Statewide Survey on New Graduation Requirements. These results were disseminated in different venues, including a community report back meeting hosted at the college. During this report back to the community, a significant outcome emerged—a moment of participatory policy making (Fine, Ayala, & Zaal, 2012). Members of the collective strategically invited key people from their home communities to attend. As a result, an audience of 75 were present: Parents, students, department of education officials, educators, and community activists. The presentation itself was a collective effort—youth presented alongside adult members of the NJUYRI, presenting the process of the work, the findings and implications using multiple modes of delivery, including academic reporting, video, spoken word, visuals in the form of post cards and slogans, and finally dialogue. The young woman who presented last, ended with her perspective and with a question to the audience about what they were now going to do about the issues that had been raised. What followed was a dialogue, a participatory policy making moment, as audience members took up the challenge with pointed questions and constructive suggestions for the education officials, along with praise and support for the young people who created the space for this discussion with their work. Materials, such as the postcards and the report, were distributed to all the audience members, including the education officials. Some time later, we found that some of the issues that were brought up in this report-back, and in the report itself, appeared in other documents; for example, a Q&A section of the state department website, and a piece that seemingly made it to a report for the incoming governor at the time.

Actions occurred throughout the research process and not simply through this one community event. Partnering with CBOs ensured that actions continued locally even after the project ended. One of the Newark organizations, ALI, had expertise in the media arts and produced documentary films during the span of the project. They did this separately from NJUYRI, as part of their own independent local action, but were informed by the research and analysis produced as part of the collective. Youth from Paterson presented to their local board of education and Jersey City youth were invited to present to middle school students in their district. Some of the methods also doubled as actions (Tuck, 2009). For instance, when the youth publicly interviewed a high level education official in one of the camps, it was an action as well as a method. They asked informed, critical questions publicly serving to both collect data and to raise the issues of concern shared by the collective.

Assessment

One question to consider as we in engage in PAR as pedagogy within an education context is how to translate social justice work to a framework that can be used to assess learning and evaluate outcomes. Another question to consider is: In what ways do we honor the work that is accomplished, and acknowledge the time and commitment that is devoted by young people—elements that are not easily measured. In order to lend further legitimacy to the efforts put into this work, we were able to offer high school youth the opportunity to earn three college credits for their participation. A syllabus was created with ideas for assessment of the materials and shared with the group of adult allies prior to the first camps. Youth participants were then enrolled in a course called *Current Social Problems* that was specific to this project. At one of the camps, team members participated in a BlackBoard workshop as a way to gain exposure to online courses as well as a means to communicate and collect or share materials between camps. From an academic skill development perspective, the work in which we engaged involved producing and consuming research: we read policy documents, analyzed graphs and charts with data from site high schools; we created and analyzed surveys; conducted interviews with high school youth and adults; and triangulated data from varied sources. On what then, did we base assessment? Ultimately, we based it on a range of activities: Participation in the camps and meetings; reflections on the process of the research; engaging in the different phases of the research, including data collection; creating a portfolio of the products; and a final reflection of the overall work. At the completion of the project, 15 of the initial 19 high school youth researchers earned three college credits.

Reflections on Participation, Balance Points, and Relationships

Connecting back to the guiding principles, this PAR example focuses primarily on the approaches and dilemmas related to participation, knowledge co-construction, and transformational actions through what Lopez and Valenzuela term "engaged policy" (Valenzuela, 2016). One of the critical components of a PAR project is this notion of participation, and there are varying degrees of participation depending upon the project. In some projects, the starting point may be a community and from there, a decision is collectively made about what may be the issue or question. In this particular case, the starting point was an issue, the new graduation requirements, and around that issue a collective was organized. As this was a multi-site project with a specific time-frame, there were aspects that were not as fully developed as all would have wished.

There are a series of decision points and balances to navigate. One balance point involves recognizing the power differentials that exist, particularly in this project where youth researchers were also students working towards college credit and a final grade. Additionally, as facilitators we worried about how much support to provide in the research process without undermining the spirit of participation. In our case, given the time constraint, we tended to provide more scaffolding. In terms of data collection tools, youth and adults in small groups constructed the questions and after the camps, the university members combined them and did some editorial revisions. We then shared these finished tools from which the entire team worked. In terms of the data analysis, we first drafted some potential themes as examples and even provided some of the quantitative analysis. In the camps, the teams took this information, added, revised or subtracted categories, then coded the transcripts. The initial codes then were changed based on this participation. We could have gone through many drafts and revisions of the data collection tools with the full team, or simply offered transcripts without any ideas of potential analytic categories when it came to analysis; this would have made the process more participatory. In the time frame we worked from, this was difficult to achieve; nonetheless, it was a concern we had.

The collaboration with the CBOs as first an advisory board was another important point in the participatory process. The research camps themselves were devised with input from this initial group. Draft agendas were distributed and discussed at meetings with the larger group, and revised according to their feedback. For instance, the need for activity, and paying attention to the body during the long days of work, were addressed. We therefore incorporated games of volleyball with members of the college volleyball team, and a salsa class, into the camps. We also decided on college credits instead of stipends as compensation for the youth researchers based on these conversations. Ideally, youth representatives could have been present at these initial meetings.

Working as a collective means that it is important to build in time for establishing relationships and creating community—particularly if members are coming together from different places for the first time (Torre, 2005). Each of the camps tried to incorporate this type of space, where we brought together youth and adults from three different areas of New Jersey. One difficulty with a multi-site project like this is that it can be more difficult to forge strong bonds with youth when you do not see them regularly. The youth experienced continuity with their respective site facilitators and other team members, thus sustaining these relationships beyond the project (as was intended), but it was still a loss for us, the university team members personally, not to have been able to engage more consistently with young people from other sites. However, the benefit of these kind of multi-site projects was that with these larger numbers and multiple schools, individual students and schools were not as vulnerable. For instance, if there is a troubling finding or question that youth bring up in a presentation, individual school teachers or administrators may become angry or defensive towards the young people, concerned with how the findings make the school (or themselves) appear. If presented in the context of multiple sites, couched as an issue that occurs across schools, individual schools are less vulnerable.

We discuss this project here, not as a model for others to follow, or a perfect example of how PAR should be done, or even how we have conducted all of our own projects (in terms of starting points, etc). Here, we share one way we attempted the process and pedagogy of PAR, highlighting our intentions and struggles so that others who attempt it can reflect on their own strategies and approaches as we strive for a PAR EntreMundos.

Epilogue: Life After NJUYRI

This project began close to a decade ago as an intergenerational collective concerned about the changing graduation requirements and attendant influx of standardized tests taking place in New Jersey. What follows is a multi-voiced update on life after NJUYRI, from both a personal and policy level.

Francisco de Jesus

Several years have passed since I was a part of the Urban Youth Research Initiative at Saint Peter's University, known then as Saint Peter's College. The program was a great experience for me, having had the chance to work with students from different schools throughout New Jersey, and learning from professors of various institutions. Together, we focused on gathering data involving the changes in the high school curriculum, and confirmed whether they would be beneficial to students. Through the program, I gained skills in research gathering, learned to communicate with other people, and developed leadership skills that I would use in my college career. Having gone through such an experience, I can honestly say that without it, I would not be where I am today.

Since the program, I have graduated from Henry Snyder High School, and earned my Bachelor's Degree in Communications from Saint Peter's University. Now, I work at my Alma Mater in the IT Service department, helping students and staff with media and tech-related issues. In a way, without the Urban Youth Research Initiative, I would never have gotten to this point, being the first in my family to graduate, and providing for them as they have always done for me. Being involved with Saint Peter's during high school gave me an early look at college life, and because of my positive experience, I applied and became a student at the school. There, I experienced many opportunities along the way, such as studying abroad. The program has helped make me who I am today, and for that, I will be forever grateful.

Stan Karp

The policy debate on NJ's graduation requirements, which served as the context for the PAR project described herein, continues today. NJ did increase the math and science credit requirements for a high school diploma, but the end of course "competency assessments" that were the focus of NJUYRI's research were ultimately abandoned. In the summer of 2010, the State Board backed away from a proposal to make passing end-of-course exams in Algebra and Biology a graduation requirement. Results from several years of pilot testing made it plain that too many students would fail. Instead, NJ continued to use the 11th grade HSPA and a modified version of its alternative assessment as graduation tests. This helped sustain the state's high school graduation rate which has risen steadily to nearly 90%, third highest in the nation despite persistent gaps across communities and subgroups.

But the testing impulse remains strong, and the familiar policy debate resurfaced, this time in the context of the "common core state standards" and its "college and career ready" assessments. In 2015, NJ replaced its state tests with PARCC (Partnership for the Assessment of Readiness for College and Careers) exams, assessments developed by one of two federally-funded consortia at a cost of some $380 million. NJDOE adopted a complicated system of "transitional" graduation rules that will eventually make passing several PARCC exams a diploma requirement. But common core and PARCC ran into a buzz saw: the largest test resistance movement in US history. More than 100,000 NJ parents and students "opted out" of the PARCC tests, including large numbers of high school students. The legislature overwhelmingly passed bills seeking to delay or defer the use of PARCC scores for high stakes accountability purposes, though Governor Chris Christie refused to sign them. Parents represented by ELC and the ACLU-NJ sued the Department for failing to follow required legal steps before imposing its new graduation policies.

As the fight over high school exit testing in NJ continues, nationally the tide may have turned. Today, less than half the states tie diplomas to test scores, down from a peak of 27 a few years ago. FairTest (2016) reports that in recent years "at least seven states ended their tests or imposed a moratorium". Several states decided to issue diplomas retroactively to students denied them on the basis of tests that were discontinued. Even some common core supporters signed on to "The Case Against Exit Exams" (2014). The voices of young people helped create this debate, in NJ and across the nation. They may ultimately determine who wins it.

References

FairTest. (February, 2016). Time to Abolish High School Graduation Tests.

Fine, M., Ayala, J., & Zaal, M. (2012). Public science and participatory policy development: Reclaiming policy as a democratic project [Special issue]. *Journal of Education Policy, 27*(5), 685–692. doi:10.1080/02680939.2012.710023

Fine, M., Roberts, R., & Torre, M. (2004). *Echoes of Brown: Youth documenting and performing the legacy of Brown v. Board of Education*. New York, NY: Teachers College Press.

Hyslop, A. (2014). The case against exit exams. New America Education Policy Brief.

Torre, M. (2005). The alchemy of integrated spaces: Youth participation in research collectives of difference. In L. Weis & M. Fine (Eds.), *Beyond silenced voices*. Albany, NY: State University of New York Press.

Tuck, E. (2009). Re-visioning action: Participatory action research and Indigenous theories of change. *The Urban Review, 41*(1), 47–65.

Valenzuela, A. (2016). *Growing critically conscious teachers: A social justice curriculum for educators of Latino/a youth*. New York, NY: Teachers College Press.

Zaal, M., & Ayala, J. (2013). "Why don't we learn like this in school?". One participatory action research collective's framework for developing policy thinking. *Journal for Curriculum Theorizing, 29*(2), 159–173.

6

EDUCATION IN OUR BARRIOS PROJECT, #BARRIOEDPROJ

Edwin Mayorga

#BarrioEdProj is a youth-centered, digital, critical participatory action re-search (D+CPAR) (Mayorga, 2017) project about, and working with, Latino core communities (Morales, in press). In the pilot version of the project, the primary goal was to map the circuitry of urbanism and its material and racio-cultural effects within the East Harlem neighborhood of New York City (El Barrio) and its schools. While gentrification has taken hold in popular dis-course, it is but one aspect of what I have come to describe as racial neoliber-al urbanism (RNU) (Mayorga, 2016) that emphasizes a market-logic and an exploitative use of cultural diversity to shape the city, its neighborhoods and institutions, including schools. It is at the intersection of RNU, El Barrio, and education reform that the Education in our Barrios project (#BarrioEdProj) came to be.

I work and think as an educator-scholar-activist (Suzuki & Mayorga, 2014) whose work is rooted in the scholarly, political and pedagogical com-mitments of PAR EntreMundos. PAR EntreMundos is situated in the wisdom of local communities, and combines critical inquiry and activism for the pur-poses of collective transformation (see Chapter 1 of this book). As such, PAR EntreMundos is committed to engaging communities in a process of what Gloria Anzaldúa described as conocimiento (Keating, 2000). Conocimiento is a theory of consciousness in motion, where the inner life of the mind and spirit is connected to the outer worlds of action within the struggle for social change. While not always explicit, the connective work of conocimiento is pedagogical in nature. There is an "instructional dynamic" (Ball & Forzani, 2007) in this work that emphasizes processes of teaching and learning as collaborators "interpret one another and their environments over time" (p. 531) through a PAR process.

The pedagogical dimension of #BarrioEdProj is what is of particular interest in this chapter. In what follows, I provide background on El Barrio and its public schools, and the creation of #BarrioEdProj. Specifically, I map year one of the project pointing to the ways the project is a materialization of the principles of PAR EntreMundos. I will briefly discuss our research findings focusing on how RNU advances material, cultural and affective forms of dismemberment, where local people are dismembered, or disconnected, from power, knowledge, and place. I will also point to how conditions under RNU force individuals and institutions to create ways of navigating and transforming these conditions. I conclude by reflecting on the impact the project had on the youth co-researchers, and I consider how #BarrioEdProj might serve as a "guide for action". I argue that by involving youth and community members in research, storytelling, and social media engagements, #BarrioEdProj became a transformative way of expanding our critical consciousness and re-membering ourselves to our histories, to each other, and to place, as a means of survivance (Vizenor, 2008).

Background: El Barrio and Its Public Schools

El Barrio has always been a community that is being reinvented. This was particularly evident with the mass migration of Puerto Ricans from their U.S. controlled island starting in the early 20th century and peaking in the 1950s (Sharman, 2006). El Barrio had become a Latino core community or "codified … homeland (both real and imagined) for Puerto Ricans, and by extension many other Latino immigrant groups, not only through demographic and sociological analysis, but also through a tropicalization process transmitted through literature, music, and visual art" (Morales, 2017, p. 334).

In the midst of demographic change, El Barrio would become a symbol of urban poverty (Cayo Sexton, 1965; Freidenberg, 1995) and a site of political struggle, as people dealt with varying cycles of organized abandonment

(Gilmore, 2008) and urban renewal. Renewal in the 1960s would come to El Barrio through an ambitious construction of multi-block (super blocks), high-rise, public housing that would make El Barrio the neighborhood with the highest concentration of public housing in the city.

The city faced its worst financial crisis in the mid-1970s, which would most adversely affect the already economically and racially marginalized populations of the city. By 1990, the economic and political power of El Barrio and the Puerto Rican population had been in decline though it's cultural and historical significance for Latinos continued (Rodríguez, 1994). Economically, "40% of the total population was below the poverty level and, of those, 62% were below 200% of the poverty level" (Freidenberg, 1995, p. 6) by 1990.

As El Barrio underwent economic and social change, the local schools also experienced significant change. During the first half of the 20th century, El Barrio schools were deemed some of the worst performing schools in the city (Fliegel & MacGuire, 1993; Nieto, 2000). Between the late 1950s and the 1970s, Black and Puerto Rican parents and activists criticized the school system for failing to educate their children, and began to demand more local control over the school system. In El Barrio and Central Harlem, this struggle would play out at Intermediate School 201 (I.S. 201), as parents and activists sought to have control over the school (Lee, 2014). While successful in galvanizing activism between Blacks and Puerto Ricans, the community control movement would be ended by the implementation of a decentralized, governance formation that dispersed bureaucracy and gave families limited but varied forms of choice between 1970 and 2002 (Lewis, 2013).

During decentralization, El Barrio would undergo an educational renaissance that had a profound impact on the schools. Through the leadership of savvy, political superintendent Anthony Alvarado, District 4 would launch a bilingual education program and a "progressive" small schools movement in the district (Fliegel & MacGuire, 1993; Meier, 1995; Pedraza, 1997). While these strategies would not transform the entire school district, it encouraged innovation by individual schools and school leaders to meet the needs of a broad range of learners. This "East Harlem miracle" (Fliegel & MacGuire, 1993) would move the whole district from the bottom rungs of school performance rankings (around 30th) to the middle rankings (around 14th) and ushered school choice as a way of improving urban school districts (Kirp, 1992; Schneider, Teske, & Marschall, 2000). Still, the heavy reliance on strong leadership, the weakness of the district as a whole, and the ongoing financial struggles of the city, were among a number of factors that undermined the sustainability of the miracle (Lewis, 2013).

In 2002, newly elected Mayor of New York City, Michael Bloomberg, New York Governor George Pataki, and other elected officials stood in the Patrick Henry School, located in El Barrio. They were convening to announce the signing of a new state law that would give the Mayor primary control of the public school system. The Mayor was optimistic that day and noted that in the near future he hoped to be able to show everyone "a system that is getting better and working and that will give the mayor and the city an awful lot more muscle in getting the changes that we think are necessary to continue the progress" (Steinhauer, 2002). Announcing this major change in school governance structure made clear that the direction of the city would be inextricably linked to the future of the schools. It also reflected the circulation of a brand of urbanism that would materially and discursively contribute to the remaking of the city and the school system over the eleven years of the Bloomberg administration.

The Roots of #BarrioEdProj

Unlike participatory action projects that begin with a group of individuals from a community who articulate a set of questions, #BarrioEdProj emerged from my own political commitments and vivencia as an Asian-Latino-educator-scholar-activist (Suzuki & Mayorga, 2014). Vivencia is a term Fals-Borda used to describe as the full experience of an event with all its possibilities that comes through direct participation (see Glassman & Erdem, 2014). As such, "vivencia cannot be observed; it can only be lived, felt, and experienced" (Glassman & Erdem, 2014, p. 212). During the Bloomberg era, I engaged personally and politically in the city as a teacher in the public schools, an education activist, and as a doctoral student. Over the course of that decade, my thinking with *and* through activism increasingly centered on understanding the brand of urbanism that operated within this era of racial capitalism (Mayorga & Picower, 2012; Melamed, 2011; Robinson, 1983).

I found that the global, material, effects of RNU were primarily damaging, and in some cases fatal, for already racialized and marginalized communities, including Latino communities. I am committed to working alongside these communities because I recognize myself as a Latino, I understand that our struggles are bound up in each other's, and participating in efforts for liberation will contribute to all of us "getting free" (Taylor, 2016). Engaging in research by, for, and with Latino core communities and schools was thus needed to understand and disrupt the cultural and material consequences of contemporary urbanism. What, I asked, did urbanism look like during the Bloomberg era in Latino core communities, in the schools and the city overall? And, how did people navigate this brand of urbanism?

The Design of the Project

#BarrioEdProj, was designed to be a form of Digital, Critical Participatory Action Research, of D+CPAR (Mayorga, 2014). In this project, digital technologies and ubiquitous social media tools were leveraged to support and animate a form of public social science. CPAR is

> rooted in notions of democracy and social justice and drawing on critical theory (feminist, critical race, queer, disability, neo-Marxist, indigenous, and poststructural) and is an epistemology that engages research design, methods, analyses, and products through a lens of democratic participation. (Torre, Fine, Stoudt, & Fox, 2012, p. 171)

CPAR places the processes of problem posing, research, analysis, and data sharing, in the interlocking hands of adults and youth, of the focus community, and partnering scholars and activists. CPAR is thus not solely method, but a reimagining of the research process. It is a recasting of the "researched" as participants in the design of research, the production of knowledge, and the sharing of knowledge with the broader publics. From this premise, the collaborative was created.

Digital social science is an emerging area, but it draws from various traditions and is used in #BarrioEdProj as a means to amplify the analytical and political dimensions of this form of public science. The Economic and Social Research Council, a British organization, defined DSS as social research aimed at:

> developing innovative and more powerful, networked and interoperable research tools and services that make it easier for social scientists to discover, access and analyse data, and to collaborate so that they may tackle increasingly complex research challenges. (as quoted in Spiro, 2014)

Data gathering and data sharing were the aspects of DSS that were of most importance to #BarrioEdProj. Early on in the implementation of the project, the overall research design moved from an online community engagement to digital historical ethnography. Digital historical ethnography is, like traditional ethnography, about gathering, sharing, and analyzing stories (Murthy, 2008; Underberg & Zorn, 2013). In this project, the focus was on gathering archival materials and video recorded interviews. Hunter (2013) asserts that "[t]he goal of historical ethnography, as with any other ethnography, is to gather and convey an internally valid description of a site and the peoples therein" (p. 231). As a process, historical ethnography relies on the construction of temporally, and spatially, situated narratives that are triangulated through archival materials. This approach enabled a contextual understanding of change in El Barrio and its schools, as well as the actions of individuals to these changing social conditions. Digital tools, in this case, do not supplant traditional historical ethnographic methods, instead it pushes how data would be organized and used to teach and engage the public.

#BarrioEdProj would seek to collect, analyze, and share barrio stories through digital video cameras and online video tools (Vimeo/YouTube). We launched http://barrioedproj.org (Wordpress site via OpenCUNY.org) to serve as an information clearinghouse and interactive space to create an evolving archive and to invite discussion. The bulk of the data came from digital video recorded, semi-structured interviews, with a multi-generational group of stakeholders connected to El Barrio education. We asked participants about their relationship to El Barrio and its schools, their perspectives on cultural and economic change, and, finally, their views on the future of the neighborhood and the schools.

Building With El Barrio

New York's Latino population has grown and changed over the last century, with over 2 million Latino New Yorkers (27.3 percent of the city's population) forming Latino core communities in different parts of the city by 2010 (Haslip-Viera, 2017). #BarrioEdProj could have been initiated in a number of these core communities, but having connections to educational institutions and fellow activists in El Barrio, and the neighborhood's long history as a cradle of Latino New York, El Barrio became the first project site. Moreover, with funds awarded to me by the Graduate Center of the City University of New York's (CUNY) Digital Initiatives grants program, I was able to offer a small stipend for two youth researchers. Using social media platforms, I posted an advertisement calling for El Barrio youth who wanted to develop research and social media skills and, most importantly, have a stronger voice in their community. Within a week, several young people had contacted me, as did colleagues who worked with high school and college aged youth. One colleague, Blanca E. Vega, who was then director of the Higher Education Opportunity Program (HEOP) at Marymount Manhattan College in New York, would connect me to Mariely and Honory. After conducting interviews where we spoke about the project and why they were interested in doing this work, Mariely Mena, then age 19, and Honory Peña, then age 23, were hired as project co-researchers to form #BarrioEdProj research collaborative.

Mariely is a Chicana from New York who went to public schools throughout her K–12 career, including The Young Women's Leadership High School (TYWLS) in East Harlem. Honory is a Dominican-American who, as a child, split her time between schools in New York and the Dominican Republic. She went to a high school in the city. Both Honory and Mariely were students at Marymount Manhattan College in New York, where they were very active in the college's Higher Education Opportunity Program (HEOP).

Partnerships

As a pilot version with limited funds and still underdeveloped relationships, we kept decision making power amongst the three of us until we as a group felt we could engage more people in steering the project. To cultivate our fledgling relationships we continued to do outreach in the neighborhood and online to build partnerships and our presence in the community. The outreach was geared toward raising awareness about the project, identifying potential interviewees, and building relationships where we would offer to promote events and make note of issues that were of concern to these individuals and organizations. In building these partnerships, we sought to create an interactive dynamic where our partners could provide us feedback on the work, connect us to other stakeholders, and collaborate with us in crafting more questions.

Our partners varied in who they represented, and how they partnered with us. The local Community Board (CB11) was supportive and provided space to conduct interviews. East Harlem Preservation, a volunteer advocacy group dedicated to promoting and preserving the vibrant history of East Harlem, under the direction of Marina Ortiz, endorsed the project, participated in interviews, and shared relevant information and events with #BarrioEdProj on an ongoing basis. La Casa Azul Bookstore, an independent bookstore and community space in El Barrio, under the leadership of Aurora Anaya-Cerda, supported our work by providing space for events and inviting us to partake in education-centered events. And Marie Winfield, an El Barrio parent and advocate for, among other things, parks equity, educational justice, dual language instruction, and local tech incubators for youth, was one of our early interviewees and now remains in close contact with the project.

A Curriculum of Conocimiento

Wright (2015) notes that PAR projects are "adult-supported learning contexts that promote young people's involvement in project decision-making, planning and design", and that "entail[s] providing a curriculum and skill-building instruction to student researchers" (p. 25). As the collaborative was taking shape, I had begun to design the curricular framework to get us started, and as an educator-scholar-activist my approach to curricular design drew heavily from the traditions of critical pedagogy. Duncan-Andrade and Morrell (2008) remind us that critical pedagogy is:

> an approach to education that is rooted in the existential experiences of marginalized peoples; that is centered in a critique of structural, economic, and racial oppression; that is focused on dialogue instead of a one-way transmission of knowledge; and that is structured to empower individuals and collectives as agents of social change. (p. 1)

Critical pedagogy is a twining of critical reflection and action, or praxis, for the purposes of inciting participant's conscientization, or critical consciousness. Along the same lines, Gloria Anzaldúa spoke of the notion of conocimiento as a "state of awakeness" that "connects the inner life of the mind and the spirit to the outer world of action" (Keating, 2000, p. 178). In this case, the curricular goal was to engage in a process of awaking all participants to the operation of social injustice and to El Barrio and its schools, specifically, as a means to transform our collective future.

Critical pedagogy is actualized through the curriculum. Curriculum is defined here as the "series of things" a group of people must do and experience in order to unfold the development of some dimension of individual and collective capacities (see Flinders & Thornton, 2012). As a place-based project, the content of the project was El Barrio, its history, institutions, and people. My initial design of the curriculum prioritized reading materials about the neighborhood, like Arlene Dávila's *Barrio Dreams* (2004), and literary works like Ernest Quiñonez' *Bodega Dreams* (2000). Having taught in the public schools doing teacher education work for over a decade at the time, it was rare to see students exposed to this literature prior to college. As such it was critical to teach about El Barrio and to weave in key sociological themes that the literature has focused on.

While literature was our starting point, it was important to me that we connect that to people and places that make El Barrio what it is, and to develop the research and media skills needed to evolve our project. As such, I engaged the group in developing plans for outreach and engagement. Together we identified local community events to attend and built relationships with local institutions like the archives at the Center for Puerto Rican Studies. In addition, we identified the research, video and social media production skills we felt we needed and organized trainings for the group. This included trainings on conducting interviews and observations, video production, and using social media tools to engage the public.

Team Meetings

Another key aspect of the curriculum was the building of a sense of community. The collaborative would meet between one and four times a month to discuss readings, do trainings on research methods or social media practices, and reflect on our work in the field. More, meetings were an opportunity for reflection and community building. Routines were established where we opened with personal "check-ins", which gave us an opportunity to share and discuss things happening in our personal lives. Reflections on readings and our field experiences also included examinations of the affective dimensions of our fieldwork. By making the social emotional development of each of the collective members a part of the curriculum, we established a familial dynamic within the group that honored personal knowledge, feelings and perspectives, as an equally legitimate aspect of the curriculum.

Findings: Dismemberment and Survivance

Over the course of a year of being in the neighborhood and the archives, and conducting interviews, doing social media work, and team meeting discussions, we began to organize our findings. In documenting the way RNU had worked its way through El Barrio, two major findings that emerged were the affective effects of RNU, and the varied strategies of survivance the people of El Barrio enacted to navigate RNU.

It was clear that the gentrification of the community was central to residents' views, as was the often-punitive characteristics of a Mayor-controlled education system. One similarity between El Barrio and school are the damaging affective and material effects of RNU. Fullilove (2005) poignantly notes that

> ...all people—live in an emotional ecosystem that attaches us to the environment, not just as our individual selves, but as beings caught in a single, universal net of consciousness anchored in small niches we call neighborhoods or hamlets or villages. (Chapter 1 Section 2, para 16)

For many of our participants and the co-researchers, the remaking of El Barrio and its school came as a root shock (Fullilove, 2005) that produced feelings of dismemberment or loss. As one of our interviewees noted, "the history, the historicalness of East Harlem is diminishing for the simple reason of the push that's coming into our community on the development level" (Nazario, 2013). We felt that the feeling of losing one's neighborhood was reflective of what we also had been reading from the literature about the community and urban change--namely feelings of disconnection from place and political voice.

At the same time that we had documented this brand of urbanism, we paid close attention to survivance. Native scholar Vizenor (2008) says that survivance "is greater than the right of a survivable name. Survivance stories are renunciations of dominance, detractions, obtrusions, the unbearable sentiments of tragedy, and the legacy of victimry" (Chapter 1, Section 8, para 9). In this project we learned about how people in El Barrio navigated dominance. Our interviews and observations of public events, for example, demonstrated that some individuals and local institutions focus on complicity, while others engage in local politics with the hopes of disrupting dominance. The data we gathered connected to our reading of secondary literature and archival materials where the lives of community advocates, like activist Antonia Pantoja, were powerful examples of activism. Through our interviews and coming to know the history of the community, we came to appreciate the actions people have taken in response to living with, for and against social conditions.

We continue to be in the process of writing up our findings, but we have been committed to using the findings as a tool for teaching. For example, we have shared our findings, and lead workshops on some of our methods, at research and educator activist conferences. Most importantly, we organized a community event at La Casa Azul Bookstore to share some of our work with the local community to receive feedback from participants to help us craft more formal reports and online blog posts.

Assessing the Impact of #BarrioEdProj

#BarrioEdProj has not made a profound impact on the redistribution of resources or changes in urban policy on a systemic level in El Barrio, yet. Still, I argue that as a pedagogical tool, #BarrioEdProj has had a transformative impact on those who have crossed paths with the project.

Our two youth co-researchers Mariely and Honory, I contend, felt the most profound effects of the project. My intention was to give them opportunities to become engaged community scholars who were aware, or consiente, of the social, structural issues and be able to use research to inform and incite social transformation. Their responses and ideas over the course of the first year of the project suggest that the project had a positive impact on their emerging critical consciousness and research skill development. But what I want to pay particular attention to is the impact the work had on their own conocimiento, or critical consciousness.

Having been members of the East Harlem community for most, if not all, of their lives, Honory and Mariely were being exposed to East Harlem-focused social science and archival information for the first time. This elicited feelings of surprise, dissatisfaction and some anger. The fact that this material was not part of school curriculum for many people, including themselves, lead them to express feelings of missing out and asserting that Latinos were somehow seen as less. On top of all these feelings, there was also a growing anger as they began to think more about the devastating impact gentrification and education reform were having on their lives, and the lives of others in the neighborhood. In short, they had become critically conscious of the varied ways that education and urbanism had dismembered them from their histories and their community.

Doing the archival work and conducting interviews also served as a counter to dismemberment, as they engaged in work that afforded them opportunities to re-member themselves to these narratives. They were pleased to learn about the rich history of the neighborhood. As they began to read through

the archives about the work of organizations like ASPIRA or United Bronx
Parents, and individuals like Antonia Pantoja and Evelina Antoinette, their
pride was observable.

While Honory and Mariely's analyses were honest and often propelled
by feelings of anger and despair, by re-membering they were engaged in the
empowering and joyful compelling. She notes,

> My whole perspective of my own community has changed a lot, especially because I
> feel like when I was younger I didn't really pay too much attention. Or at least, me,
> mentally, I wasn't worried about anyone else, but myself and what I had to do. Now
> with the project, it's more like every day no matter what when I walk out of my house
> and I'm around East Harlem, I'm always consciously thinking about what's going on.
> (Mena, 2014)

Mariely's comments are suggestive of an important distinction between
remembering and a politics of re-membering. In engaging in our research
process, teaching and action were processes that were "active rather than re-
active, prescient rather than nostalgic, abundant rather than lacking, social
rather than solipsistic, militant rather than reactionary" (Eng & Kazanjian,
2002, p. 2). Re-membering is thus a political act, rather than an apolitical
recollection.

Re-membering is also a path to action. In the midst of our research, one
of the questions we often asked ourselves was fundamentally one about taking
action: The community is in trouble, so how can we help people realize what's
going on? We drew from all aspects of our projects as we wrestled with this
question, including the archives. When reflecting on examining the archives
from ASPIRA and our interviews, for example, Honory asked, "A lot of the
interviewees have been talking about parent involvement, how can we spread
what ASPIRA is doing into the community?" (Peña, Meeting Notes, 2013).
In this question, Honory was engaging in her own process of re-membering
herself to the history, and strategies, of struggle that ASPIRA represents. At
the same time that she was connecting the past to contemporary struggles,
she was looking to the past for guidance. The question that Honory posed
here became an essential question that continues to animate the work of the
project in the present.

During an interview toward the end of the first year of the project, Honory would also extend her thoughts on taking action based on our research
into schools. Here she was speaking about how students were underserved by

the education system, and how the work of the project might contribute to working against these conditions:

> It's a battle because they're just used to that. I feel like maybe doing some of that kind of connection in the neighborhood, or even if it's not the school principal, someone whose involved, even if it's a parent. If they're involved, what do they see?… and getting their point of view. Not even just the interviewing in the neighborhood, but coming into these schools or into these programs or even just community spaces, it's like, *what's the scoop? What's happening?* [Italics added] (Peña, 2014)

Honory had come to recognize that there are people very much involved in the struggle to create more just educational conditions, but the emphasis on the individual within RNU meant a solidification of already present divisions. Part of her solution to interrupting that individualization was to further expand the reach of our D+CPAR into the schools by sharing information for the purposes of inspiring conocimiento.

#BarrioEdProj as a Guide to Action

More, by learning from, with, and through the project, #BarrioEdProj can also be understood as a "guide to action" (Le Blanc, 1996) for others to use against adaptive racial neoliberal urbanism. Perhaps the most important lesson is that we can all participate in a PAR EntreMundos to actualize social change. The notion of EntreMundos refers to "in-between spaces of our own creation since we cannot fit neatly into categories made for us" (See Chapter 1). Latino core communities and we, as Latino educator-scholar-activists, live and struggle in the in-between, formed by multiple histories and futurities from the south and the north.

To do research, teaching and political action from this in-between space is challenging and necessary work. It is a means of educating each other and ourselves in order to move toward liberation. Further, by rooting our work with and through a barrio, PAR projects become a tool of empowerment. I return to our co-researcher Honory's description of research within our structure:

> I definitely see research differently now and I do hope to one day do some research of my own. I've noticed that is more than just reading what's already out there but is also about going straight to the sources themselves and make connections/research that way. All my life I've been told what is that I need to get done and what tasks I

need to finish and that's what I thought this experience was going to be like, but it has actually taught me that I can bring my own ideas and i[t']s ok to brainstorm and talk about what I like to see be done and how my thoughts can be integrated into the project. (Peña, 2014)

It is our hope then that #BarrioEdProj serves as a valuable and accessible guide to action to use in establishing their own work in their own contexts, and working toward social change.

References

Ball, D. L., & Forzani, F. M. (2007). 2007 Wallace foundation distinguished lecture—what makes education research "educational"? *Educational Researcher*, 36(9), 529–540. http://doi.org/10.3102/0013189X07312896

Cayo Sexton, P. (1965). *Spanish Harlem: Anatomy of poverty* (1st ed.). New York, NY: Harper Colophon.

Dávila, A. M. (2004). *Barrio dreams: Puerto Ricans, Latinos, and the neoliberal city*. Berkeley, CA: University of California Press.

Duncan-Andrade, J. M. R., & Morrell, E. (2008). *The art of critical pedagogy: Possibilities for moving from theory to practice in urban schools* (Vol. 285). New York, NY: Peter Lang. Retrieved from http://books.google.com/books?hl=en&lr=&id=Xd6AtJ3EhK8C&oi=fnd&pg=PP11&dq=%22critical+pedagogy.+In+our+joint+efforts+we+have+worked+across+multiple%22+%22center,+that+we+cotaught+for+three+years.+We+begin+with+the%22+%22that+is+rooted+in+the+existential+experiences+of+marginalized+peoples%3B+that%22+&ots=YICCwIDJW8&sig=P7n8md0-Adpq7fWBPMyFlHsDshU

Eng, D. L., & Kazanjian, D. (Eds.). (2002). *Loss: The politics of mourning*. Berkeley, CA: University of California Press.

Fliegel, S., & MacGuire, J. (1993). *Miracle in East Harlem: The fight for choice in public education*. New York, NY: Times Books.

Flinders, D. J., & Thornton, S. J. (Eds.). (2012). *The curriculum studies reader* (4th ed.). New York, NY; London: Routledge.

Freidenberg, J. (1995). *The anthropology of lower income urban enclaves: The case of East Harlem*. New York, NY: New York Academy of Sciences.

Fullilove, M. T. (2005). *Root shock: How tearing up city neighborhoods hurts America, and what we can do about it [Kindle edition]*. New York, NY: One World/Ballantine Books.

Gilmore, R. W. (2008). Forgotten places and the seeds of grassroots planning. In C. R. Hale (Ed.), *Engaging contradictions: Theory, politics, and methods of activist scholarship*. Berkeley, CA: University of California Press.

Glassman, M., & Erdem, G. (2014). Participatory action research and its meanings: Vivencia, Praxis, Conscientization. *Adult Education Quarterly*, 64(3), 206–221.

Haslip-Viera, G. (2010). The evolution of the Latino community in New York City: Early seventeenth century to the present. In S. Baver, A. Falcón, & G. Haslip-Viera (Eds.), *Latinos in New York: Communities in transition* (2nd ed., pp. 17–56). Notre Dame, IN: Notre Dame Press.

Hunter, M. A. (2013). *Black citymakers: How the Philadelphia Negro changed urban America*. Oxford; New York, NY: Oxford University Press.

Keating, A. (Ed.). (2000). *Interviews/Entrevistas/Gloria Anzaldúa* (1st ed.). New York, NY: Routledge.

Kirp, D. L. (1992, November). What school choice really means—92.11. *The Atlantic Monthly*, 270(5), 119–132.

Le Blanc, P. (Ed.). (1996). *From Marx to Gramsci*. Amherst, NY: Humanity Books.

Lee, S. S.-H. (2014). *Building a Latino civil rights movement: Puerto Ricans, African Americans, and the pursuit of racial justice in New York City* (1st ed.). Chapel Hill, NC: The University of North Carolina Press.

Lewis, H. (2013). *New York City public schools from Brownsville to Bloomberg: community control and its legacy* New York, NY: Teachers College Press.

Mayorga, E. (2014). Toward digital, critical, participatory action research: Lessons from the #BarrioEdProj. *Journal of Interactive Technology & Pedagogy*, (5). Retrieved from http://jitp. commons.gc.cuny.edu/toward-digital-critical-participatory-action-research/

Mayorga, E. (2016). Education in our Barrios, #BarrioEdProj: Mapping dominance and survivance in contemporary racial capitalism (Dissertation).

Mayorga, E., & Picower, B. (2012, June). *What's race got to do with It?: Exploring the intersections of institutional racism and neoliberal school reform*. Paper presented at the Critical Race Studies in Education Association, New York, NY.

Meier, D. (1995). *The power of their ideas: Lessons for America from a small school in Harlem*. Boston, MA: Beacon Press.

Melamed, J. (2011). *Represent and destroy: Rationalizing violence in the new racial capitalism*. Minneapolis, MN: University of Minnesota Press.

Mena, M. (2014). Reflection form.

Morales, E. (2017). Latino core communities in change: The erasing of an imaginary nation. In S. Baver, A. Falcon, & G. Haslip-Viera (Eds.), *Latinos in New York: Communities in transition* (2nd ed., pp. 333–362). Notre Dame, IN: University of Notre Dame.

Murthy, D. (2008). Digital ethnography: An examination of the use of new technologies for social research. *Sociology*, 42(5), 837–855. http://doi.org/10.1177/0038038508094565

Nazario, H. (2013). Interview. Retrieved from http://barrioedproj.org

Nieto, S. (2000). *Puerto Rican students in U.S. schools. Sociocultural, political, and historical studies in education*. Mahwah, NJ: Lawrence Erlbaum Associates.

Pedraza, P. (1997). Puerto Ricans and the politics of school reform. *Centro: Journal of the Center for Puerto Rican Studies*, 9, 74–85.

Peña, H. (2014). Year one, evaluation form.

Quiñonez, E. (2000). *Bodega dreams*. New York, NY: Vintage Contemporaries.

Robinson, C. J. (1983). *Black Marxism: The making of the black radical tradition*. London; Totowa, NJ: Zed; Biblio Distribution Center.

Rodríguez, J. (1994). *Spanish Harlem*. Washington, DC: National Museum of American Art.

Schneider, M., Teske, P., & Marschall, M. (2000). *Choosing schools: Consumer choice and the quality of American schools*. Princeton, NJ: Princeton University Press.

Sharman, R. L. (2006). *The tenants of East Harlem*. Berkeley, CA: University of California Press.

Spiro, L. (2014, April 9). Defining digital social sciences. Retrieved from http://acrl.ala.org/dh/2014/04/09/defining-digital-social-sciences/

Steinhauer, J. (2002, June 13). As Bloomberg takes over schools, Pataki takes center stage. *The New York Times*. Retrieved from http://www.nytimes.com/2002/06/13/nyregion/as-bloomberg-takes-over-schools-pataki-takes-center-stage.html

Suzuki, D., & Mayorga, E. (2014). Scholar-activism: A twice told tale. *Multicultural Perspectives, 16*(1), 16–20. Retrieved from http://doi.org/10.1080/15210960.2013.867405

Taylor, K.-Y. (2016). *From #BlackLivesMatter to Black liberation*. Chicago, IL: Haymarket Books.

Torre, M. E., Fine, M., Stoudt, B. G., & Fox, M. (2012). Critical participatory action research as public science. In H. M. Cooper & P. M. Camic (Eds.), *APA handbook of research methods in psychology*. Washington, DC: American Psychological Association.

Underberg, N. M., & Zorn, E. (2013). *Digital ethnography: Anthropology, narrative, and new media*. Austin, TX: University of Texas Press.

Vizenor, G. (Ed.). (2008). *Survivance: Narratives of native presence [Kindle edition]* (Kindle edition). Lincoln, NE: University of Nebraska Press.

Wright, D. E. (2015). *Active learning: Social justice education and participatory action research*. New York, NY: Routledge.

7

OUR WILD TONGUES

Language Justice and Youth Research

Jenna Cushing-Leubner and Jennifer Eik

Context

In 2011, Eleanor High School's administration sent out a survey request to students and families. After years of being marked as a failing Midwest school, having failing teachers from across the city's district shuffled into its ranks, and going severely under-resourced again and again, Eleanor was experiencing a climate shift. Its new principal was working closely with a former teacher who was now working towards her Ph.D. at the local university. As a result, Eleanor had become the site for a budding and tenacious school-university partnership unlike anything else in its state of Minnesota. Up until this point, this had meant mostly recruiting top teachers out of the university's licensure program, improving support for collaborative teaching, and providing mentorship and professional development for teachers in their first few years until they, too, became mentors. The goal was to recognize and recruit the best teachers at the start of their careers, and to retain teachers who were willing and able to grow a critical and collaborative pedagogy atmosphere.

While Eleanor had miles to go, they were also starting to feel the effects of the partnership working. Its cadre of young teachers were bringing with them strategies for critical pedagogies, collective learning, and integrations of the arts. In part as a result of this and in part because of its efforts to support younger teachers who had spent time with students and teachers at Eleanor throughout the licensure program and were making Eleanor their top-choice to teach, students were calling Eleanor a school where there were teachers who cared about them, a school where they (at least at times) liked to be. In 2009, only 32 incoming freshmen had chosen the school as their first choice for attendance. By 2015, the number of first-choice freshman had soared to 278 (Principal, personal communication, 2015).

Still, Minnesota's failure to recruit, be responsive to, support, and retain teachers of color and multilingual teachers meant that the majority of its teachers continued to be white and monolingual English-speakers. At the same time, Eleanor experienced a wealth of languages and ethnic backgrounds across its student body. Forty percent of its students identified as new diaspora Latinx, 35% as African and African-American, and the rest a combination of Southeast Asian, Native American, and U.S.-born European descent. Across these groups, more than half of the students qualified as English learners, with even more speaking multiple languages at home, in their communities, and in school (Minnesota Department of Education, 2015). Still, due to the racial, ethnic, and linguistic mismatch between teachers and students, Eleanor's wealth of linguistic and cultural practices continued to be painfully restrained. Moreover, with few exceptions, its curriculum ached to be released from the limits of the Eurocentric content and teacher-fronted pedagogical models.

Because Minnesota's school funding structure applies funds based on each student who attends the school, as its student body increased, Eleanor also saw an increase in its budget. The principal was using this to reinstate the myriad courses that had been canceled in earlier years and forcefully replaced with remediated math, sheltered English language, and remediated English literacy classes. He had hired an arts-coordinator whose job included writing grants to bring in community-artists to collaborate with students and to organize tri-annual school-community arts-crawls with music, dance, and visual arts. He had reinstated the music and theater programs. As a former ESL teacher, he had made increasing language electives his next goal.

In the spring of 2011, Eleanor's principal asked the students: "If you could study a language other than English, would you?" and "What language class would you take?" Overwhelmingly, the response from students was: "Spanish for us"—the "us" being youth who came from homes, communities, and transnational families where Spanish was spoken, but who entered a school environment day after day where English was their only option. For these youth, Latinx, their experiences in the United States ranging from a year to their whole lives, speaking different regional varieties of Spanish from across the Americas—almost none of them had been provided the opportunity to learn outside of the narrow, Eurocentric curriculum that pervades our U.S. schools; to use Spanish or the variety of Indigenous languages spoken across the generations of some of their families to connect community knowledge to academic definitions of intellectualism, or to develop their languages and literacies in those languages alongside the primarily school-based development of English. "Spanish for us" was more than recognition that spending a semester learning how to ask for directions and introduce themselves in a traditional Spanish as a Foreign Language class was not worth their time. For the Latinx youth at Eleanor, "Spanish for us" was a rallying cry.

This chapter documents the development of *Jóvenes con Derechos* (JcD), a collective of multilingual Latinx high school students, which started at Eleanor High School in the 2012/13 school year. JcD was born out of the creation of a series of Spanish as a Heritage Language classes in response to this student demand from the school to provide Spanish language electives designed specifically for multilingual Latinx youth. Using a cohort model and a sociocultural approach to language and literacy development, youth and their teachers spend two years together. In this time, youth use and develop their multiple varieties of both Spanish and English to study critical race theories, justice movements across Latinx, Chicanx, and Indigenous communities across the U.S. and the Americas, borderlands identities, and arts-based approaches to collective action and transformational voicing of selves and communities. In their second year together, students draw on this shared knowledge base to engage in youth participatory action research projects. They develop critical and community-based research techniques, digital storytelling skills, and arts-based methods for data gathering and dissemination. Youth draw on their angers and dissatisfactions with suppressive schooling experiences, micro-aggressions, and linguistic constraints in schools and broader social contexts. They utilize their multiple languages to engage in a local-global nexus of transnational community-based research to speak back to these oppressive realities and to draw multilingual community knowledge into the often flat-affect monolingual and Eurocentric spaces of schools.

Jóvenes con Derechos

Jennifer was hired to teach these Spanish as a Heritage Language classes and, as a first year teacher, reached out to Jenna, a Ph.D. student at the University who had worked closely with her as a teaching supervisor and graduate assistant mentor during her licensure program. Spanish Heritage Language (SHL) education in high schools exists in response to the linguistic stripping perpetrated against multilingual Latinx youth through the predominantly English monolingual environments of U.S. public schools (García, 2005; Valdés, 2005; Valenzuela, 1999). Despite growing interest, SHL continues to lack critical holistic and nuanced examples in either educational research or in the form of instructional tools (Harklau, 2009). In particular, we found almost nothing illuminating instructional practices, curricular content, or student experiences in successful SHL classes—particularly in New Latinx Diaspora contexts (Wortham, Murillo, & Hamann, 2002), such as in Northern and Midwestern U.S. states. Together, we instead drew on examples of justice-oriented education around the country that was flipping the script of failure perpetrated by U.S. schools against Latinx youth (e.g. Cammarota & Romero, 2014; Irizarry, 2011, 2015). We sought out the arts and pedagogies of the contact zone (Pratt, 1991).

Similar to much of the United States, in the political and raciolinguistic climate (Flores & Rosa, 2015; Malsbary, 2014) of New Latinx Diaspora states, subtractive schooling (Valenzuela, 1999) has resulted in ethnic, linguistic, and cultural erasure amongst Latinx youth, as well as broad-stroke xenophobic racialization of native Spanish-speakers. Latinx youth experience high rates of school push-out, dehumanizing school climates, and active denigration of rich and varied language resources. Because Latinx youth come to Minnesota from many geographical homes across the Americas, because time in Minnesota and the U.S. ranges from third generation to recently arrived, and because nearly all of our youth are in constant transnational interactions thanks largely to social media, the varieties of Spanish spoken in New Latinx Diaspora spaces are incredibly rich and reflective of the scope of ethnic and cultural roots across the larger Latinx community. Alongside our youth, entering the multi-ethnic, translingual, transcultural, and multiracial(ized) contact zone, Jennifer is multilingual in Spanish and English, of African descent, and not Latina, and Jenna is multilingual, of European descent, and not Latina. Together, we came to view the classroom and the community learning spaces where youth and adults engaged in most of their research and actions as a contact zone (Pratt, 2007).

The contact zone has been extremely helpful in thinking about challenging institutionally imposed spaces that rely on constraining youth and adults alike, particularly in schools which have so long functioned as a core tool of colonization and marginalization. Youth and adults—both institutionally positioned as being powerful/disempowered, legitimate/illegitimate in very different ways—come into contact in an institutional space built to marginalize them. There, they draw from multiple languages with varying prestige and legitimacy due to the social and political constructions of languages as proper/ improper, standard/substandard, academic/social. Conceptualizing the SHL classroom as a contact zone makes sense, as it is a "messy social space where very differently situated people [can] work together across their own varying relationships to power and privilege" (Torre, 2009, p. 110). Furthering this, in the contact zone entremundos, hybridity is embraced and valued, encouraging those who gather there to be explicit about "varying identities, communities, relationships to power and privilege, experiences, desires and vulnerabilities" (Torre & Ayala, 2009, p. 390). With this in mind, we utilized dialogic and problem-posing approaches to explore with youth what the content and pedagogies of a SHL-as-contact-zone educational space should include.

In line with participatory action research EntreMundos (Cammarota et al., 2016; Torre & Ayala, 2009), we asked youth and ourselves to "theorize from the flesh" (Anzaldúa, 1987). We attempted to usurp the sterility and oftentimes violence of the classroom and to claim it instead as a place to offer ourselves to one another and to "[expose our] rawest wounds and deepest desires to write, theorize and reclaim that which has often been denied" (Torre & Ayala, 2009, p. 388, referencing Moraga & Anzaldúa, 1981). PAR EntreMundos became the life-force of our contact zone. We planted ourselves in Freirian traditions of the praxis of critical reflection and creative, conscious actions—and we fertilized our praxis with the intersectionalities of critical race theory, feminist theorizing and the ancestral knowledges that live in us despite attempts made to silence them. Over the first two years, this took shape as intra-ethnic studies content that utilized translanguaging (García & Wei, 2014) and focused on eco- and educational-justice, Indigenous land rights across the Americas, social justice youth development (Ginwright & Cammarota, 2002), arts-based expression, community-based local text production, and youth-led participatory action research (YPAR) (Cammarota & Fine, 2008; Mirra, Garcia, & Morrell, 2015). It was in the second year of the program, when students were undertaking their first YPAR projects around curricular representation and language rights in schools that they decided to name themselves. As Josué, a junior, put it, "If we've got something to say, people need to know our name. And it's got to say what we stand for". And *Jóvenes con Derechos* (JcD) (Figure 7.1) was born.

Figure 7.1: Jóvenes con Derechos Youth-Created T-shirt Design

Source: Erika "Castro" Palacios (Jóvenes con Derechos)

Our Languages, Our Schools, Nuestrxs Derechos

On November 5, 2014, Jóvenes con Derechos took part in their first of many collective actions and orchestrated a multilingual linguistic rights summit at Eleanor High School. The youth who planned and organized the summit were students in their second year of the class. Conference attendees included teachers, students, administrators, school district officials from the multilingual department, local political figures, and university professors in the city's teacher education and licensure programs. The purpose of the conference was for youth to share narratives that had been collected through interviews of family members, classmates, teachers, and community members discussing their experiences surrounding the topics of linguistic conflict and linguistic discrimination. In addition, they were looking for a commitment from attendees to make changes to the raciolinguistic climate of their schools across multiple levels.

Feeling Out the Rabbit Hole: JcD's First Attempt at YPAR

This was the first time both Jennifer and JcD youth had taken up YPAR. And at times YPAR's effects of "lead[ing] the student 'down the rabbit hole' past the layers of lies to the truths of systematic exploitation and oppression as well as possibilities for resistance" (Cammarota & Fine, 2008, p. 1) could not feel more real. Youth interviewed classmates, teachers, and community members; gathered autoethnographic accounts of their own experiences; and did document analyses of school, district, and international language-in-education policies. Thinking about YPAR as "an innovative approach to positive youth and community development in which young people are trained to conduct systematic research to improve their lives, their communities, and the institutions intended to serve them" (UC Berkeley, 2015), the decision was made to focus efforts on the school as one of the primary institutions that impacted all participants' lives.

We began our research by co-constructing definitions of the term "right". As a class, we discussed questions such as, "What is a right?" "What is a human right?" "What is the purpose of defining rights?" "What is the distinction between a right and a privilege?" "Who are rights for?" etc. Once we had developed a running definition of the term that the majority of the class agreed upon, we then asked ourselves the question, "What is a linguistic right?" For our purposes, we explored this as "What are the rights of people whose first language is something other than English?" and "What are the rights of people who speak more than one language?" Together, we came to the conclusion that a linguistic right is a right that protects people from being treated unjustly because of language, dialect/variation, and/or accent. Then youth developed three essential questions to drive their research:

1) How do language, accent, and dialect affect how people are treated?
2) How can we ensure that our school is a place where all languages are respected?
3) In what ways is being multilingual an asset?

Overcoming Silence: Talking to Each Other, Talking Back

Youth decided that interviewing would be an effective way to collect the stories and data that would assist us in answering our essential questions. Every student in the class knew someone closely who could speak to the experience of navigating the world through multiple languages. Many students opted to choose a friend or classmate as their interviewee. In addition to friends, the majority of youth had access to family members who could share experiences of linguistic conflict, discrimination, and success. As criteria for choosing an interviewee, we decided it should be someone who was currently living in the United States and a) spoke a first language other than English or b) spoke multiple languages regularly.

In order to generate five interview questions that everyone across two different class periods of students would use to interview one person of their choice, we divided the classes into groups of three and each group came up with three interview questions that would help us conduct our research. These were then compiled into a list of sixteen questions that youth discussed in terms of overlaps, focus, and range of topic linked to our research questions and then collectively ranked. The top five were used for our interviews.

The five interview questions were:
1) Have you ever been treated unfairly because of the way that you speak?
2) Have you ever been confused for/assumed to be someone of another race/ethnicity for the way that you looked or spoke?
3) Has speaking another language ever been an advantage for you?
4) Have you ever been belittled because of the way that you speak?
5) Have you ever been able to help someone by using two different languages?

Students were given one week to conduct their interview and were instructed to take notes and pay special attention to the stories that their interviewees shared, as those would be the stories that we would present (with their permission) during our linguistic rights summit.

Nuestrxs Derechos Lingüísticos: Speaking Truth to Power

Once the interviews had been conducted, the data were brought to class for us to analyze as a group. Students brought the stories that had been collected from their classmates, teachers, neighbors, and family members. We broke into small groups to read the stories and to discuss each situation individually. Most stories had to do with cases of microaggressions and/or overt discrimination based on race, ethnicity, belief system, language and/or language variation/dialect. When asked the question, *¿Te han hecho sentir menos por tu forma de hablar?* (Have you ever been made to feel "less than" for the way that you speak), one interviewee responded, "Yes, I was interpreting in a hospital and the nurse spoke a different dialect of Spanish so she made fun of me and that did bring me down". Across community interviews youth and adults alike shared experiences of raciolinguistic discrimination and aggressions. JcD youth shared numerous examples in their presentations, including the following:

> Ej: *Una joven fue a la cafetería para el almuerzo, se sentó con un grupo que no era de su raza. Rápido las jóvenes la hicieron mover porque fue distinta de las otras y que se fuera sentar con las mexicanas.* [Translation: One girl went to the cafeteria for lunch and sat down with a group of people who weren't the same race as her. The group at the table got up quickly and moved because she was different from them and she should be sitting with the Mexicans.]
> Ex: Erick was going through the McDonald's drive-thru. The operator didn't understand what Erick was trying to order because of his accent and asked him to pull up to the window. The operator told him that he should learn how to speak like an American because he's in America.

In examples such as these, youth found evidence of white supremacy as it plays out in raciolinguistic ideologies, such as when one young Salvadoran woman was othered, racialized through mechanisms of linguistic whiteness (wherein Spanish-speaking equates to being "Mexican", unless one is white-skinned or racialized first as black), and told to move at a lunch table when the group of students she sat down with who did not speak Spanish and she did not believe to be Latinx told her to "leave and sit with your Mexican friends". Similarly, Erick's story of being told to "learn how to speak like an American because he's in America" reflected ways that "being American" is conflated with a constantly moving target of "appropriate English" speech, which can never be achieved, in particular when coming from the mouths of brown and black speakers. Linguistic discrimination, racialization of language use, and being socially and academically reprimanded for using languages other than English not only resonated amongst JcD youth, it linked their experiences to larger race-language policies and practices in schools (Malsbary, 2014). These data that JcD collected showed that suppressive language environments were not unique to those one might expect to find in states like Arizona, with their overt restrictive and English-only school policy environments (e.g. Cammarota, Berta-Ávila, Ayala, Rivera, & Rodríguez, 2016; Iddings, Combs, & Moll, 2012). Indeed, in a northern Midwest state that could be seen as particularly progressive in comparison, multilingual youth reverberated with the English-dominant, monoglossic ideologies of what it means to be an "American" in the United States today.

In addition to collecting narratives of prejudice and discrimination, we chose as a class to word the research and interview questions in a way that that would also allow stories of resilience and empowerment to emerge. One interviewee shared such a story when asked the question, *¿Alguna vez hablar español fue una ventaja para ti?* (Has speaking Spanish ever been an advantage for you?) Her response was, "Yes, when I needed to help someone who didn't speak English. At that time it was an advantage". Throughout the community interviews, people consistently offered examples of linguistic and cultural brokering (Morales & Hanson, 2005; Orellana, 2009) only available to them thanks to their ability to move across multiple languages, communication styles, variations of languages, and cultural norms. While these stories were present, JcD found great determination in the need to bring to light the stories of raciolinguistic profiling and discrimination they felt continued to go under the radar in their schools and in the preparation of predominantly English-speaking and monolingual teachers who youth viewed as having limited race-language consciousness.

Our next step was the result of one student's comment during a class discussion following the initial reading of the narratives that emerged from the interviews: "Yes, we know that happens, but, what can we actually *do* about it?" A silence fell upon the class as some students nodded in agreement and others seemed to shift. We seemed to be in the "rabbit hole" and for a time, we reflected on just how sticky the "layers of lies" and "truths of systematic exploitation and oppression" really were. Several students mentioned feeling defeated and overwhelmed in that moment. But through this, we also talked our way to recognizing the "possibilities for resistance". For JcD, the first iteration of their resistance had already taken place—they had rejected the narratives of linguistic and intellectual deficiencies placed on them as U.S. Latinx youth and become researchers and documentarians of lived experiences. For the next iteration, it was time to speak truth to power. Out of the question "so what we do with this now?" came the idea to draft a list of "linguistic rights" to voice and lay claim to the protections people should have from raciolinguistic discrimination and aggressions. As part of an impromptu, large-group discussion, we created a "right" that corresponded to each case to protect people who were members of racial, ethnic or linguistically marginalized groups from situations of discrimination and unjust treatment. For example, in response to the above anecdote concerning the interviewee who was mocked and looked down upon in the hospital because of the variation of Spanish that she spoke, the following right was drafted: "Todos tienen derecho de no ser discriminados debido a su lenguaje, acento, o dialecto". (Everyone has the right to not be discriminated against based on his or her language, accent or dialect.)

JcD then returned to their interviews. As they poured over their data, they conducted narrative analysis and thematic coding in small groups. Each group then brought the stories and anecdotes they had highlighted along with their thematic analyses all together. After compiling and compressing similar themes, they ranked them by number of occurrence. They also considered the impact of the stories shared and collectively determined which stories were best representative of the different themes. These themes were then translated into their own list of rights (see Figure 7.2).

Figure 7.2: JcD's Declaration of Linguistic Rights

Nuestra Declaración de Derechos Lingüísticos

1) Todos tienen el derecho de no ser categorizados por el color de su piel o su lenguaje
2) Todos tienen el derecho de hablar el idioma que quieran en público
3) Todos tienen el derecho de no ser juzgado a la forma de actuar, color de piel o como se ven
4) Todos tienen el derecho de pedir un intérprete
5) Todos los estudiantes tienen el derecho de hablar en cualquier idioma con sus compañeros
6) Todos tienen el derecho a comunicarse con alguien que entienda su idioma en el trabajo

Source: Jenna Cushing-Leubner & Jennifer Eik

Many of their rights reflected the conflation of racialization, language, and white supremacist discourses of "being American" in the United States and in Minnesota. JcD put forth that everyone has the right to

1) not be categorized by the color of their skin or by their language
2) to speak the language they want to in public
3) not to be judged by the way they act, what color they are, or how they appear
4) to request an interpreter
5) as students, to speak in any language with peers
6) to communicate with someone who understands their language at work

Figure 7.3: Bilingual Invitations to JcD's Linguistic Rights Summit

Las Invitaciones

Estimada Maestra,

De parte de la voz de los alumnos de clase de español con maestra Eik. La invitamos a usted Maestra, [nombre], que venga asistir a una reunión que vamos a tener de los derechos lingüísticos. Los derechos lingüísticos son derechos de jóvenes que debería ser escuchado por todos los demás. Protegen los derechos que los estudiantes (a todos en general) que hablan más de un lenguaje en los Estados Unidos. La estamos invitando usted por queremos que se haga justicia con todos los derechos contra religión, color de piel, creencias.

Ustedes como maestra pueden ayudarnos a que se cumpla nuestros derechos que nosotros sabemos que son muy importante. Con su apoyo, puede ver más voz a nuestro favor. Este evento se llevará a cabo el 5 de noviembre a las 12:45 del día y nos encontraremos en la biblioteca nos vemos alla. Gracias

Sinceramente,

We would like to invite you to our Spanish heritage class on November 5th in the media center at [name of school] at 12:45pm to give us your opinion on what you think of our linguistic rights. Also so you could support us in maintaining our identity in our community.

From our side, we think linguistic rights are when people have the right to talk in their own language and not be discriminated for when they talk their language. We are inviting you because we want you to know that it happens sometimes in school or outside of school like our community. That affects our learning in school and how to interact with people.

Source: Jenna Cushing-Leubner & Jennifer Eik

Once the list of rights had been drafted, our next step was to decide who needed to know what we knew, how the findings and analysis should be presented, and who would be our spokespeople. We came to the consensus to hold a summit at our high school and to invite school administration, teachers, community stakeholders, and politicians as we felt that they were people in positions to affect change concerning how language rights and injustices played out across multiple levels in educational institutions. Along the way, JcD developed their community and events organizing skills. They developed a calendar of key dates, a list of key decision-makers as invitees. They discussed the ways language variation, rhetoric, and presentation (oral, written, supported visually, etc.) can either limit participation or welcome it across community members and made decisions to use everyday language; to preserve the integrity of the language used by interviewees when they shared their stories; to incorporate multiple variations of Spanish, English, and Spanglish and not "clean up" the natural translanguaging that carries knowledge and experience in their own communities (Anzaldúa, 1987). They agreed to design the summit to be multilingual, with the option to participate in predominantly English, predominantly Spanish, and translanguaging (Spanglish) spaces (see Figure 7.3).

Collecting Ourselves, Creating Change

On the day of the summit, JcD members led participants through their experiences of conducting research in their communities and working to create a collection of school-based language rights. Youth organized and led everything from finding space, seeking a small budget, organizing food from a local Mexican family-owned restaurant, presenting, videotaping, and leading subsequent discussions. Following their presentations, youth engaged attendees in a conversation about their commitment to taking action on language rights in their own lives.

Attendees commented about being prompted to think in a way that they hadn't before. Many noted they had never been provoked to consider the assumptions that they made about other people based on their accent, language, and/or variation/dialect. The conversation also prompted attendees to consider how systems of raciolinguistic white supremacy can use a person's speech and language to limit access to opportunities. Each person who attended the conference was also responsible for filling out a commitment form before leaving (see Figure 7.4).

Figure 7.4: Sample Commitment Forms

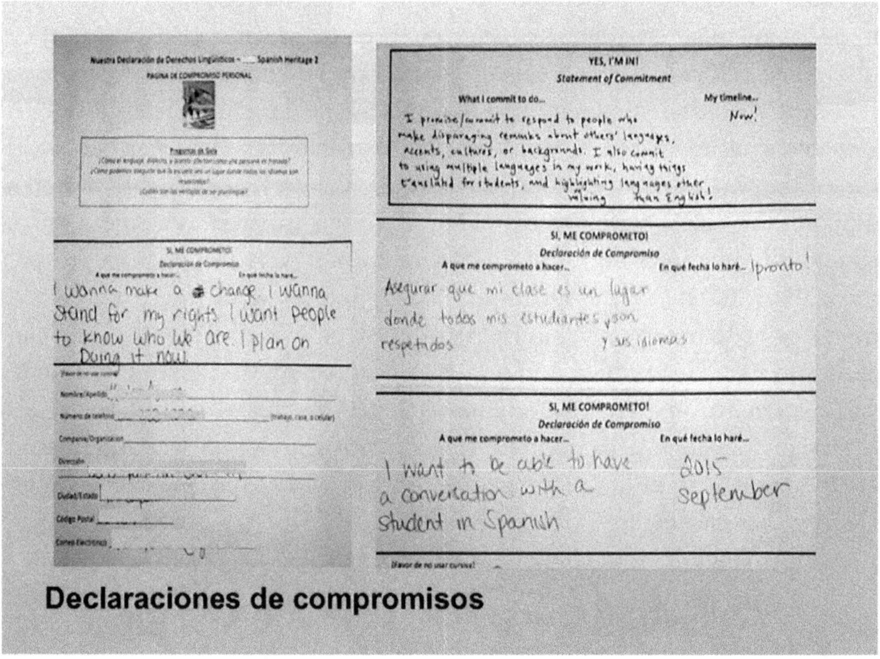

Declaraciones de compromisos

Source: Jenna Cushing-Leubner & Jennifer Eik

The commitment forms were a way for people to pledge to making a change in their lives—whether it was in the classroom, in the halls at school, at work, or at the district level—to assure that other's linguistic rights were being recognized and defended.

This Is Who We Are Now

In recent years, we have been provided numerous examples of ways that YPAR provides opportunities for youth to engage in personal, communal, and transnational transformations and social movements (e.g. Cammarota & Fine, 2008; Duncan-Andrade & Morrell, 2008; Ginwright, 2008; Mirra et al., 2015). In line with all of this, we saw JcD youth exhibit civic and educational leadership, creative expression, activist and grassroots organizational skills, research prowess, and deep commitments to themselves, each other, and movements for justice for and from within their communities. Most importantly, we saw and heard "this is who we are now".

Several months later, as Jenna was driving three of our JcD youth to a preparation session to get ready to present their research at the Allied Media Conference in Detroit, Amelia and Daniela began reflecting on their friendship, the past year, and the possibilities of college. One of the biggest concerns that day was from Amelia: "Now that I know this, how am I going to find my people when I'm there?" Daniela agreed, "I don't want to just go from this to nothing, you know". Hearing this from them, and knowing what they were preparing to do in a few weeks—to facilitate a workshop with a group of 30 strangers from all over the country—was especially striking. On the day of the summit, as we were cleaning up, a group of students had come into the media center where one of the sessions had been held. The students—Somali, Eritrean, Salvadoran, Guatemalan, and Mexican—were part of a Level 2 English as a Second Language class and their teacher had mixed up the invitation time. As the adults were trying to think of an alternative time to meet, Amelia and Daniela pulled up one of the presentations and did it on the spot. Neither of them had prepared as spokespeople. In fact, both of them had been adamantly against taking on that role, preferring instead to prepare the visuals and tweak the scripts. Afterwards, Daniela couldn't stop laughing and pointing out how shaky her hands and arms still were. "I didn't think I could do that, you know? I mean. I wouldn't have if Amelia hadn't made me. But it's good. I feel good. It's going to be better next time, even, you know?" That spring, the two of them were part of a subgroup of JcD that conducted youth workshops about linguistic rights and youth organizing at multiple schools and local conferences, and that summer they would be part of a group to travel to both the AMC and Free Minds Free People to do the same.

The centrality of PAR EntreMundos in JcD's understanding of who they are now cannot be understated. Youth-led participatory action research can be leveraged for many things. It can be an impactful pedagogical strategy, an opportunity for transformation and development of youth leadership, and a means of enacting public policy through truth-telling and focused collective actions. PAR EntreMundos draws together the embodiment of critical consciousness, hope and love, lived joys and pains, tensions and choques, deeply rooted knowledge and traditions, and the creative force of languages in motion. It is fertile ground for telling it how it is, for resistance, for finding and amplifying voices, and for embracing one another. Through it, youth counterstories can challenge dominant narratives and lies that masquerade as truths. For Jóvenes con Derechos, PAR EntreMundos was both a portal and a promise. A portal between being silenced, laying realities bare, envisioning, and crafting a present and future more deserving of them. A promise that this is who you/they are now—and there's no going back after that.

References

Anzaldúa, G. (1987). *Borderlands/La frontera: The new Mestiza*. San Francisco, CA: Aunt Lute Books.

Cammarota, J., Berta-Ávila, M., Ayala, J., Rivera, M., & Rodríguez, L. (2016). PAR entremundos: A practitioner's guide. In A. Valenzuela (Ed.), *Growing critically conscious teachers: A social justice curriculum for educators of Latino/a youth*, (pp. 67–89). New York, NY: Teachers College Press.

Cammarota, J., & Fine, M. (Eds.). (2008). *Revolutionizing education: Youth participatory action research in motion*. New York, NY: Routledge.

Cammarota, J., & Romero, A. (Eds.). (2014). *Raza studies: The public option for educational revolution*. Tucson, AZ: University of Arizona Press.

Duncan-Andrade, J. M. R., & Morrell, E. (2008). *The art of critical pedagogy: Possibilities for moving from theory to practice in urban schools*. Bern: Peter Lang.

Flores, N., & Rosa, J. (2015). Undoing appropriateness: Raciolinguistic ideologies and language diversity in education. *Harvard Educational Review, 85*(2), 149–171.

García, O. (2005). Positioning heritage languages in the United States. *The Modern Language Journal, 89*(4), 601–605.

García, O., & Wei, L. (2014). *Translanguaging: Language, bilingualism and education*. Basingstoke: Palgrave Macmillan.

Ginwright, S. (2008). Collective radical imagination. In J. Cammarota & M. Fine (Eds.), *Revolutionizing education: Youth participatory action research in motion* (pp. 13–22). New York, NY: Routledge.

Ginwright, S., & Cammarota, J. (2002). New terrain in youth development: The promise of a social justice approach. *Social Justice, 29*(4), 82–95.

Harklau, L. (2009). Heritage speakers' experiences in new Latino diaspora Spanish classrooms. *Critical Inquiry in Language Studies, 6*(4), 211–242.

Iddings, A. C. D., Combs, M. C., & Moll, L. (2012). In the arid zone drying out educational resources for English language learners through policy and practice. *Urban Education, 47*(2), 495–514.

Irizarry, J. (2011). Buscando la libertad: Latino youths in search of freedom in school. *Democracy and Education, 19*(1), 4.

Irizarry, J. (2015). *Latinization of US schools: Successful teaching and learning in shifting cultural contexts*. New York, NY: Routledge.

Malsbary, C. (2014). "Will this hell never end?": Substantiating and resisting race-language policies in a multilingual high school. *Anthropology & Education Quarterly, 45*(4), 373–390.

Minnesota Department of Education. (2015). Minnesota report card. Retrieved from http://rc.education.state.mn.us/

Mirra, N., Garcia, A., & Morrell, E. (2015). *Doing youth participatory action research: Transforming inquiry with researchers, educators, and Students*. New York, NY: Routledge.

Moraga, C., & Anzaldúa, G. (1981). *This bridge called my back: Writings by radical women of color*. New York, NY: Kitchen Table Women of Color Press.

Morales, A., & Hanson, W. E. (2005). Language brokering: An integrative review of the literature. *Hispanic Journal of Behavioral Sciences, 27*(4), 471–503.

Orellana, M. F. (2009). *Translating childhoods: Immigrant youth, language, and culture*. New Brunswick, NJ: Rutgers University Press.

Pratt, M. L. (1991). Arts of the contact zone. *Profession*, 91, 33–40.

Pratt, M. L. (2007). *Imperial eyes: Travel writing and transculturation*. New York, NY: Routledge.

Torre, M. E. (2009). Participatory action research and critical race theory: Fueling spaces for nos-otras to research. *The Urban Review, 41*(1), 106–120.

Torre, M. E., & Ayala, J. (2009). Envisioning participatory action research entremundos. *Feminism & Psychology, 19*(3), 387–393.

UC Berkeley. (2015). YPAR Hub [Online resource center]. Retrieved from http://yparhub.berkeley.edu

Valdés, G. (2005). Bilingualism, heritage language learners, and SLA research: Opportunities lost or seized? *The Modern Language Journal, 89*(3), 410–426.

Valenzuela, A. (1999). *Subtractive schooling: US-Mexican youth and the politics of caring*. Albany, NY: State University of New York Press.

Wortham, S. E. F., Murillo, E. G., & Hamann, E. T. (2002). *Education in the new Latino diaspora: Policy and the politics of identity* (Vol. 2). Westport, CT: Greenwood Publishing Group.

·PART III·

PAR ENTREMUNDOS IN THE CONTEXT
OF GROW-YOUR-OWN INITIATIVES

Presented in this third section of the book is a discussion of how PAR was uti-lized within the context of two different grow-your-own teacher education in-itiatives. We begin with Irizarry's FUERTE project, addressing the underrep-resentation of people of color in the teaching profession through high school classroom PAR experiences which invite a critical examination of education. This experience, in turn, helps inspire critically conscious students of color to consider teaching as a social justice profession. Developed, in part, as a result of the previous work on a PAR EntreMundos framework with NLERAP, Bak-er and Berta-Ávila's chapter offers portraits of teacher candidates participat-ing in the Bilingual Multicultural Education Department (BMED) of Teacher Credentialing. They articulate the ways in which PAR approaches can be used in teacher education, as part of a cohesive social justice-oriented curric-ulum. Following this is a next generation application of PAR from a teacher education course to a high school classroom, with Gonzalez's reflections on the work of PAR EntreMundos in his experience as a high school educator. Taken together, Chapters 9 and 10 provide a snapshot of PAR EntreMundos as a multilayered experience shared between generations of students and ed-ucators.

· 8 ·

PARTICIPATORY ACTION RESEARCH AS A PATHWAY INTO THE TEACHING PROFESSION FOR LATINX AND AFRICAN-AMERICAN YOUTH

Jason G. Irizarry

Latinxs and African-Americans account for more than one-quarter of the U.S. population and more than one-third of all students enrolled in public schools, yet they represent less than 11% of all teachers (Ahmad & Boser, 2014). In contrast to the deepening racial/ethnic texture of the United States, the teaching force remains relatively homogenous, with the overwhelming majority of teachers identifying as White, middle-class, monolingual females. Although the benefits teachers of color bring to the classroom have been lauded in the research literature (Dee, 2004; Foster, 1991; Irizarry, 2011b; Irvine, 2003; Monzó & Rueda, 2001; Ochoa, 2007; Quiocho & Rios, 2000; Villegas & Lucas, 2004), the pool of Latinx and African-American teachers remains woefully undernourished.

Several theories have been forwarded in the literature to explain the dearth of people of color in the teaching profession. Some argue students of color don't see themselves reflected in the teaching force and therefore choose other professions (Milner, 2010a). Others have suggested that teachers of color actually dissuade students of color from considering careers in education (Gordon, 2000). Relatively low salaries, working conditions, and challenges navigating teacher preparation programs have all been forwarded as variables that depress the representation of people of color in the teaching profession (Irizarry, 2011b; Watt & Richardson, 2008a, 2008b). While each of these certainly has value and helps to explain at least some of the variation between the presence of White teachers and teachers of color, it is important to note that the types of educational experiences offered to students in districts with high concentrations of students of color differs significantly from the experiences of their White, often suburban, counterparts. The skill and drill approaches to education that are often employed in urban schools in an effort to boost achievement scores often alienate students from school and make the teaching profession seem unattractive to young people (Irizarry, 2011a). That is, even if students of color can overcome some of the institutional barriers that often inhibit their ability to pursue postsecondary education, they recognize that the system is set up to maintain the status quo and underserve the masses, as evidenced by the astronomical dropout/pushout rates found in many schools that serve large concentrations of students of color. Moreover, most students of color don't see themselves or groups with which they identify reflected in the curriculum and often have to deal with insensitive teachers and other school personnel (Hawley & Nieto, 2010). How, then, might we get young people from minoritized communities to consider teaching as a possible career option? How might teacher diversity be considered as an integral part of school reform efforts? Drawing from a three-year ethnographic study of Latinx and African-American teachers, this article explores the potential of Youth Participatory Action Research (YPAR) as a vehicle for engaging youth in a critical examination of education that has the potential to contribute to a more diverse, more socially conscious teaching force committed to transforming schools so that they work in the best interests of all students.

Drawing from data collected as part of a multi-year longitudinal study, this chapter documents how a group of African-American and Latinx high school students who were apathetic about the teaching profession modified their professional aspirations to consider education-related careers, including teaching, after engaging in a systematic, critical examination of the policies and practices that negatively impact the educational experiences and outcomes for urban youth of color. It highlights students' evolving perceptions of teaching as an act of resistance and challenges oversimplified notions of teacher diversity that seek proportionate representation without preparing all teachers to challenge the social reproductive function of schools.

Project Overview

In an effort to engage young people more deeply in the study of education, I created a research collaborative comprised of high school students, a university-based researcher, and graduate students. Project FUERTE (Future Urban Educators conducting Research to Transform Education), as we referred to our group, was a multi-generational research collaborative that aims to engage urban youth of color in meaningful, co-constructed research that will enhance their academic skills and address issues related to the material conditions of their lives. A primary goal of the study was to familiarize high school students with the conventions of ethnographic research as a means of exploring the ways in which power and opportunity manifest themselves in urban schools. While there is a wealth of research that explores urban teacher preparation, very little draws from the experiences and forwards the recommendations of urban youth. Instead of being positioned as the "problem" within school reform efforts, urban youth served as researchers developing and delivering recommendations to enhance the professional development of preservice and inservice teachers. Another significant feature of this project is that it aimed to familiarize urban youth of color with the teaching profession in part as a means to get them to consider becoming urban educators. The project was embedded in a course I offered at the participants' schools. The first year the project was located at Metro High School, an interdistrict magnet school in the northeast United States and the following year the project moved to Rana High School, a more traditional comprehensive high school in the same state. Students were recruited randomly and any student who expressed a desire to participate was invited to join the group. The group at each school was pared down when student availability to take the course in which the project was embedded was considered.

The project at Metro High School spanned an entire academic year, from September of the students' 12th grade year through their graduation. I remained in contact with the students after the conclusion of the project. At Rana High School Project FUERTE was active for two years, the students' final two years of high school. This chapter draws from data sets collected in both settings and shares findings emerging over a three-year period.

Findings

When examining the educational experiences of African-American and Latinx youth from a Critical Race Theory and Latinx Critical Race Theory perspective, the reluctance of youth of color to consider teaching as a career choice, and the resulting paucity of teachers of color in the profession, seems logical and highly predictable. That is, schools serving large populations of youth of color often exalt cultural assimilation over quality education, subordinating their histories, experiences, and cultural identities (Campano, Ghiso, & Sanchez, 2013; Kirkland, 2013; Valenzuela, 1999). Urban youth of color are most often relegated to overcrowded, underfunded, and underperforming schools (Noguera, 2003; Ravitch, 2010), and many of their teachers are unprepared to meet their academic and social needs (Milner, 2010b). And while they may not be able to explicitly name CRT or LatCrit, youth of color can and do apply the tenets of the theory to evaluate the opportunity structure at their schools. From this perspective, "the official school curriculum" can be seen "as a culturally specific artifact designed to maintain a White supremacist script" (Ladson-Billings, 1998, p. 10). Overall, the findings from this study underscore that attempting to attract urban youth into the teaching profession by appealing to their sense of altruism or highlighting the intrinsic rewards associated with careers in education is largely ineffective. In contrast, the voices of the participants suggest that engaging youth of color in critical examination of schooling, exposing racialized power dynamics and explicitly confronting the social reproductive function of schools—or as one student put it, "keepin' it real"—is a far more effective strategy for attracting African-American and Latinx youth into education-related professions. Finally, the findings highlight the potential of Youth Participatory Action Research (YPAR) to serve as a vehicle to foster the critical examination of schooling and help foment the critical consciousness necessary for teachers (and future teachers) to work with youth and their communities to transform schools.

YPAR: Exploring Potential Selves

During my first meeting with the students at Metro High School, after the customary introductions and overview of the course and the possibilities associated with PAR, I began to speak on the dire need for more Latinx and African-American youth to consider teaching as a profession and extol the benefits of becoming an urban educator. Without hesitation, Shawn, an African-

American student in his senior year, interjected and initiated an intense conversation where the students clearly rejected the notion of becoming a teacher and unapologetically shared their aversion for the teaching profession.

> **Shawn:** Become a teacher? That's not for kids like me.
> **Irizarry:** What do you mean?
> **Shawn:** C'mon Dr. I. You know the deal. That's not for us. That's for them (pointing toward the hallway).
> **Crystal:** What do you mean? Like girls?
> **Shawn:** Yeah, but you know, White girls. Look at who is teaching all the time.
> **Tony:** That's true when you think about it. There really aren't too many minorities teaching… a few but not many… and no dudes all girls… or women.
> **Irizarry:** Why do you think that is?
> **Shawn:** Like I told you, 'cause teaching ain't for us.

For this group of young people, and many others like them, the teaching profession was raced as a White endeavor, off-limits to "students like them". When asked to consider the possibility of teaching as a career choice, students didn't cite low salaries or a lack of respect for teachers, typical explanations for the lack of teachers of color within the profession, as deterrents but rather referenced the "overwhelming presence of whiteness" (Sleeter, 2001) within teaching and teacher education as having the most profound impact on their professional aspirations.

Beyond the lack of representation of people of color within the teaching profession, students also noted the impact of their interactions with school personnel and a feeling of disconnection from the curriculum as additional factors shaping their perceptions of teaching as a potential career path. The students at RHS were especially vocal about the ways in which faculty and staff within their school treated Latinx students, creating a school culture and climate that was not conducive to learning or supporting their professional aspirations.

> **Taína:** The teachers here make you feel like less than… They put Latinos down all the time and treat us like dirt. To be a teacher, that is like saying you want to work with that. I have to deal with that crap as a kid, as a student, like I have to come to school, but I wouldn't deal with that as an adult. I would flip on one of those teachers. I wouldn't last as a teacher for one day. As soon as a teacher tried to say something bad or be racist to Latinos, I would just flip on them. If I was a teacher here, I would be fighting all the time. Matter of fact, I am a student here and I am always fighting against the teachers and how they treat us. Imagine then…

Taína's interactions with teachers at her school were largely negative. As the demographics of the school were shifting, mirroring the national trend of the "Browning of America", school personnel were largely unprepared, and according to the participants, unwilling, to modify their teaching practices to meet the needs of a burgeoning, multilingual Latinx population at the school. These cultural collisions, or *choques* (Torre & Ayala, 2009), between a predominantly White, monolingual teaching force and a multilingual, predominantly Latinx student body were often hostile and adversarial, leaving students feeling like they had to maintain a state of constant vigilance, as they believed that teachers and other school personnel were not acting in their best interests.

While students at Metro High School described their experiences and interactions with teachers far more favorably than students at Rana High School, they nevertheless felt largely disconnected from important aspects of school life and were reluctant to consider joining the teaching profession. In a journal entry completed as part of a class assignment, Tenika, an African-American student, described her antipathy toward teaching as follows:

> On some level, becoming a teacher seems like a good thing to do. I would have the chance to help kids directly. I would be able to provide that support they need to reach their goals. At the same time, to be perfectly honest, school is boring. All we do is learn about White people, White history, White literature from mostly White teachers. Sure we have to know those things. It is important. But what about Black people and Latinos and others? I can play the game as a student, but I am not going to be a teacher if that is what they want me to teach.

Schools have been racially oppressive spaces for Taína, Tenika, and students of color, more generally. Forced to endure insensitive teachers and a Eurocentric curriculum, at the inception of the project the participants were, understandably, reluctant to pursue careers within the very institutions that have marginalized them and underserved their communities. Asking them to consider becoming teachers was viewed by the participants as synonymous with asking them to identify with the culturally insensitive practices that often characterize the schooling experiences for youth of color. Students' persistence in their schooling, despite often being made to feel "less than" by teachers and school policies, demonstrates a commitment to their education and the high value they place on schooling. However, because of their negative experiences, the Project FUERTE students had concluded that there was little space for them to have their identities affirmed and bring their unique perspectives, developed over more than twelve years of navigating schools as students of color, to the teaching profession. Because of their experiences, the students were, consequently, dissuaded from seriously considering teaching as a possible career choice. Alienating students of color from the teaching profession initiates a vicious cycle whereby the teaching profession, and by default K–12 schools, continue to be largely characterized by Whiteness, even though students of color will soon be the numeric majority within schools, and we lose out on the resources and skills students of color can potentially bring to bear on transforming the current system of education.

The role of race and racism, and how these constructs interact with other identity categories, within schooling and, more specifically within the recruitment and retention of students of color into teaching, must be more closely examined and interrogated. As the students' passionate voices demonstrate, it is unlikely we can increase teacher diversity without seriously considering and addressing racism and racialization within K–12 education. Subjecting students of color, or any students for that matter, to a narrow curriculum that is largely disconnected from their lived experiences, forcing them to subordinate their identities, and failing to privilege issues of diversity will not lead to substantive improvements in the educational experiences and outcomes for students of color, nor will it result in those students identifying with the teaching profession. The students in this project, through their lived experiences and work on the project, are well-positioned to enter the teaching profession with a heightened sociopolitical awareness and skills to navigate oppressive educational institutions. Who better, then, to become educators, particularly in schools and school districts that have underserved communities of color?

YPAR: Interrogating Inequality

Through their participation in the research project, students were able to identify issues they wanted to explore further, develop strategies for collecting data to inform their perspectives, analyze that information, and forward empirically-based recommendations to improve schooling for students like themselves. Students who were largely apathetic about school—not to be confused with a lack of passion for learning—participated at high levels when the content was relevant to their lives. More specifically, students' level of engagement peaked when they examined issues of inequality relative to their schooling experiences. Speaking to an increased level of engagement and rigor in their studies associated with investigating how power and opportunity were manifested at their school, Carmen shared the following during an interview about her experiences:

> I never really liked school. I like came [to school] and went through the motion… like I was physically here but my heart wasn't here. With this research, I am working to make things better for me, my family, other Latinos. Right now the system isn't fair. Like we discovered that Latinos are not getting access to Algebra early enough, which messes you up for going to college. It's hard, you know, but I like to do the work. It's a lot. I will stay up late, come to school early, come here during vacations because this is important. I learned a lot about research and Latinos and Education, but I think I read better, too. I'm better at speaking, just smarter all around. I have done more work in this class than all the others combined. I've loved it. I've learned a lot.

Carmen and her colleagues in Project FUERTE felt a connection to the research project and appreciated the real-world application of their findings. Most school improvement efforts tend to narrow the curriculum, increasing focus on those topics of study that are covered on standardized tests. For this reason, many urban schools serving students of color have decreased course offerings such as social studies, physical education, and the arts (Ravitch, 2010). Innovative approaches to increasing student engagement, a precursor to increasing academic achievement, are often overlooked in favor of scripted curricula that are believed to increase student performance on standardized tests. In contrast, students like Carmen (above) reported learning more from this experience than they did in other, more "traditional" classes.

Carmen was a student for whom school had worked reasonably well, or so she thought prior to her participation in the project. She received good grades and was generally thought of by teachers and administrators as a good student. However, she was rarely, if ever, challenged or encouraged to take higher level classes. Over the course of time she realized that she, like many of the Latinx students at her school, was not getting an education that would make her a viable applicant to a four-year institution of higher education. Moreover, she and her colleagues in the research collaborative were unprepared to meet the rigors of college. As evidenced by the following exchange from a class at the end of the first year of the project, students connected their study of inequitable educational opportunities with increased passion and commitment for their own education.

> **Jasmine:** This [role as researcher] makes me feel like a real student, like for the first time I feel like I belong in school, like I can really go to college and be somebody.

Ramon: We see how we are not getting a good education, how they are treating us here… like we are nothing. Before I thought teachers were cool when they don't make you do work, so you can chill in class and no homework. I thought that was good. Now I see how that is hurting us. I want education, like more than ever. I need it. I want it.

Jasmine: That's right! We see that [the way were are being educated] is wrong. Now we fight back by taking our education more serious, by working harder and getting what we need from the school… to change the school.

Alberto: That's how I feel. I can't really say it right, but basically I want to do better in school. This makes me want to reach higher. I see what's wrong and I want to make it right.

Students became more aware of the ways institutional racism worked to shape their educational aspirations and attainment and decided to push back against the system by shifting the focus of analysis from students—who are often blamed for "failing schools" and other problematic educational outcomes—to the institutions that structure opportunities in ways that foster social reproduction. However, critique in and of itself is insufficient for bringing about social change. It is not enough to criticize and deconstruct practices in schools. Project FUERTE was committed to developing and forwarding a vision for what education could look like for youth of color and develop recommendations to achieve their vision for schools. Students in Project FUERTE forwarded a vision of schooling where students' cultural identities and language practices are validated, where they have access to courses that will prepare them for college, and where teachers and administrators are invested in their success. Thus, through their work as researchers, the students acquired a unique skill set and perspectives that are often lacking among teachers and not necessarily fostered in teacher preparation programs or professional development efforts.

YPAR as a Pathway Into the Profession

At the outset of the project, none of the students at either site had becoming an educator as a career goal. In fact, most harbored antipathy for the teaching profession. Their experiences in schools were largely negative and popular perceptions of teaching as a relatively low-status and low-pay profession prompted them to aspire to become professionals in fields outside of education. Through their engagement in the research project and their increased familiarity with participatory action research methods, students began to expand their options to include education related professions, including but not limited to teaching. In a journal entry recorded as part of the class in which the research project was embedded, Tamara and Jasmine expressed the connection between youth participatory action research and their consideration of teaching as a career choice:

> **Tamara:** If I could teach how this class runs, I would become a teacher. With participatory action research, students are the experts. I have never felt like an expert at school. Teachers act like they are the experts and we have nothing to teach them or each other. We are only here to learn. Participatory action research lets student take responsibility for what they learn and how they learn. I wish more teachers would use this method with students. We would do better. I now am thinking about going to college and becoming teacher.
>
> **Jasmine:** I never thought of myself as a researcher or a teacher. At first, I didn't see how those two things go together. Now I want to become a teacher and teach my students how to do real research. I want to teach them to analyze the world, and if they don't like something, to change it. That's really what education should do. It should prepare you for the world. It should teach you how to shape your environment. Education should give you choices. With the research skills I have, I now have more choices. I want all kids to have choices. I can be the teacher that I always wanted to have.

Students' engagement with participatory action research helped them imagine new possibilities for their futures, including the teaching profession. They spoke to the personal and communal transformation that can occur through participatory action research projects grounded in minoritized communities and aimed at improving educational opportunities.

While YPAR facilitated a process whereby students could become more critically conscious and engage more deeply in their formal education, the research project did not completely eliminate barriers preventing students in Project FUERTE from pursuing careers in teaching. All of the students who participated in the project graduated from high school, a level of success that far exceeded graduation rates in both districts. However, YPAR was not a panacea, erasing all of the institutional barriers that impede students from reaching their academic potential. Many of the students were tracked into the least academically rigorous courses at their school and did not have the necessary prerequisite courses necessary to make successful application to college. The best case scenario for most of the participants was to begin their pursuit of higher education at a community college, taking remedial courses that will not count for credit at a four-year institution. Nevertheless, several students still pursued this option. Jasmine, for example, has completed her Associate's degree in Early Childhood Education and is now in the process of transferring into a Bachelor's degree program leading to educator licensure. Others, like Ramon, found balancing work and cours-es at a community college too difficult, particularly when those courses will not be applied to a four-year degree. Other students were undocumented, and as such would have to pay out-of-state tuition rates at their local state college, which is three times the rate of in-state tuition. In addition, because of their undocumented status, they were not eligible for federal financial aid or loans to subsidize the cost of their education. Several students, however, remained passionate about the transformative potential of education and pursued teaching related professions. Kristina, for example, who participat-ed in the first cohort at Metro High School, recently became a school coun-selor at Rana High School and remains committed to using YPAR to help students empower themselves to achieve at higher levels and transform the system so that it works for other members of their communities. Similarly, her colleague, Erika completed her undergraduate studies and plans to at-tend law school and specialize in educational policy. Whether their paths led them to college or directly into the workforce, all of the students have a more profound commitment to education and community development, and they attribute this shift to their participation in the research project. They are better advocates for themselves, their families, and other members of their communities. The utility of YPAR is perhaps best evidenced by the following response Kristina gave to an audience member at one of the con-ferences where the students shared findings from their research:

> Audience member: What is your biggest takeaway from your project?
> Kristina: No matter where I go or what I do, Project FUERTE will always be a part of me. It has shaped the way I think and see the world. I am going to use this to make a change in education, to work with kids differently. I still have a lot to learn but I feel confident about what I can accomplish now. This research project has giv-en me confidence. It has taught me so much. I want to share that with others.

Implications for the Field of Education

All of the student participants spoke to the positive impact the project had on their lives. The findings shared in this chapter also present significant impli-cations for the field of education writ large. Most notably, they underscore the importance of teacher diversity, the utility of YPAR as a pedagogical practice, and the potential to leverage YPAR as a vehicle to inform educational policy.

Significant attention has been given to issues of teacher diversity in the educational research literature. Many of these studies speak to the value of a more diverse teaching force, highlighting the importance of proportional representation. Having the demographics of the teaching force more closely align with those of the student body is certainly a laudable goal. However, if teachers are not trained to challenge the status quo, then the system which stymied the progress of the students in Project FUERTE and limited their ability to pursue higher education and the professions for which a college degree is necessary remains unchanged, and future generations will continue to inherit schools that do not operate in their best interests. The students in Project FUERTE have experienced the shortcomings of the educational system first-hand and after participation in the research project, several aspired to use teaching as a platform to redress their maltreatment and ensure that loved ones and other people of color are not forced to endure what they had to endure. In contrast to teachers who enter the profession as an act of altruism, Project FUERTE students aim to enter the profession as an act of resistance—to change the system and challenge deficit perspectives regarding communities of color.

As demonstrated in this chapter, critical consciousness can be enhanced through participation in YPAR. The students in Project FUERTE have unique lived experiences as students of color who have successfully navigated schools. These experiences, combined with their familiarity of research methods that can speak to their lives and offer them a vehicle to address problems in their communities, uniquely positioned this group to enter the teaching profession and work with students and their families to transform schools. In short, nominal representation is insufficient. We need teachers with unique skill sets that are willing to challenge the status quo and work differently with students.

In addition to being a valuable research method, Youth Participatory Action Research can also be leveraged as a pedagogical strategy, one that aligns intellectual pursuit with the needs of students and communities. As schools serving large percentages of students of color and low-income students become increasingly organized to increase standardized tests scores, which are usually the primary indicator of quality, YPAR offers an important and necessary alternative. Because it is explicitly designed to challenge inequality, YPAR centers students and positions them as experts of their own lives, and speaks to the lived experiences of young people; it offers a model for teachers, administrators, researchers, and others genuinely invested in the lives of urban youth to create opportunities for students to develop the skills necessary to positively shape their life trajectories, while simultaneously challenging the multiple forms of oppression that limit them and reproduce social inequality. As educators are constantly looking for ways to more effectively engage parents, YPAR also has the potential to foster improved school-community relations, as students are natural liaisons between their schools and the communities in which they live. Engaging the community more effectively and systematically can lead to gains in academic achievement.

Finally, YPAR can also be leveraged to develop or inform educational policy. This unique approach to research positions participants as experts of their own lives rather than passive "subjects" in someone else's research project. It honors the funds of knowledge (Moll, 1992) and lived experiences of community members. The perspectives of communities of color, and particularly young people in these communities, are often rendered silent in policy creation and educational reform efforts. Inserting the perspectives of those most directly impacted by these policies and practices increases the likelihood for success.

The findings shared in this chapter suggest that traditional explanations and methods for attracting Latinxs and African-Americans into the teaching profession are largely inadequate because they fail to account for the disparate experiences of minoritized communities within a system of public education that is designed to reproduce race and class-based stratification. It is imperative that we rethink how teachers of color are attracted to the profession and prepared for this work. Youth Participatory Action research can, and should be, a part of that process.

References

Ahmad, F. Z., & Boser, U. (2014). *America's leaky pipeline for teachers of color*. Washington, DC: Center for America's Progress.

Campano, G., Ghiso, M. P., & Sanchez, L. (2013). "Nobody knows the . . . amount of a person": Elementary students critiquing dehumanization through organic critical literacies. *Research in the Teaching of English, 48*, 98–125.

Dee, T. (2004). Teachers, race, and student achievement in a randomized experiment. *Review of Economics and Statistics, 86*, 195–210.

Foster, M. (1991). "Just got to find a way": Case studies of the lives and practice of exemplary Black teachers. In M. Foster (Ed.), *Qualitative investigations into schooling* (pp. 273–309). New York, NY: AMS Press.

Gordon, J. (2000). *The color of teaching*. New York, NY: Falmer Press.

Hawley, W. D., & Nieto, S. (2010). Another inconvenient truth: Race and ethnicity matter. *Educational Leadership, 68*(3), 66–71.

Irizarry, J. G. (2011a). *The Latinization of U.S. schools: Successful teaching and learning in shifting cultural contexts*. Boulder, CO: Paradigm Publishing.

Irizarry, J. G. (2011b). En la lucha: The struggles and triumphs of Latino/a preservice teachers. *Teachers College Record, 113*(12), 2804–2835.

Irvine, J. J. (2003). *Educating teachers for diversity: Seeing with a cultural eye*. New York, NY: Teachers College Press.

Kirkland, D. (2013). *A search past silence: The literacy of young black men*. New York, NY: Teachers College Press.

Ladson-Billings, G. (1998). Just what is critical race theory and what's it doing in a nice field like education? *International Journal of Qualitative Studies in Education, 11*(1), 7–24.

Milner, H. R. (2010a). What does teacher education have to do with teaching? Implications for diversity studies. *Journal of Teacher Education, 61*(1–2), 118–131.

Milner, H. R. (2010b). *Start where you are, but don't stay there: Understanding diversity, opportunity gaps, and teaching in today's classrooms*. Cambridge, MA: Harvard Education Press.

Moll, L. (1992). Funds of knowledge for teaching: Using a qualitative approach to connect homes and classrooms. *Theory into Practice, 31*(2), 132–141.

Monzó, L. D., & Rueda, R. (2001). Professional roles, caring, and scaffolds: Latino teachers' and paraeducators' interactions with Latino students. *American Journal of Education, 109*, 438–471.

National Center for Education Statistics. (2006). *Schools and Staffing Survey (SASS) 2003–04, Public Teacher File*. Washington, DC: U.S. Department of Education. Retrieved February 3, 2011, from http://nces.ed.gov/pubs2006/2006313.p

Noguera, P. A. (2003). *City schools and the American dream*. New York, NY: Teachers College Press.

Ochoa, G. L. (2007). *Learning from Latino teachers*. San Francisco, CA: Jossey Bass.

Quiocho, A., & Rios, F. (2000). The power of their presence: Minority group teachers and schooling. *Review of Educational Research, 70*(4), 485–528.

Ravitch, D. (2010). *The death and life of the great American school system*. New York, NY: Basic Books.

Sleeter, C. E. (2001). Preparing teachers for culturally diverse schools: Research and the overwhelming presence of whiteness. *Journal of Teacher Education, 52*, 94–106.

Torre, M. E., & Ayala, J. (2009) Envisioning participatory action research entremundos. *Feminism & Psychology, 19*, 387–393.

Valenzuela, A. (1999). *Subtractive schooling: U.S.-Mexican youth and the politics of caring*. Albany, NY: State University of New York Press.

Villegas, A. M., & Lucas, T. (2004). Diversifying the teacher workforce: A retrospective and prospective analysis. In M. A. Smylie & D. Miretzky (Eds.), *Developing the teacher workforce: 103rd yearbook of the National Society for the Study of Education* (pp. 70–104). Chicago, IL: University of Chicago Press.

Watt, H. M. G., & Richardson, P. W. (2008a). Motivation for teaching. *Learning and Instruction, 18*, 405–407.

Watt, H. M. G., & Richardson, P. W. (2008b). Motivations, perceptions, and aspirations concerning teaching as a career for different types of beginning teachers. *Learning and Instruction, 18*, 408–428.

· 9 ·

PAR ENTREMUNDOS

A "Critical" Approach for Latinx Teacher Preparation

Susan Baker and Margarita Berta-Ávila

Context

The glaring mismatch between teachers and students in terms of race and social class background is a major factor in the poor academic achievement of low-income students of color. While this mismatch exists nationwide, it is especially stark in California, a state in which 29% of teachers are White and 73% of students are children of color, and from which a disproportionate number come from low-income households (National Center for Education Statistics [NCES], 2013). The California Latinx population is especially hard hit by this mismatch; in 2011/12, 17% of California teachers were Latinx versus 51% of students (NCES, 2013). The discrepancy between teacher and student background does not show signs of abating; the percentage of children in California public schools has risen 8% over the last 10 years while the percentage of Latinx teachers has risen only 4% during the same time period (DataQuest, 2015).

While it is well documented that White teachers can be effective teachers of students of color (Garza & Garza, 2010; Ladson-Billings, 2009), there is also a great deal of evidence that many White teachers hold deficit views of students of color (Bomer, Dworin, May, & Semingson, 2008; Marx, 2008) and that these views contribute to classroom practices that are deleterious for low-income students of color. Teachers of color serving students of color, on the other hand, have been found to be more successful than teachers who come from mainstream backgrounds. Not surprisingly, these teachers are less likely to hold deficit views of students of color and are more likely to hold students accountable to high standards, use culturally responsive teaching practices, and forge caring relationships with their students and their families (Villegas & Irvine, 2010).

There are myriad reasons for the unacceptably small numbers of teachers of color and Latinx teachers in particular, including poor recruitment, teacher education programs that silence Latinx students (Irizarry, 2011), and the disproportionate number of teachers of color who leave because of job dissatisfaction (Ingersoll, 2002). This chapter explores a project designed to address the above challenges to Latinx teacher recruitment and retention: the "Grow Your Own" (GYO) Latinx Teacher Pipeline project at California State University, Sacramento (CSUS).

The GYO project emerged from the National Latino Education Research and Policy Project (NLERAP), which was begun in 2000 by a group of Latinx educational leaders with the goal of increasing the volume of research focused on Latinxs in education. Originally named the National Latino/a Education Research Agenda Project, in 2003 project leaders expanded the effort to include policy work and community action projects and renamed the project so as to reflect its larger vision. Focus groups of Latinx educators met over a two-year period, creating a far-reaching research agenda focused on Latinxs and education.

NLERAP uses the lens of critical race theory, among other theories, to inform its research agenda and resultant research efforts. Critical Race Theory is based on three central tenets: first, that racism is endemic to political and other institutional systems in the U.S., and that while it shifts form, it remains an underlying organizer of individual behavior and institutional structures; second, in our society, opportunities to acquire all forms of property are organized by race and other social markers, and race itself constitutes a type of property in that it is currently and historically tied to privilege and power; and third, that education is a form of property, opportunities for which are also organized by race (Ladson-Billings & Tate, 1995). An essential aspect of critical race theory is an inclusive approach toward research methodology and the stance that current (within academia) research methodologies often serve to perpetuate and justify racial and other social inequities. Congruent with Critical Race Theory, NLERAP uses a "research approach that seeks to uncover the emancipatory potential of education" (p. 5). Such an approach would be impossible without the participation in the research process of those who are the targets of oppression, not as "subjects" but rather as agents of their own liberation. As such, NLERAP champions the use of Participatory Action Research (PAR) EntreMundos to further the important work of using research to support education for liberation.

NLERAP approached Dr. José Cintrón and proposed the Bilingual Multicultural Education Department (BMED) of Teacher Credentialing at CSUS as a pilot site for a PAR project. BMED was chosen as the pilot site, as the program served a majority of teacher candidates of color and the majority of the faculty was of color.[1] The department had an explicit social justice agenda and strove to shape our teacher candidates to be change agents within their schools and their communities. It also made sense to choose Sacramento as a pilot site for a "grow your own" program, as the area, like the rest of California, has a disproportionately low number of teachers of color compared to the student population. For example, in 2012–2013, 37% of all Sacramento City Unified School District (SCUSD) students were Latinx, yet only 13% of SCUSD teachers were Latinx. Also comparable to California as a whole, Sacramento's Latinx students are not well served by the school system. In 2012–2013, only 31% of Latinx Sacramento County high school graduates were eligible for entrance to the California State University (CSU) or University of California (UC) systems.

With the support of NLERAP, in 2012, the first group of NLERAP candidates was launched, consisting of eight Latinx Bilingual Single Subject teacher candidates who were placed in schools across Sacramento. While it was important the candidates were Latinx, we also knew, from past experience, that it was crucial to raise their level of political awareness and instill a view of themselves as social change agents. Therefore, we created a robust training program within and alongside coursework with the twin goals of learning to approach the curriculum through the lens of social justice as well as how to teach the PAR EntreMundos process. During the second year of the program, Dr. Berta-Ávila, co-author of this chapter, was granted a sabbatical to support and document the progress of that year's NLERAP teacher candidates. This chapter is a portrait of that effort. It is told through recounting the journeys of two NLERAP participants—Maribel and Martiliano—so as to provide the reader with an insider perspective of the PAR EntreMundos project and process.

Portraits of Maribel and Martiliano

In the spring of 2014, five of the ten NLERAP candidates participated in implementing PAR EntreMundos in their student teaching classrooms. These five NLERAP candidates are further referred to as "PAR educators". The selection criteria for the candidates was based on subject matter knowledge and the willingness of their cooperating teachers to allow the PAR EntreMundos process in their classrooms. Due to personal circumstances, only two of the five PAR educators fully completed PAR EntreMundos projects.

Maribel

In the academic year of 2013–2014, Maribel student-taught in a rural high school in Northern California. In 2011–2012, over half the students at this school qualified for free and reduced lunch (Education Data Partnership, 2012). In 2012–2013, approximately 1,000 students were enrolled in the high school, with Latinxs comprising over half the student population, Whites comprising about 30%, American Indians/Alaskan Natives approximately 5%, Asian/Pacific Islanders close to 15%, Black/African Americans averaging 5%, two or more races 3%, and about 2% did not report their race (California Department of Education, 2013b). Out of the 196 graduates in 2012, only 25% met the California A-G requirements, making them eligible to enter the UC and CSU systems. Out of 98 graduating Latinx seniors, only 20% of them met the A-G requirements.

Maribel was assigned to teach U.S. Government and Economics, and both were subjects of which she had a deep knowledge. From the onset, it was important for her to use a social justice frame from which to approach her lesson planning. Moreover, what made Maribel passionate about her teaching was that she could personally relate to the demographic, economic, and immigrant experiences of her students. Maribel's strong sociopolitical stance is also revealed in the following quote from our first PAR training of the year:

> This is my corrido. I am from Guanajuato Mexico. We came from El Norte and migrated to the U.S. in search of work. We left because of political issues with corn and my family was no longer working. My mom, brothers, and I—we crossed the river. This was a key event that shaped my life because we got held up at the detention center. As a result, we got sent back. To return, a female coyote brought us back. We got caught again and I remember riding in the Migra (immigration) van. They sent us to Nuevo Mexico. I am not sure what happened but we were living in a barn. Later on we ended up in Stockton....around the time of prop 187. My mom would always

tell me "hide if you see the van". I remember it because I saw it before when I was 4. These experiences impacted my schooling. I didn't understand I was undocumented until 187 came around and I was called "wetback" growing up in south Stockton. Every morning I wake up with a healthy outrage!!!!

Martiliano

Martiliano student-taught at an urban high school near Sacramento. It is one of the oldest schools in the area and serves students from a variety of socio-economic, linguistic, and racial backgrounds. In 2013–2014, approximately 1,500 students were enrolled, with Asians comprising close to 40% of the student population, Pacific Islanders approximating 2%, Filipinos averaging 3%, Latinxs estimating 30%, African-Americans comprising 15%, Whites 8%, and two or more races 2%. Of the entire school population, over three fourths are considered socioeconomically disadvantaged (California Department of Education, 2013a, 2014).

Martiliano student-taught ninth grade ELD/language arts and 11th grade English. Similar to Maribel, Martiliano had a deep knowledge of both his subjects and could relate personally to the backgrounds and lived realities of his students. As a result, he planned lessons that incorporated literature relevant to the experiences of his students while teaching/reinforcing common core/ELD skills. Like Maribel, Martiliano noted it was important to him to build relationships with his students and foster an environment in which they would trust him and themselves to master grade level expectations. As well, both Martiliano and Maribel stated that it was crucial they teach students to use a critical lens in their learning of content area knowledge and skills. During the first PAR EntreMundos training, Martiliano revealed his understanding of students who had difficult life experiences when he shared the following with his cohort:

> In Kinder, I was put in speech therapy because I couldn't say certain words and letters. Up to the 4th grade I was a good student. However, I received my first referral in the 4th grade and that began to change everything. I went through a personal change. I became the black sheep of the family and didn't fit in. In the 6th grade I would go clean homes with mom when I got suspended. My dad, on the other hand, would beat my ass. I struggled with grades all the way through high school. I got kicked out of school my sophomore year and all my mom could ask me was "where did I fail you in raising you". I tried to go back but I was behind on credits. So I went to the community college and took night time classes. I had a 3.5 GPA when I finally decided to apply myself.

When reflecting upon the backgrounds of the two PAR educators, three shared personal factors emerge: both entered the program with a social justice disposition, personal knowledge of their students' lived experiences, as well as a strong foundation in their subject matter. The combination of these elements coupled with our program's instruction in pedagogy allowed the educators to successfully plan and implement their PAR EntreMundos projects. Below we describe the programmatic features that supported the educators' PAR EntreMundos projects as well as further developed their social justice lens and classroom pedagogy.

Credential Program Structure and PAR EntreMundos Support

The CSUS credential program spans two semesters. The first semester consists of a student teaching practicum as well as the following courses: Theoretical Foundations of Teaching in a Multicultural Democratic Society (Foundations), Fundamentals of Lesson Planning and Curriculum Design, Academic Literacy, ELD/SDAIE, and a Seminar course to support student teaching. The second semester builds upon the first in the continuation of the courses above, with a stronger focus on subject matter pedagogy. Below, we detail the aspects of coursework that directly supported the candidates' PAR EntreMundos projects.

Theoretical Foundations of Teaching in a Multicultural Democratic Society

NLERAP goals include preparing Latinx teachers to be highly qualified to teach in their respective content areas and also to be proponents of social justice. Our findings suggest that the course that most fostered growth in these two areas was *Theoretical Foundations of Teaching in a Multicultural Democratic Society*, also known as "Foundations". This course guides students to critically analyze the purposes and processes of U.S. public schooling. It also calls on students to "examine the sociopolitical contexts of public schools and society, educational theories, philosophies, notions of culture, community, and educational practice" (Allender, Berta-Ávila, Cintrón, & Coughlin, 2014, p. 1). More specifically, the Foundations course assists students in grounding their new pedagogical understandings in a social justice framework.

For students like Martiliano and Maribel who already came to our program with strong foundations in social justice, this course allowed them to
apply their political framework to the context of the public school setting.
Additionally, Foundations taught the PAR educators how to teach subject
matter content within a social justice framework by utilizing the approaches
for multicultural/social justice teaching developed by Christine Sleeter and
Carl Grant (2007). Students were guided through each approach (Human
Relations, Single Group Studies, Multicultural, and Multicultural/Social Justice Education) and required to develop and teach social justice lessons using
these approaches. Overall, this experience demonstrated to the student teachers (specifically those integrating PAR EntreMundos) how to write and teach
subject matter lessons through a social justice framework.

Requiring the PAR educators to teach integrated lessons in the fall semester provided a forum for the PAR educators to discuss macro sociopolitical themes that could (a) emerge as their students engaged with PAR
EntreMundos in the spring and (b) strengthen their students' political lens
and knowledge base regarding their own lived experiences. As a result of
having already explored these themes at the university, with the guidance
of the PAR university professors, the PAR educators then taught specific
lessons in their placement sites addressing social justice concepts through an
analysis of self, society, and the institution of education. The PAR educators
developed the following diagram to visually depict their approach.

Figure 9.1: Overarching Sociopolitical Themes: Values, Culture, Immigration, Stereotypes,
Racism, Poverty

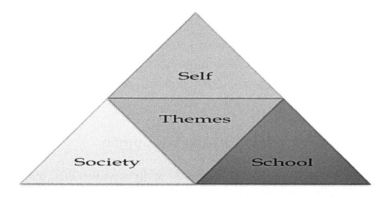

Source: (PAR educators, 2014)

The PAR educators came to call this specific approach the "Frontloading" phase to PAR EntreMundos. This new phase proceeds the former phase one, that of "constructing the PAR collective". This addition is an important expansion of the PAR EntreMundos phases because it refines the processes to inform implementation at the high school level, where students may not have the necessary sociopolitical knowledge base to discern the themes that emerge from their "educational journeys" or "I am" poems. Examples from the classroom of this new phase are outlined below.

The importance of this additional phase of frontloading sociopolitical knowledge became apparent to the PAR educators when they began PAR EntreMundos in the spring. After sharing their educational journeys, students were asked to reflect on their lived experiences and then deepen their analysis by referencing sociopolitical concepts addressed during the front loading phase. This process allowed students to contextualize and understand that their individual experiences did not exist in isolation but rather were part of larger political systemic structures. The essence of these classroom dialogues, informed by the front loading phase, eventually guided the identification of the research questions the students would choose to investigate. For instance, Martiliano's class identified the following research question, *Why do students at Francisco High segregate themselves based on race and language?* and Maribel's first class decided to focus on the research question, *How does bullying exist at San Lucia High School?* while her second class chose to explore the research question, *What about high school causes depression in students?* In addition, once the topic/research questions (phase 2 and 3) for the PAR EntreMundos project were identified, the PAR educators led classroom discussions linking the research topics to social justice concepts and knowledge gained during the frontloading phase. In planning the discussions, the PAR educators drew from their learnings from the Foundations course. The frontloading phase also informed students' choice of research methods in that they were able to choose methods that would specifically illuminate larger issues they had learned about earlier.

Academic Literacy/ELD-SDAIE/170 Course

Three additional courses that especially supported the PAR educators' lesson planning and instruction were the "Academic Literacy", "ELD/SDAIE", and "Bilingual Education" courses. The Academic Literacy course focuses on literacy content and strategies that are content-area specific, while the ELD/

SDAIE course teaches candidates how to identify the academic language demands of a lesson, how to address those demands through sheltered instruction, and adaptations of process and products within the classroom. The Bilingual Education course is a survey course focusing on the history, theory, and politics of educating English learners in the U.S. While the course is a survey course, content is taught using strategies appropriate for EL students, so as to model those practices for our teacher candidates.

Both Maribel and Martiliano stated that during the PAR EntreMundos projects, they asked students to read material that was at a higher level of complexity than what they normally read and to synthesize reading materials written from various perspectives, a task which their day-to-day textbooks assignments did not require of them. As a result, the PAR educators found themselves using strategies from their Academic Literacy and ELD/SDAIE classes in order to make the readings accessible and support student success with reading tasks. For example, Maribel scaffolded complex readings through creating anticipation guides as well as by asking students to generate their own questions about the reading, before, during, and after the readings. To promote discussion as well as divide up the readings, Maribel also created jigsaw activities so students could teach each other about the different articles they had read, creating an authentic purpose for discussion. The jigsaw activities also helped students synthesize the readings in that students were prompted during their discussions to compare and contrast the readings, including the point of view of the authors. To promote academic language use during discussions, Maribel taught her students constructive conversation skills (Zwiers, 2014). Using the constructive conversation skills allowed students to think not only about the content they were discussing and how it related to their research question, but also promoted metacognition in that students were asked during discussions to build upon each other's utterances in purposeful ways. Conversational "building" included asking others for evidence for their claims from the readings, asking for clarification, and agreeing or disagreeing with what another student had said, using evidence to back their point of agreement or disagreement.

Martiliano also used a number of strategies learned during the Academic Literacy and ELD/SDAIE classes. As in the case of Maribel, these strategies also involved scaffolding students' reading, writing, listening, and oral language production. Martiliano provided sentence frames for students' oral and written language use, gradually pulling them away as students began internalizing them and using them on their own. He also frontloaded difficult vocabulary from the readings and adapted online articles by bolding and glossing vocabulary and shortening sentences without changing the meaning of the text. Students were provided with text-dependent questions to answer after the readings as well as questions to be answered during the readings to help teach them annotation skills. In addition, both PAR educators used audio and video clips as additional texts, providing close notes for the students to complete while listening and viewing, with questions to be answered afterwards to guide discussion. An example of this was an excerpt of a Tim Wise speech on institutional racism used during a study of housing discrimination.

Martiliano, like Maribel, engaged the students in Socratic Seminars, thus allowing them authentic opportunities to discuss the readings in small group and whole group formats and an opportunity to synthesize various readings through the discussions. Martiliano heavily scaffolded the process of the Socratic Seminar, showing the students videos about the format and the student roles, and provided them with graphic organizers to help them organize their thoughts about the readings. The Socratic Seminar supported students' leadership abilities, too, in that students were placed in groups of three (one leader with two "pistoleros/pistoleras") that discussed the same reading and proposed points that the leader could take to the whole class discussion. After a short time, the students would switch off from the leader role to become one of the "pistoleros". Students were heterogeneously grouped according to English language proficiency as well as achievement, with the stronger students acting as models for the less proficient students.

In sum, the two university courses provided strategies that allowed Martiliano and Maribel to make difficult texts accessible to their students and provide support for difficult academic tasks such as synthesizing complex pieces of text. The PAR EntreMundos project provided an authentic reason for the PAR educators to apply these strategies and also gave them multiple opportunities to refine them. The PAR educators shared that such opportunities were scarce when they taught the "regular" curriculum and also that students were not as motivated to speak in front of the class, read complex text, or accomplish difficult tasks as part of the regular curriculum, no matter what type of scaffolding they received. In contrast, students' interest in the PAR EntreMundos project, the authentic nature of the readings—about racism, segregation, etc.—created a situation in which students were willing to go the extra mile to understand the readings and speak in small and large group settings, and the PAR educators were ready to support them with the strategies and scaffolding techniques they had learned during their university program.

PAR EntreMundos Ancillary Support

PAR EntreMundos Training

In addition to regular coursework, NLERAP teacher candidates also received extra support in the form of two Saturday workshops and monthly "check-in" sessions with NLERAP professors. The Saturday workshops, begun in the fall and led by the NLERAP professors, provided a theoretical and sociocultural foundation for the PAR EntreMundos process before the PAR educators began their PAR EntreMundos processes in the classroom. During the first session, candidates learned about the PAR principles and the theoretical frameworks undergirding PAR EntreMundos efforts. They also took part in sharing their own educational journeys and "I am" poems. This process had a three-fold goal: (a) to create community and trust between the NLERAP candidates, (b) to learn the process by doing the process so as to better be able to lead their own students in these activities, and (c) to further their own sociocultural understandings of racism and other "isms" and their institutional roots. Indeed, candidates remarked that they "thought they were the only ones" until they saw similar obstacles, including suppression of their home language, domestic violence and drinking, and low expectations from teachers. After sharing about their own lives, the candidates identified common themes undergirding the obstacles that emerged from the journeys, such as linguicism, institutionalized racism, and sexism. At the end of the first session, the candidates created a "timeline" for their own PAR EntreMundos projects in their placement classrooms.

The second PAR EntreMundos workshop took place in January and focused on PAR research methodologies to be used in the placement classrooms. The candidates had completed the educational journeys and theme identification process with their own students and now needed to be able to lead their students in gathering information about the manifestations of that theme (e.g., the low number of teachers of color). PAR research methodologies taught during the workshop included: (a) creation and administration of a survey as well as the analysis of survey data, (b) identification of interview questions that would shed further light upon the identified problem as well as interview techniques, (c) use of observation to collect ethnographic data, (d) archival research (current and historical) on the identified problem, using the Internet and other sources. The workshop training was comprised of modeling the research methodologies and then candidates' direct application—the candidates identified a research problem (a different one than that identified by their placement students) and then created and carried out a survey gathering information about the problem as well as created interview questions and carried out an interview. Archival research was not a process practiced during the workshop, as it is a method with which the candidates are already familiar and have been instructed in how to teach during program coursework.

During the weeks before and after each workshop, the NLERAP professors held "check-ins" on the CSUS campus with the candidates to gauge their progress and offer support. The check-ins were also useful in that the candidates learned about each other's processes and supported each other with ideas and encouragement. Two check-ins were held after the last workshop, with the final check-in serving the purpose of a wrap-up to the process, lessons learned, and in some cases, to support getting ready for a final presentation of the data collected to the key stakeholders at the school sites.

The Strengthening of Pedagogy via PAR EntreMundos Support Guide

As previously mentioned, in spring 2014, I, co-author Margarita Berta-Ávila, went on sabbatical and documented Maribel and Martiliano's YPAR journeys. I observed the PAR EntreMundos/content-integrated lessons on a weekly basis, and observations were followed up with one-on-one debriefings of their teaching and PAR EntreMundos phases. This refined how the PAR educators thought about their lesson plans and instruction and provided them with an opportunity to explore content lesson planning/curriculum development via PAR EntreMundos. For instance, during various sessions, I helped the PAR educators refine their students' research questions and identified how they would teach their students research methods (phase 4 Research Protocol). In Maribel's case, we often reflected upon different sequencing of teaching the research methods, such as frontloading all the methods and then collecting data or teaching each method one-by-one. During our dialogues, I helped Maribel think about her own students and how to best approach the teaching of the research methods. Through our conversations, she was able to reach the conclusion that her seniors were able to learn about all the research methods before trying them out on their own. In contrast, my dialogue with Martiliano led to a different conclusion; he decided, upon being guided to think about his students and their level of maturity, that his ninth graders would need to apply each method immediately after teaching it.

During our debriefings, the knowledge and skills Maribel and Martiliano were learning in their credential program were constantly reflected upon in the context of PAR EntreMundos. As their PAR EntreMundos guide, I became that bridge between university coursework and their high school placements in the field. The PAR educators and I would always cycle back to the program's course content and intentionally select strategies and practices that supported making the phases accessible for the students. For instance, Martiliano was cognizant that his ninth graders were going to need a tremendous amount of scaffolding. As a result, we brainstormed scaffolding techniques he could use to make content concepts and the PAR EntreMundos process clear to his students. For example, when he started with the first method (observation), Martiliano developed a graphic organizer to help guide the students in their observations and taught them how to write "raw notes" and transpose them to "expanded notes".

In helping the PAR educators conceptualize and carry out scaffolding techniques for their students, a sense of trust between the students and the PAR educators was built; students realized their teachers were going to do everything necessary for them to gain content area knowledge and skills and carry out the PAR EntreMundos process. Interestingly enough, this sense of trust the PAR educators established with their students also occurred between the PAR educators and me. Maribel and Martiliano understood the debriefings would help them refine their pedagogy and write well-developed lessons. They trusted me to hold high expectations of them. Those high expectations included "checking them" when it was noticeable that time and thought had not been taken into consideration with their lessons. It also meant nudging them beyond their comfort zones to take chances with their pedagogy. For example, when Maribel and Martiliano felt overwhelmed juggling their university courses and student teaching requirements, I helped them negotiate and prioritize their time and energy.

Another outcome of PAR EntreMundos was my ability to guide the educators in learning how to advocate for themselves during the inevitable "pushback" situations they faced. For example, this was most evident when Martiliano shared that he would be facing a difficult experience in the future and trusted us to support him. He explained to me that being in our program, and specifically being involved with NLERAP, has helped him name what he experienced as a student of color and what he hopes to change in the future. Because of that, he planned to go full force with PAR EntreMundos in his class. However, he honestly felt some apprehension because the assistant principal of the school wrote the unit/outline for the literature piece with which he planned to integrate PAR EntreMundos. He was concerned about how she would react to his approach because he was definitely planning to go deeper.

Maribel faced a similar difficult situation in which I taught her how to strategically integrate PAR EntreMundos as she experienced resistance from White students. She had a White male student making discriminatory comments toward the students of color in class and acting aggressively toward her. Maribel was scared. She was nervous that she would be the one to get in trouble and be called into the principal's office. Immediately, I reassured Maribel that feeling nervous is normal with this kind of work, especially when people are socialized to not speak against the system. At that point, we analyzed the situation and strategized next steps. For example, the PAR guide asked Maribel several questions like how did her CT react if she had connected all her Inquiry and PAR EntreMundos lessons to the standards of economics/government and Common Core, and what plan did she have to integrate an activity to address norms? As the PAR guide and Maribel discussed/analyzed the questions posed, next steps were determined:

1. She would have a conversation with the student after class to emphasize that all voices will be respected.
2. She will stop the PAR EntreMundos process in order to integrate this mini lesson on norms by utilizing "charged" conversation scenarios and, via a fishbowl experience, have the students act out a before/after situation utilizing sentence starters with the "after". She would participate as well.
3. She will make sure all lessons are supported with government/economics Common Core standards.

Statements like Martiliano's and experiences like Maribel's led me to be explicit and outline with PAR educators the following: (a) how to broach a conversation with their administrators and other stakeholders about PAR EntreMundos, (b) how to explain PAR EntreMundos in the context of California Common Core and mandated content standards, and (c) how to foster alliances to support the PAR EntreMundos work.

The personal transformation that Martiliano and Maribel underwent reaffirmed that they could challenge an inequitable structure, be strategic in how to navigate challenges, know through it all they were part of a collective that "had their back", and were truly willing to engage in a movement of "hope"

(Darder, 2014). Moreover, in teaching the educators how to advocate for themselves, they learned resilience. Research suggests that educators of color leave the profession at higher rates than their White peers. By teaching the educators how to advocate for themselves, we hope to be proactive in keeping them in the field and keeping them from burning out. In sum, my presence as the PAR EntreMundos guide was essential in the success of the two PAR educators. Our process together led the PAR educators to an authentic view of education—education for emancipation—and importantly, it created a shift in their pedagogy and how they viewed their profession. Martiliano shared:

> Now, I am aware of how to strategically work against and challenge institutional structures at the department and school wide levels that result in, and perpetuate, inequitable outcomes for students based on race and class. Prior to this experience, I viewed myself more as a classroom teacher who worked toward social justice through my curriculum and instruction. Now, I see myself as an educator that uses the classroom and curriculum as a starting point, but must also work at a structural and institutional level to achieve social justice for all students. This experience allowed me to learn strategically how to identify who truly holds power in these structures, not going by the title individuals hold (e.g., principal, department chair, etc.), and how to approach stakeholders in working toward transformative change. Moreover, knowing how to position myself within these structures and amongst these stakeholders in order to better advocate and work for a more equitable and socially just education for students.

Conclusions and Next Steps

Action-Accomplishments of the PAR EntreMundos Efforts

The accomplishments of our PAR EntreMundos efforts had a strong effect on the PAR educators in YPAR classrooms. The selected PAR educators were exposed to a transformative pedagogy (PAR EntreMundos) that put the academic and social needs of prospective classroom students at the forefront. Moreover, they learned how to integrate the PAR EntreMundos social justice framework with their subject matter content. Ultimately, the educators gained skills in (a) connecting subject matter content to local and national social issues identified by the students in the classroom and (b) implementing and refining strategies and methods they learned through the single subject program. Lastly, because of their participation with PAR EntreMundos, they had the opportunity to participate at three professional 2015 conferences (Multicultural Education Conference at Sacramento State, California Association for Bilingual Education, and Association of Raza Educators); they have written and proposed English language development social justice courses integrating PAR EntreMundos in the districts where they teach; one of them has assisted their students in implementing a Social Justice Collective (club) at the school site; and both continued to integrate PAR with their content as first-year teachers in the field.

Personal Transformation

What became clear from the close exchange of ideas, questions, and responses with the PAR educators was that PAR EntreMundos would not only foster a pedagogical shift but also a personal transformation. PAR EntreMundos facilitated a liberating experience in which the challenges facing PAR educators of color were confronted and alleviated. Thus, the PAR EntreMundos journey became a political awakening. PAR educators felt affirmed to be in the NLERAP cohort supporting a liberatory pedagogy like PAR EntreMundos; they knew they were not alone. The feeling of reassurance ("we have their back") and learning how to navigate inequitable school structures became part of the transformational process and fostered an environment of trust.

Recommendations/Next Steps

The PAR EntreMundos project described above has implications for teacher education and inservice teacher support. Given the transformative nature of the project for the teacher candidates and their high school students, our goal is to include all of our bilingual students in the PAR EntreMundos effort. This would mean training our content area teacher educators in PAR EntreMundos theory and practice and co-planning PAR EntreMundos support across the content areas. Under our current structure, teacher candidates have received targeted support in their Foundations/Social Justice course, Academic Literacy course and their ELD/SDAIE course with respect to PAR EntreMundos. It is crucial that the students' specialized content area methods courses also be taught in such a way so as to support PAR EntreMundos work. It would be powerful for our science candidates to receive support on how to use their knowledge of science to help students identify inequities that are science-based, such as food deserts, contaminated water, and environmental racism. It would be helpful if math candidates were taught how to guide students in effective data display and other uses of math that can be leveraged for social change.

A further goal is for our university supervisors to reflect upon how to integrate their guidance of the PAR EntreMundos process with their supervision. As such, supervisors can offer just in time advice on how to use course content to support PAR EntreMundos work in the field. University supervisors can dialogue with each other as to candidates' progress with PAR EntreMundos and give feedback to professors as to how the University coursework can be better tailored to support the PAR EntreMundos process.

Finally, we hope to create an induction process so we can specifically support our graduates in their use of PAR EntreMundos in their own classrooms. Induction can be leveraged as an important support of PAR EntreMundos work; in supporting first-year teachers in their nascent social justice work, we can create cohorts of inductees who can support each other and provide each other guidance on PAR EntreMundos projects. The induction mentor can provide the inductees with support in pedagogy and content and can also provide the university with important feedback as to the competencies of first-year teachers and their success with PAR EntreMundos projects.

Note

1. In 2012, BMED merged with the larger Teacher Education Department, to form a new department (the Department of Teacher Credentialing), which adopted many of the social justice practices and expectations of BMED. While initial planning for Sacramento NLERAP began under the BMED program, the first year of implementation of the project was under the Department of Teacher Credentialing.

References

Allender, D., Berta-Ávila, M. I., Cintrón, J., & Coughlin, M. (2014). *EDTE 364A/01: Theoretical foundations of teaching in a multicultural democratic society syllabus.* Sacramento, CA: California State University, Sacramento, Department of Teaching Credentials.

Bomer, R., Dworin, J. E., May, L., & Semingson, P. (2008). Miseducating teachers about the poor: A critical analysis of Ruby Payne's claims about poverty. *Teachers College Record, 110,* 2497–2531.

California Department of Education. (2013a). *Enrollment by ethnicity for 2012–13 school enrollment by ethnicity.* Retrieved from http://data1.cde.ca.gov/dataquest/Enrollment/EthnicEnr. aspx?cYear=2012–13&cGender=B&cType=All&cChoice=SchEnrEth&cSelect=346731 43430477,Florin

California Department of Education. (2013b). *Enrollment by ethnicity for 2012–13 school enrollment by gender, grade & ethnic designation.* Retrieved from http://dq.cde.ca.gov/dataquest/

Enrollment/EthnicGrade.aspx?cType=ALL&cGender=Byear=2012–13&Level=School &cSelect=GALT^HIGH--GALT^JOINT^UNIO—34673553433471&cChoice=SchE nrAll

California Department of Education. (2014). *Enrollment by ethnicity for 2013–14school enroll- ment by ethnicity.* Retrieved from http://data1.cde.ca.gov/dataquest/Enrollment/EthnicEnr. aspx?cYear=2012–13&cGender=B&cType=All&cChoice=SchEnrEth&cSelect=346731 43430477,Florin

Darder, A., (2014). *Freire and education.* New York, NY: Routledge.

DataQuest. (2015). *Home page.* Retrieved from http://data1.cde.ca.gov/dataquest/

Education Data Partnership. (2011–12). *School Report: Galt High School.* Retrieved from *assic/profile.asp?tab=0&level=07&ReportNumber=16&County=34&fyr=1112&Dis- trict=67355&School=3433471*

Garza, R., & Garza, E. (2010). Successful white female teachers of Mexican American students of low socioeconomic status. *Journal of Latinos and Education, 9*(3), 189–206.

Ingersoll, R. M. (2002). The teacher shortage: A case of wrong diagnosis and wrong prescrip- tion. *NASSP Bulletin, 86*(631), 16–31.

Irizarry, J. (2011). En la lucha: The struggles and triumphs of Latino/a preservice teachers. *Teachers College Record, 113,* 2806–2835.

Ladson-Billings, G. (2009). *The dreamkeepers: Successful teachers of African American children.* San Francisco, CA: Jossey-Bass Publishers.

Ladson-Billings, G., & Tate, W. (1995). Toward a critical race theory of education. *Teachers College Record, 97*(1), 47–67.

Marx, S. (2008). Popular white teachers of Latina/o kids: The strengths of personal experiences and the limitations of whiteness. *Urban Education, 43*(1), 29–67.

National Center for Educational Statistics (NCES). (2013). *Number and percentage distribution of teachers in public and private elementary and secondary schools, by selected teacher char- acteristics: Selected years, 1987–88 through 2011–12.* Retrieved from https://nces.ed.gov/ programs/digest/d13/tables/dt13_209.10.asp

Sleeter, C. E., & Grant, C. A. (2007). *Making choices for multicultural education: Five approaches to race, class and gender sixth edition.* Hoboken, NJ: John Wiley & Sons.

Villegas, A., & Irvine, J. (2010). Diversifying the teaching force: An examination of major arguments. *Urban Review, 42*(3), 175–192.

Zwiers, J. (2014). *Building academic language: Meeting common core standards across disciplines, grades 5–12.* San Francisco, CA: Jossey-Bass.

· 1 0 ·

"STUDENTS WITH BIG DREAMS THAT JUST NEED A LITTLE PUSH"

Self-Empowerment, Activism, & Institutional Change Through PAR EntreMundos

Rubén A. González

Students are seated in groups of four during their ninth grade English class. Twenty-two students diligently complete a written reflection about their experiences completing a whole-class Participatory Action Research (PAR) EntreMundos project. The scratching of pens and pencils against sheets of paper are the only sounds that break the silence throughout the classroom. Students are one day removed from the culmination of their project, a presentation to the school's Steering Committee (i.e., school leadership team composed of administrators, department chairs, counselors, and teachers), community members, parents, and other students. After five minutes, students stop writing and share what they wrote in their respective groups. The classroom bursts with the sound of voices eager to share their experiences after months of dedicated and difficult work seeking to transform their campus into a more equitable and socially just institution for all students. I ask for volunteers to share aloud to the rest of the class.

Instantly, Zaier[1] stands up:

> During this process, I've changed a lot because everywhere I go, I see things more clearly. I see the injustice when before I wouldn't... and now that I can see it, it's

easier for me to stop it. I'm glad we did PAR[2] because now I can help my school and community. I see the problems and now I have the ability to make a change.

Lorenza is the next student to speak. She looks down at her paper for a few moments, places it back on her desk, and instead speaks from the heart:

> I noticed that ever since we started PAR, I learned many things I didn't know before. I learned that there are a lot of problems in the world and we don't notice them because we don't care enough to do something about it or we're doing it ourselves—we're part of the problem. This experience changed my life because I see the two sides of how the world can be. One side is caring and one side is just full of negativity… We just need to step up and do something about it. This class started to do that… Doing PAR taught us how to try to make the world a better place. Everyone in here helped and pushed each other to do it. We are students with big dreams that just need a little push.

These testimonies demonstrate how PAR EntreMundos (this volume; Torre & Ayala, 2009) projects, rooted in critical pedagogy (Duncan-Andrade & Morrell, 2008; Freire, 1970) and critical literacy (Freire & Macedo, 1987; Gutiérrez, 2008; Morrell, 2007) have a profound influence on how students view themselves, their world, and their own positionality as change agents. Zaier and Lorenza provide a glimpse into how their experiences with PAR EntreMundos increased their civic engagement (Dewey, 1916), self-empowerment (Cahill, 2004; Camangian, 2008), and critical consciousness (Freire, 1970).

This work, critical pedagogy with a civic action component, is vital in a time where there is a focus within public education on standardized assessments and the scores derived from such measurements. Consequences of this current educational climate often include narrowed curriculum and teacher-centered classrooms (Au, 2007; Mintrop & Sunderman, 2009; Ravitch, 2010), and "teacher proof" curriculum (Delpit & White-Bradley, 2003). These policies and practices are presented under the guise of well-intentioned attempts to improve instruction and learning, yet inevitably hinder the creativity and critical thinking of students. PAR EntreMundos is a pedagogical approach that educators may employ to counter these realities in an effort to empower students to use their education as a tool for liberation through evoking institutional change while simultaneously developing competencies in various academic skill and content areas.

Literature Review

Youth Participatory Action Research (YPAR)

YPAR is a critical research methodology rooted in social justice that fore-grounds youth as experts of their lived experiences in school and larger com-munity settings (Cammarota & Fine, 2008; Morrell, 2004). This counters the traditional approach in schools that view students as objects and rarely, if ever, consult them when addressing educational policies, practices, and/or issues. Instead, YPAR has students serve as legitimate stakeholders and actors in issues that affect them (McIntyre, 2000) through knowledge co-construction between students and other affected parties such as researchers, teachers, and community members. These types of spaces and learning oppor-tunities provide students with an avenue to conduct authentic research based on their needs and lived experiences, and through the power of their own voice, work toward evoking social change (Morrell, 2008). Students accom-plish this through learning about critical social issues, identifying prevalent issues within their own communities they feel passionate about changing, and through data collection and research, provide recommendations aimed to-ward addressing the identified issues.

This pedagogical approach of positioning students as change agents seek-ing to transform their realities is grounded in the Freirean praxis of reading and speaking back to the world through critical inquiry, active reflection, and social action (1970). This constant and ongoing process allows students to develop what Freire calls "conscientização", or critical consciousness (1970), as they simultaneously develop various academic competencies across major academic content areas (Morrell, 2006a, 2006b; Rogers, Morrell, & Enyedy, 2007; Torre & Fine, 2006). The development of critical consciousness and academic competencies results in students having the skill to "read the word in order to read the world" (Freire & Macedo, 1987). Students develop these abilities and skills that transcend the traditional classroom setting, and be-come lifelong learners and change agents in society that are vested in us-ing their education as a tool for their own liberation and for the liberation of their communities. This evolves into a sense of concientización para la colectiva (see Chapter 1, this volume), a paradigm that the work students are involved in is "part of a movement, not simply separate sets of isolated actions, whose goals include critical consciousness, social justice and mutual liberation/emancipation from oppression". It is through a young person's own social development as an action research participant that this transformation into a more critical and active individual takes place.

PAR EntreMundos builds on the foundation of YPAR by taking the core principles of educational transformation through collective research and action, and integrating them with the southern tradition, critical race theory, feminist theorizing, and indigenous cosmologies (see Chapter 1, this volume). Cammarota and colleagues (see Chapter 1, this volume) foreground these four general principles in participation, critical inquiry, knowledge co-construction, power with(in), indigenous cosmologies, creative praxes, transformative action, and concientización para la colectiva.

Education for Liberation During Oppressive Times

In the context of high-stakes testing and accountability within schools, which often fail to promote civic engagement (Kahne & Middaugh, 2008), there is an increasing amount of research that focuses on the work of educators conducting critical action research projects, namely YPAR, with students in various educational settings (Burke & Greene, 2015; Cammarota & Fine, 2008; Cammarota & Romero, 2011; Duncan-Andrade & Morrell, 2008; García et al., 2015; Mirra, García, & Morrell, 2015; Mirra, Morrell, Cain, Scorza, & Ford, 2013; Wright, 2015). Although there is a large and growing body of research focused on YPAR, most of the work is limited to spaces in after-school (Burke & Greene, 2015; Cammarota & Fine, 2008; Wright, 2015) and/or summer seminar (Duncan-Andrade & Morrell, 2008; García et al., 2015; Mirra et al., 2013, 2015) settings with the guidance of researchers and/or graduate students that work in collaboration with classroom teachers.

Research that does focus on YPAR projects that occur in schools is often conducted in collaboration between a university researcher and a classroom teacher, or it is the researcher who periodically enters the classroom to solely lead and complete YPAR projects with students (Cammarota & Romero, 2011). There is also a lack of scholarly literature focused on YPAR conducted solely with teachers and students in classroom settings, much less with preservice candidates and novice teachers. YPAR integrated into the classroom curriculum, rather than an appendage that is added to the learning experience of students and disconnected from the classroom content and standards, is another area of potential inquiry that has yet to be adequately examined.

In this larger context I attempt to add to the growing body of literature focused on action research projects conducted with youth, specifically through findings related to PAR EntreMundos projects in a classroom setting. In particular, this chapter focuses on the findings of an ethnographic study conducted in three ninth grade English classes I taught over the course of two years, 2013–2015, both as a preservice candidate from a local university (see Chapter 9, this volume) and as a first year teacher at the same school site. The PAR EntreMundos projects each class completed were integrated into the mandated classroom curriculum, enhancing and enriching the overall learning experience of students. From these experiences, students became more socially and academically self-empowered, matured into advocates committed to working toward social justice, and evoked large institutional change on campus.

Positionality as Teacher-Researcher

The disposition one takes into the classroom is never neutral. Classroom teachers either teach students to work toward their own liberation and the liberation of their communities, or they teach students to become complacent in the face of different forms of oppression. I acknowledge that I have a different perspective toward education, and my role as a classroom teacher, as a result of being a bilingual Chicano[3] who grew up in a household of low socioeconomic standing and who was pushed out of high school. Unlike the vast majority of teachers who are White and grew up in middle-class households (Aud, Hussar, Kena, Bianco, Frohlich, Kemp, & Tahan, 2011; Snyder & Dillow, 2015) —experiences far removed from most of the students they serve—I have a more vested interest in the success of my students in social and academic settings because of our shared lived experiences. My lived experiences are what prepared me to enter the profession with a greater disposition toward teaching and working toward social justice, yet it was my preservice credential preparation that gave me the language and skill to engage in such work.

As a preservice candidate at a local university, I was part of the National Latino/a Research and Policy Project (NLERAP) Grown Your Own (GYO) Latino Teacher Pipeline project. This experience, entirely under the guidance of NLERAP affiliated university professors, included the completion of coursework focused on critical pedagogy, critical race theory, and teaching from a social justice paradigm (Arellano, Cintrón, Flores, & Berta-Ávila, 2016) and the participation in multiple Saturday workshops and "check-ins" over the course of the academic school year (see Chapter 9, this volume).

This support system provided NLERAP preservice candidates with, among other things, the PAR EntreMundos framework, knowledge of curriculum integration, and professional/personal mentorship—allowing preservice candidates to undergo personal transformations that helped us to actively engage in critical pedagogy and social justice work at the classroom and schoolwide levels (see Chapter 9, this volume). My disposition and desire to teach and work toward social justice based on my own lived experiences, coupled with the NLERAP-GYO initiative and knowledge gleaned from that experience, allowed me to begin my career actively engaged in working toward social justice.

Setting

Campus

Miwok High School (MHS) is made up of about 1,500 students. The student population is representative of the ethnic and linguistic diversity of the larger community setting. The ethnic demographics on campus are 42% Asian, most of whom are Southeast Asian, 35% Latinx, 14% African American, 6% White, 1% Native American, and 3% mixed race. The linguistic diversity is just as prominent, with twenty documented spoken languages and one out of four students identified as English language learners (Miwok Unified School District [MUSD], 2017). Socioeconomically, over 91% of the student population are from households identified as living below the poverty line and 100% of students on campus qualify for free-and-reduced lunch (MUSD, 2017). The Miwok area is also considered by some to be one of the most dangerous areas in the county region (Kempa, 2013). The reputation of the general area, along with Miwok being the poorest high school in the school district, results in many outsiders to the school and larger community often having a deficit viewpoint of the campus and students, unfairly viewing both as "bad" and/or "ghetto".

Classroom

The first class to complete PAR EntreMundos (2013-2014) was enrolled in a Specially Designed Academic Instruction in English (SDAIE) course for English learner (EL) students at levels three and four based on the California English Language Development Test (CELDT). Students in this class were identified as "intermediate" and "early advanced" with respect to their English language proficiencies based on their CELDT scores from the previous year. This class was composed of twenty-two students—thirteen female and nine male. The ethnic demographics were 64% Latinx, 23% Southeast Asian (all but one student was Hmong), and 13% Fiji Indian. The two other classes that make up the findings of this study were mainstream English classes during the 2014–2015 school year. These two classes had twenty-two and twenty-three students, respectively: twenty-six females and nineteen males, 40% Southeast Asian (mostly Hmong), 30% African American, 19% Latinx, 9% White, and 2% Fiji Indian.

The PAR EntreMundos Process

Content Overlay[4]

Although projects did not commence until the latter part of the fall semester,[5] all of the curriculum leading up to their initiation was instrumental in setting its foundation. The mandated classroom curriculum used was integrated (Sleeter & Grant, 2009) and frontloaded (see Chapter 9, this volume) with critical pedagogical, multicultural, and social justice approaches and perspectives. This initial phase in PAR EntreMundos was pivotal in teaching students about critical social issues that were historically and contemporarily relevant to them and their immediate communities. It fostered a space for students to engage in critical and relevant curriculum, but also provided students the ability to further develop the academic skills targeted by the mandated curriculum in contexts that were more meaningful to them. Student interest piqued as they were able to learn about "real life issues" that concerned them.

Interest in learning about their lived experiences and the intersectionalities they shared with peers fostered a classroom rooted in culturally sustaining pedagogy (Paris & Alim, 2017), a space in which Paris and Alim posit that students are able to sustain "the cultural and linguistic competence of their [own and other] communities while simultaneously offering access to the dominant cultural competence… [to] perpetuate and foster—to sustain—linguistic, literate, and cultural pluralism as part of the democratic project of schooling" (2017). This was accomplished through strategically integrating PAR EntreMundos into the mandated curriculum and Common Core State Standards (CCSS) expected to be taught to students. Instead of the projects being an appendage that were added to the curriculum, out of context to the larger content and academic skills being taught, projects were seamlessly integrated into the content and skills students were learning—enriching their overall learning experience with a critical and social justice oriented paradigm.

Construct PAR Collective

Coupled with providing students critical, relevant, and culturally sustaining curriculum, the creation and sharing of autoethnographies—cultural narratives that build toward critical social analysis (Alexander, 2005; Camangian, 2010; Carey-Webb, 2001)—were important in the development of closer learning communities and overall PAR collective. Different forms of autoethnographies included spoken word poetry, memoirs, and visual essays—each performed at various points throughout the fall semester and for various academic and social-emotional purposes. The bond fostered early in the school year as a result of these activities nurtured an environment where students were able to trust and care for one another, making collaboration between students more genuine throughout the PAR EntreMundos process.

Students presented autoethnographies in the form of spoken word poetry at the beginning of the school year in order to build community with one another, and as Camangian (2010) states, to allow students to foster an "understanding of one another by healing the various perceived differences they experience within their social contexts" (p. 179-180). Students became more comfortable with each other and formed a closer bond as a class after this activity, recognizing similarities within each other's lived experiences based on factors such as race and ethnicity, language, sexual orientation, and school experiences. I was able to foreground students' experiences as the foundation for curriculum integration from the insight gathered from this activity. Students were able to see that the class would be student-centered, and that they had a genuine voice in what was taught, rather than being taught solely what the teacher deemed valuable and/or worthy of study.

One example of students having a decision in what was taught in class was after the presentation of autoethnographic poems toward the beginning of the school year. Students identified major reoccurring issues in their collective lived experiences, which I integrated into the class curriculum and/or created stand-alone lessons that reinforced the academic skills students were learning or had already learned. Students were able to better understand these topics and how they, and their communities, were affected by them. Major topics students identified during the presentations, and which lessons were created for, included racism, sexism, linguicism, homophobia, and internalized oppression.

Identifying Generative Themes

Once PAR EntreMundos officially commenced, students presented another autoethnographic text, Educational Journeys (see this volume)—a critical and reflective narrative of academic and social experiences presented through the use of images and words. Educational Journeys provided an avenue for students to identify a topic to further investigate, which would later inform their PAR EntreMundos research question.

Figure 10.1: Student Example of an Educational Journey

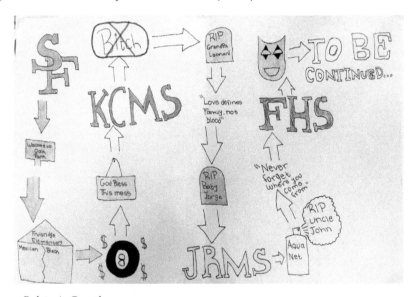

Source: Rubén A. González

Continuing with the strategic decision to integrate PAR EntreMundos into the classroom curriculum, I structured the activity in a manner that allowed students to meet the school district's speech proficiency graduation require-ment—a graduation gatekeeper for many, particularly EL students. To do so, aside from meeting the time requirement for the length of the speech, each student had to provide a general outline of their presentation, which allowed me to reinforce how to create outlines for more traditional forms of writing such as essays. The other requirements to fulfill the district's speech proficiency grad-uation policy were already embedded in the presentation (e.g., use of visuals; logical order and sequence of information; and to inform the audience about a specific topic or issue). The integration of Educational Journeys into the mandated curriculum provided students with an additional opportunity to pass this graduation requirement compared to their peers in other classes, and allowed for a more meaningful presentation opportunity—all other ninth grade English classes were limited to book report and/or demonstration speeches.

Figure 10.2: Student Example of an Educational Journey

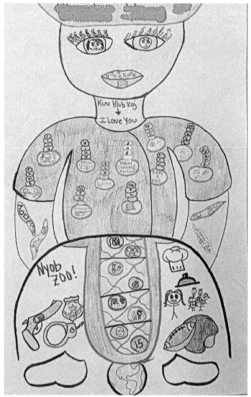

Source: Rubén A. González

As narratives were shared, students took notes of major topics that emerged from each presentation. After everyone presented, students worked individually to narrow their list to three topics they felt were the biggest issues affecting their collective lives as students on campus. Then, in groups of four, students discussed the topics each person identified and created a group list, which was then narrowed further. Each group presented the topic they felt most passionate about to the entire class. Students then came to a democratic decision regarding which topic would be selected for the entire class. It is important to note that in all three classes it was a near unanimous decision as to the topic that was ultimately selected.

Topics selected served as a general field of interest. Students felt that these topics were issues on campus, yet did not know exactly what they wanted to research. The topics selected by the three classes were modern day segregation, institutional racism, and institutional inequity. I then created lessons based on the selected topics. Gaining more insight and understanding into these topics allowed students to better understand how they were affected by them, and helped students make a more informed decision as to what they wanted to research.

Problematize Generative Themes

Students read Lorraine Hansberry's (1959) play, *A Raisin in the Sun*; a mandated text for all ninth grade English classes on campus. Integration of the topics student selected not only helped them better understand their respective issue as they progressed through PAR EntreMundos, it also allowed students to better understand the sociopolitical context of the play and what led Hansberry to write it. Once students had an understanding of these topics at a historical level, greatly reinforcing their understanding of *A Raisin in the Sun*, I provided lessons to show students how these topics were still relevant today and how they affected people of various backgrounds. Lessons incorporated information from their own school and neighborhoods to make the information more relevant to students, such as the housing patterns and restrictions of their neighborhoods and the disproportionate suspension rates of students on campus based on ethnicity.

One example of content integration and academic skill development was a lesson focused on disproportionate suspension rates of youth of color in public schools and relating that information to Miwok High. The lesson, specific to the class interested in institutional racism, integrated various CCSS Anchor Standards, but focused on close reading and evaluating content presented in diverse media and formats, and determining what texts explicitly say as well as being able to make logical inferences based on textual information.[6] Students read multiple informational texts (i.e., articles and short video) from various sources as a means to address these standards.

Students first watched a short video and took notes about the information presented, then read two sets of print texts with more detailed information about the topic. The texts were read twice: once for general understanding and a second time employing close reading strategies for a more purposeful read. On their second read, students annotated for the main idea, supporting details, and important details and/or quotes, a skill they had been practicing all year. Students then completed a descriptive outline of the texts, dividing each text into sections where the author(s) transitioned from one main idea and/or supporting detail to the next. In those sections, students wrote on the margins of their texts a one sentence summary (i.e., what is the author "saying" with the information) and one sentence explaining the rhetorical purposes (i.e., what is the author "doing" with the information) of that section.

In addition, students compared and contrasted the multiple texts they read and annotated. Student analysis of the texts focused on similarities and differences between the subject matter, purpose, and tone; how the texts helped the reader better understand the topic having read them together or how the reader's perspective might have been different if they had only read one text; and a reflection concerning what questions the textual information raised for them as readers. After engaging with the multiple texts, students participated in a Socratic Seminar to discuss what they learned and how the texts related to their own experiences on campus.

After a series of lessons for each class such as the example mentioned above, students problematized their topics. A more profound understanding of the topics each class selected allowed students to (1) better understand the root causes of these issues plaguing them on campus, and (2) be more specific in what they wanted to research for their respective projects. The problematized topics, which guided the research for each project, were student self-segregation based on race and language; teacher discrimination toward students based on race, language, and gender; and the lack of ethnic and linguistically diverse teachers on campus. These problematized topics helped students develop their respective research questions. The research questions would then guide their data collection.

Generative Research Protocol

Students were given a handout that provided them with their respective class topic and space with language frames in order to document possible research questions. This was completed the week leading up to the class discussion in which they would decide what research question their respective projects would focus on. The languages frames included examples such as "I wonder why _____?" and "Why is it that _____?" to assist students in the development of their questions, although the use of the language frames were optional. Students were encouraged to create possible research questions related to their class topic based on "feelings, experiences, and observations you have every day at Miwok High".

Much like the process students used to decide which topic to learn more about as a class after their Educational Journeys, students first worked individually on their research questions before working in groups, and then had a whole class discussion to select their PAR EntreMundos research question. Students individually chose the question they were most interested in focusing their project on, and in groups of four decided which question addressed one of the most important issues facing students on campus. One representative per group shared their group's research question and their reasoning as to why it was an important issue that needed to be addressed. After a series of discussions and combining similar research questions, each class voted to decide what would be the focus of their project. All classes unanimously agreed on their respective research question:

- Why do students at Miwok self-segregate themselves based on race and language?
- How are students affected by teacher discrimination against them based on race, language, and gender?
- How does a lack of ethnic and linguistic teacher diversity affect students' education on campus?

The research questions were not static, as classes were able to make changes throughout the research process—particularly as they analyzed and reflected on the data gathered after each research approach. Further, each research question anchored the PAR EntreMundos projects for students, as all of the data they collected would attempt to answer their question, or at the very least better inform students as to the causes and consequences related to their research question.

Data Collection

Research approaches students employed included ethnographic field notes based on campus and peer observations; written and oral surveys; semistructured interviews that were audio recorded and later transcribed; and the review of relevant scholarly literature from various online databases. Students were all taught the same research approaches, yet not every class employed observations, and the surveys and interviews were all structured and conducted slightly differently by students in each class.

All three classes gathered information throughout the data collection process in pairs. Data were collected by students from their peers around campus at various times throughout the school day: before school, during lunch, and after school. Data were also collected from a wide range of student groups based on race, gender, and grade level. Most data were gathered and recorded during lunchtime and in the quad area outside of the cafeteria, the most populated area on campus. Other prominent areas for data collection included inside the school library and inside the cafeteria during lunch time. My classroom also served as an area for students to gather data, but was mostly utilized by students before and/or after school as a space to conduct interviews.

Students learned, practiced, and employed each research method in sequential order and had an entire week outside of class to collect data for each approach. I used the Gradual Release of Responsibility (GRR) model of instruction (Pearson & Gallagher, 1983) when teaching students the different research approaches. The GRR instructional approach allowed students to complete rigorous academic tasks they had not yet developed expertise in (Buehl, 2005) and helped students learn research skills and literacies while improving their overall literacy achievement (Fisher & Frey, 2007).

Data Analysis

Once data was collected for each research method, as it was completed in sequential order, students worked in small groups to tabulate, categorize, and analyze their findings. Data such as observations from field notes were shared aloud by students while I wrote the information on a large sheet of paper with a diagram of the quad area and of the inside of the cafeteria. Survey findings were tabulated in groups of four, with students counting the responses for each question. One representative from each group tallied their respective survey findings on a large sheet of paper prominently displayed in class with each survey question written underneath their respective tally marks. The overall number of tally marks for each response was then converted into percentage points.

The interview findings were recorded in a similar manner, with students working in pairs to identify and code major reoccurring themes based on interviewee responses. Prominent themes were written on large sheets of paper and displayed on the classroom walls. The large sheets of paper for each set of data remained on the classroom walls for the duration of the projects. After each set of data was recorded and displayed in class, students had a Socratic Seminar to discuss their findings, which informed the creation of the next set of questions for further data collection.

Figure 10.3: Tabulated Survey Results

Source: Rubén A. González

Figure 10.4: Major Reoccurring Interview Themes

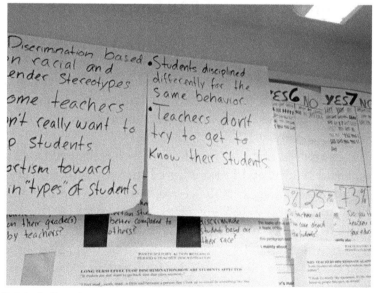

Source: Rubén A. González

Action Plans & Community Dialogues

With initial data collected (e.g., observations, surveys, and interviews), students discussed recommendations to address the issues they were researching. Recommendations were brainstormed and decided upon via Socratic Seminars. Students then found evidence from various online databases to support their overall findings and recommendations. Once all information was collected, students brainstormed possible audiences for their projects.

All three classes decided to present whole-class multimedia presentations to the Steering Committee on campus, which is in charge of all school-wide decisions and policies. Each class also invited counselors and teachers who were not part of the committee, as well as community members, parents, and fellow students to attend their presentations. Project presentations were conducted after school and in different venues such as the school theater (2013–2014) and the school cafeteria (2014–2015). The presentations to these key stakeholders included the PAR EntreMundos framework, research methodology, data findings and analysis, and detailed recommendations, respectively.

Implications of PAR EntreMundos

Major findings of the effects PAR EntreMundos had on students were derived from my own research notes: participant observations and field notes, student written reflections, and semi-structured interviews. Written reflections were completed by students throughout the PAR process, while interviews were conducted at the culmination of each project, and at the beginning and middle of the next school year.

I selected an even number of students to be interviewed based on ethnicity/race and gender, and I also selected students with a diverse set of academic and disciplinary experiences/records during the year they were in my class. I hoped this would provide a set of interviewees that truly represented the wide range of student experiences and perspectives engaged in PAR EntreMundos, and would allow me to better analyze how being part of this type of work affected students from various social and academic backgrounds.

"We Were All Moved": Social & Academic Self-Empowerment

Students fostered positive and caring relationships with one another in their respective classes over the course of each PAR EntreMundos project. The foundation for the improved interpersonal relationships among students were the presentation of autoethnographic narratives that allowed students to share their own experiences while fostering positive bonds with each other. Critical and multicultural curriculum based on student experiences strengthened these bonds, as students were able to see historical and contemporary similarities between themselves and their peers, seeing how they had all been similarly oppressed and dispossessed. Having their experiences validated while fostering classroom community at the beginning of the semester, and throughout the semester with similar activities and lessons prior to beginning their projects, situated the students and the classroom within an authentic caring framework (Valenzuela, 1999). Students were able to naturally form support groups within classes, eliminating feelings of alienation when confronting historical and contemporary difficulties in their lives.

The foundation of trust and care for one another was enhanced by the "common struggle" of completing the PAR process. Students became united in an effort to obtain the same goal—the improvement of their school—that transcended any differences between them that might have alienated students from each other in the past. Working toward this common goal allowed students to bond with one another, and taught them about the power of collaboration when seeking to evoke change. They realized that without each other, they would not have been able to complete their projects and all they entailed. The changes on campus as a result of their projects would not have been realized if it were not for the genuine trust and care students had for one another. How completing the PAR EntreMundos process brought students together as a class is encapsulated by the words of Zaier:

> As a class we've become closer because of PAR. We all began as strangers in our class and as we struggled together became a family. We are all brothers and sisters that overcame challenges and were able to complete something special together... We always had each other's back. I learned that if we work together to be heard, we can and will be.

The very nature of PAR EntreMundos, collaborative and academically rigorous, had students learn to trust each other and work together in completing difficult activities and tasks that necessitated assistance from one another. Finding and reading scholarly texts in order to support their own research would not have been possible for some students, even with academic supports and scaffolds, if they did not have each other in order to make a large and complex task into smaller, more manageable activities. Likewise, the interviewing of fellow students, transcribing, and coding of findings, was an extremely complex and academically rigorous task that was able to be completed as a result of students collaborating on the various aspects of the overall activity. Successfully completing these difficult tasks with peers helped students see that their classmates could be trusted in completing academically challenging work and were valuable co-constructors of knowledge.

As students continually engaged in the PAR process, they were able to foster trusting relationships of mutuality among each other, a power with(in) (see Chapter 1, this volume), as they recognized the important role their peers played in each other's experience and in the completion of the overall project. The constant utterance of the word "family" in various written reflections and interviews when referring to the class and each other demonstrates the power with(in) that was nurtured, specifically in the degree of success students had in collaborating and trusting one another in mutually completing tasks. Students knew they had a responsibility to someone beyond themselves and that others relied on them. Zaier explained this when he elaborated on why he called his peers helping each other "like a family".

> We had to trust each other—trust that each person did their job collecting information. I trusted that they would do their part so I could do what I had to get done… I never doubted anyone. I trusted them without a doubt. Once you know someone like how we got to know each other, you don't want to let someone down. You care too much about them to let them down.

The self-empowerment through experiences in PAR EntreMundos manifested itself clearly in class as students purposely worked toward "having each other's back" throughout the process, knowing they could count on their peers to fulfill their own responsibilities as well as assist each other throughout PAR. Students genuinely cared for each other and their overall well-being not only in class and with their PAR projects, but in larger social contexts as well. In support of students caring too much to let each other down, Zaier stated:

> Educational Journeys helped us understand each other and why people act the way
> they do, so you don't judge them in a bad way anymore…you care about people and
> worry when something is wrong…Working on PAR brought us closer because you
> know each other now; working together on something makes you a lot closer.

Students cared for each other as they learned about similarities they had, and this was reinforced by the realization that they all had the common goal of working toward the betterment of their respective realities and of their school as a whole. They showed a stronger work ethic as a result of not wanting to disappoint their peers, and wanting to do well for each other became an intrinsic motivation for many.

This newfound intrinsic motivation for someone besides themselves led students to take part in indigenous cosmologies (see Chapter 1, this volume), another tenet of PAR EntreMundos, as the work they were engaged in was a healing process for the individual and the community, in this case the classroom and larger school community. As Zaier shared with his classmates during the reflections at the end of the school year, "I'm more considerate of other people now. I believe I changed in the way I see things now compared to how I did before… I used to not care and say hurtful things to some of you and just not care. Now that I realized I was doing wrong. I don't do that to people now because I see how it hurts them". What initially started as a common struggle to work together for the betterment of their campus through PAR projects gradually came to encompass caring and helping each other along the way to their ultimate goal. Students learned that it was not possible to transform their campus unless they first began by transforming themselves as individuals and their interactions with others. The overall self-empowerment students felt as part of the PAR collective had internalizing effects on them, and how they viewed themselves and others.

At the completion of their projects and throughout the subsequent academic year, many students viewed themselves in a more positive light. Students viewed themselves as much more socially and academically capable than what had usually been expected of them by others, and frankly, what they had come to expect of themselves. They began to counter the belief that many of them had that they were academically inadequate as a result of the negative perceptions others had of Miwok and its students. Zaier clearly demonstrated how students began to view themselves in a more positive manner as a result of their experiences in PAR EntreMundos:

> I've never done work like PAR before and it was great getting to work on something that we actually care about… I've built more character and learned that I'm capable of doing difficult work and accomplishing higher level work…This process showed me to not give up and that I can do anything I put my mind to… I now have more confidence in myself inside and outside of class. When things are difficult in class or life, I tell myself, 'I can do it, come on, don't give up.' I know I'll get it done now. Before I doubted myself and gave up a lot.

This testimonial is a sample of how students often walked away from completing PAR EntreMundos projects feeling self-empowered both socially and academically. Many students stated they had never taken part in anything for such an extended amount of time that was both engaging and rigorous. Completing their projects was a proud and major accomplishment for students. Putting in a great amount of time and effort, and seeing the results of their work as recommendations began to be implemented, led students to view themselves differently: as leaders on campus who are critical change agents capable of achieving great accomplishments both socially and academically.

Many students shared the ideas of "coming out of their shells", "being more outspoken", and having an overall increased confidence in themselves. Toward the end of each respective project, students began to become more vocal and speak out when they disagreed with something happening in class, on campus, or in larger social settings. Students were not afraid to speak up for themselves or others in the face of what they believed to be injustice. They ultimately developed the critical consciousness to reflect upon and question things around them, along with the confidence and skill to speak up and take action as needed.

Increased self-empowerment in social settings translated into viewing themselves as more academically capable. Throughout their projects, students completed tasks that were academically demanding and difficult for them, even with scaffolds and supports provided. Examples of this included comprehending, analyzing, and synthesizing multiple texts in written and spoken form, such scholarly texts and the data collected during their own research. While rigorous and far in excess of what other ninth grade students were being asked to produce, students were able to successfully complete these and other tasks, being proud of the work they accomplished and allowing themselves to see that they are capable of academically rigorous tasks.

The success students had in completing difficult academic tasks, as well as learning the skills required of them to complete these tasks, led students to begin to not shy away from demanding and rigorous academic work, but instead, to embrace it. Supported by various scholars (Camangian, 2015; Finn &

Voelkl, 1993; Newmann, Wehlage, & Lamborn, 1992; Steinberg, 1996), student's improved self-confidence led to higher levels of engagement in their learning and willingness to complete academically rigorous tasks, which in turn resulted in higher academic achievement as students were willing to take part in tasks that benefited them as learners.

The overall confidence students had in themselves contributed to higher academic achievement and success compared to students in other classes. Students engaged in PAR EntreMundos had a pass rate of 90%, compared to the average of 69% for students in other ninth grade English classes. The level of engagement in the curriculum and confidence in themselves allowed for a more genuine investment in their learning, evident with their commendable work ethic in completing various activities and assignments outside of class. The enjoyment and overall investment in their learning allowed students to rise to the higher expectations and academic demands placed on them.

I attribute the success students had in my class in comparison to their peers in other classes to the above mentioned investment and overall engagement they had in their own learning. PAR EntreMundos made the curriculum more meaningful for students in comparison to the mandated curriculum their peers were exposed to all year. The investment and engagement in their learning is what allowed students to not falter in class. It allowed students to be more willing to engage in learning and further develop their academic skills. Further, students had developed a support system with their peers that influenced their willingness to further engage in their learning, regardless of the level of difficulty. All of this translated into higher levels of academic achievement and success.

In acknowledging the higher pass rates of my students, one must also recognize that grades and pass rates may reflect different grading policies and practices between myself and my colleagues. While this may be true, as grading in the areas of English is subjective, this may not have been as strong of a factor. In major writing assignments all teachers used the school district's writing rubrics. The rubrics are painstakingly detailed in what constitutes an overall grade for students, and provide specific grading guides for categories such as reader orientation, evidence selection and integration, and correct sentence structure. Common assessments as a result of the mandated curriculum created a sense of continuity among teachers, as teachers graded all students based on the same criteria. Not only were students who took part in PAR EntreMundos feeling more confident about themselves, they were in fact producing at a higher level academically than their peers in different classes based on the same mandated curriculum and assessments.

A Pedagogical Approach for Nurturing Critical Student-Activists

As students progressed with their projects and began to prepare for their presentations to various key stakeholders, they recognized how their own critical consciousness and academic skills not only benefited themselves but also served a larger social purpose (Camangian, 2015). Their commitment to "making our school and society a better place" was solidified after presenting their findings and recommendations to audiences who took them seriously and began to implement what was proposed. Students now viewed themselves as change agents who had made their campus more equitable for their peers and also became committed to continuing to engage in working toward social justice.

This was a major theme in the written reflections and interviews after the completion of their projects, and also in interviews the following school year. Lorenza was a clear example of how students were transformed via their experiences with PAR EntreMundos, specifically in developing concientización para la colectiva. In an interview during her tenth grade year, Lorenza talked about how PAR EntreMundos changed how she viewed herself as a person and her positionality as a student on campus. Lorenza now saw her purpose of working toward social justice as a lifelong duty:

> I don't think I would be encouraged or have confidence to speak for myself or others if it wasn't for PAR. I always cared about issues in society but I didn't know how to do anything to fix the problems... [Now] I feel more dedicated to go out there in the real world and help those who are afraid to speak up... As a student here at MHS, I learned that I am capable of many great things. I am capable of changing the school and society, small steps at a time. I am capable of inspiring others... The presentation really made me realize that this isn't the end, it's just the beginning.

Lorenza, like many of her peers, became self-empowered, with a new sense of confidence to speak up and take action. She realized that she had the knowledge and skill to work toward the elimination of societal issues she always felt passionate about. What was telling about her words was how she situated herself as a student on campus capable of making change "small steps at a time". Lorenza realized that she had the ability to evoke change, and took this as a responsibility to her immediate community to work toward making change in any way she could. This sense of responsibility to herself and her community was evident when Lorenza said she realized she must go beyond PAR EntreMundos, and not be complacent with one moment of activism. She recognized that this was "just the beginning" of a lifelong journey of working toward social justice.

Lorenza had already been superficially involved on campus, being part of the associated study body (i.e., student government), yet she realized that "coloring and hanging posters for rallies and assemblies" would not evoke a critical change that would benefit her peers. She demonstrated great critical consciousness in realizing how she was part of maintaining the status quo by not doing anything to benefit the campus in a critical manner, and also, realizing that many of her peers possibly lacked the critical consciousness and skill to work against different forms of oppression.

Lorenza, like many of her peers, began to create and join different school organizations in order to build the critical consciousness and skill of their peers, with a focus on seeking to transform their school and larger community settings through critical, civic activism. Students became core members and leaders of these groups focused on issues of social justice, and viewed their standing within these entities as a space for them to "give back and improve Miwok High" and to begin to "change society" by helping peers grow their own critical consciousness, civic engagement, and activism. In the case of Lorenza, she became a founding member of a student-led group on campus focused on building more positive interpersonal relationships among students and addressing issues related to school climate such as bullying. Lorenza continued her involvement in student government, but now employed a more critical paradigm regarding activities that were organized and conducted on campus, and also seeking to address the lack of inclusivity of students in activities and who participated in student government.

Many students who participated in PAR EntreMundos projects departed with a newfound confidence and view of themselves as capable of evoking change. More importantly, students positioned themselves in various student-led groups on campus and in historically adult-dominated spaces at the district level in order to work toward change. Students have consequently done a lot of tremendous work in addressing various forms of injustice on campus, transforming Miwok at many macro and micro levels the last few years.

Inciting Institutional Change Through Critical Student Activism

Every PAR EntreMundos project has resulted in significant institutional change on campus, and has organically built on each other to nurture and grow student activism. Student recommendations proposed to key school

stakeholders have varied in their level of success with respect to implementation, yet students have continued to maintain a strong commitment toward
having each of their recommendations become a reality on campus. This high
level of dedication and engagement has led students to obtain at some level,
and to continue to strive for, the PAR EntreMundos tenet of transformational
action—a commitment to conscious action and social change on campus via
creative praxes and engaged policy (see Chapter 1, this volume). Manifestations of this have included organizing and protesting against inequitable
learning conditions and institutional racism on campus, presenting at a school
district board meeting to demand an end to inequitable district transportation policies and practices, regularly meeting with campus administrators and
district superintendents regarding issues of equity and social justice, and positioning themselves as student voices that must be taken into account regarding school and district-wide decisions.

The primary recommendation posed by the students in the 2013–2014
project has by far had the most profound influence on both students and the
campus as a whole, particularly at the institutional level. In response to student self-segregation, students recommended the creation of a student-led
organization to address critical issues affecting students on campus. Students
wanted a space to voice their concerns and to address issues related to equity
and social justice. This was vital as there was a profound lack of student voice
on campus in regard to school-wide decisions, as well as a lack of space for students to address issues affecting them. The Social Justice & Equity Collective
(SJEC) was proposed and created the next academic school year. I, along with
two colleagues,[7] became advisors. This marked the first time in school history
that there was a student organization focused on critical issues related to social
justice, and the first attempt at positioning students as key stakeholders on
campus with a voice in the decision-making process.

Since its founding, SJEC has been a prominent fixture on campus that is
increasingly considered by various stakeholders, becoming a critical voice for
students seeking to transform their school. One such example is how SJEC
and its members were able to advocate for, and obtain, a new school schedule
that made the educational experience of many students, particularly African-
American and Latinx students, more equitable by drastically improving their
ability to graduate from Miwok High. Students met with various teachers and
campus administrators to address the need for a new schedule and to voice
their concern regarding a lack of student voice in this school-wide decision.
Students also took part in various protests to voice their displeasure toward

teachers initially voting down the proposed schedule change, even though teachers had data over the course of multiple years to prove such a change would benefit all students. This data included the fact that Miwok was pushing out one out of every three African-American students and two out of every five Latinx students. The proposed schedule would decrease these numbers with more opportunities for credit remediation and academic support courses, a major reason many students were being pushed out.

Another critical moment of activism for students in SJEC was their own PAR EntreMundos project the following school year, 2015–2016. After a campus policy instituting an hour-long detention for each tardy to school and an out-of-school suspension if detentions were not served, students conducted research with respect to those affected by this policy and found that many students were tardy to school as a result of a lack of access to transportation. Upon further research, SJEC members discovered that the high schools within the school district with the largest number and highest percentage of affluent and White students were provided school buses. The school buses were paid for by the school district. This troubled students, as schools like Miwok that mostly serve low-income students of color do not receive these services, forcing students to walk up to five miles to get to school or pay fifty dollars every month for a bus pass in order to take public transportation to school.

SJEC members culminated their PAR EntreMundos project with a presentation to the school board, citing the greater need for Miwok High students to receive transportation services compared to their more affluent peers, and explaining how the current transportation policies and practices were unjust and possibly a civil rights violation (Macdonald, 2016). School board members and district officials were "called out" and forced to put equity into practice— not simply include the word in their mission statements. The school board members heeded the recommendations of students and subsequently called for the creation of a transportation committee, which would include Miwok students, teachers, community members and parents, in order to create a new district-wide transportation policy.

This marked the first time in the history of the school district that students would serve on a district committee. In addition, two district superintendents expressed the possibility of free bus passes for all Miwok students, which was the minimum SJEC students wanted after their presentation. Overall, this was a victory for the members of SJEC and their entire high school, but it was also not enough, as the goal of SJEC is still to continue to work toward Miwok receiving their own school bus system.

The recommendations posed by the class that researched teacher discrimination against students have led to multiple meetings between students, campus administrators, district superintendents, university professors, and Miwok teachers to discuss implementation of professional development for all staff members focused on topics such as microaggressions, implicit and racial bias, and social justice. This work has been spearheaded by SJEC members, who have discussed possible topics and structure of the professional development and have met with various campus and district leaders to share the importance and urgency of this work.

The call for more ethnically and linguistically diverse teachers on campus has also been acknowledged and acted upon by adult stakeholders. Administrators partnered with a local university to primarily place on campus preservice credential candidates of color and candidates who are earning their bilingual authorizations. This was a profound first step toward potentially hiring more diverse teachers, as there is a long history of hiring their own preservice credential candidates to full-time positions at Miwok High. Moreover, there has been an increase in teachers of color who have been hired since the recommendation by students was proposed. While one cannot say for certain that the recommendation posed by students directly influenced who has been hired on campus, one can acknowledge that students brought up the issue of the trend of hiring mostly White teachers to those who interview candidates and make hiring decisions, placing the need for change in their purview.

These are a few of the recommendations students have proposed. While students have had some level of success implementing some of their recommendations, and have received some level of support from individuals in positions of power, this is far from the norm. Each presentation and subsequent set of recommendations has received resistance from teachers and administrators. Some examples include White teachers becoming angry at students as a result of feeling that a desire for more teachers of color means that White teachers are unfit to teach students of color; teachers having a deficit viewpoint of students and believing that students did not—could not—conduct the research in their presentations, and subsequently disregarding students entirely; and administrators not providing students and student-allies with access to institutional structures and supports to begin to implement proposed recommendations. In other words, what students have implemented thus far has been hard fought.

With that being said, some recommendations have yielded immediate results and others continue to be a work in progress that will take an arduous
amount of dedication, time, and effort by all of those involved. Yet, students
have not withered in their dedication and commitment to these recommendations and the larger goal of transforming their campus into a better place
for all current and future students. Teachers, administrators, and superintendents are now also "on notice" that there is a strong and active student voice
on campus that is critical of policies and practices that affect them. Moreover, now that multiple different groups of students have taken part in PAR
EntreMundos and have gone on to pursue other endeavors rooted in critical activism, student activism is becoming normalized on campus. Students
are committed to working toward social justice and show no signs of slowing
down their plans or actions toward improving Miwok High.

Conclusion

The findings presented provide a glimpse into the transformative potential
and overall benefits of youth engaged in PAR EntreMundos. I challenge educators to use this framework in classroom settings: to integrate this pedagogical approach into what is already being taught in the classroom, to create
more critical and relevant learning experiences for students, and to foster an
environment in which students can engage in activism while simultaneously
developing critical consciousness and academic competencies.

Creating curriculum and integrating content with critical and social justice pedagogical approaches will not be easy, nor will implementing PAR EntreMundos. Lessons and projects will not be pre-packaged in textbooks or in
teacher-proof curriculum. It will require moral courage and professional skill
to do well, and will result in various forms of resistance: pressure from administrators to not "cause trouble", anger and resentment from colleagues when
students present difficult findings for staff to confront, and other systemic constraints such as mandated curriculum and pacing guides. These are just a few
of the many obstacles one is sure to encounter in this type of work, or frankly,
any time you teach and work against the status quo.

As classroom teachers, one of our primary tasks is to ensure that students
learn. Yet, we must not become complacent is doing the bare minimum—in
helping students learn the basic academic skills and content knowledge associated with what we teach. This results in becoming solely a content teacher;

someone who limits the possibilities of what is learned in the classroom and who hinders how students engage in their learning. Instead, it becomes imperative for us to become critical educators who teach students through a critical and social justice paradigm. We must seek to create meaningful learning opportunities for critical, civic engagement and action that allows students to challenge and address different forms of oppression while developing their academic skills. Ultimately, we must strive to become critical educators who stand in genuine solidarity with our students.

Notes

1. All student and school names are pseudonyms.
2. Students refer to their PAR EntreMundos projects as "PAR".
3. Refers to a man of Mexican ancestry who was born and/or raised in the United States.
4. The following subheadings are the phases of PAR EntreMundos. This serves as a general outline/guide for practitioners, not a formulaic or standard approach (see Chapter 1, this volume).
5. Projects began in the middle of December and ended in late May.
6. CCSS referred to are CCSS.ELA-LITERACY.CCRA.R.1 and CCSS.ELA-LITERACY. CCRA.R7.
7. One veteran African-American female and one veteran White male teacher, both with a long history of classroom success and working toward social justice at institutional levels. This provided SJEC members with a diverse set of advisors based on race, gender, age, and social backgrounds.

References

Alexander, B. K. (2005). Performance ethnography: The reenacting and inciting of culture. In N. Denzil & Y. Lincoln (Eds.), *The sage handbook of qualitative research*. (3rd ed., pp. 411–441). Thousand Oaks, CA: Sage.

Arellano, A., Cintrón, J., Flores, B., & Berta-Ávila, M. (2016). Teaching for critical consciousness: Topics, themes, frameworks, and instructional activities. In A. Valenzuela (Ed.), *Growing critically conscious educators: A social justice curriculum for educators of Latino/a youth*. New York, NY: Teachers College Press.

Au, W. (2007). High-stakes testing and curricular control: A qualitative metasynthesis. *Educational Researcher, 36*(5), 258–267.

Aud, S., Hussar, W., Kena, G., Bianco, K., Frohlich, L., Kemp, J., & Tahan, K. (2011). *The Condition of Education 2011 (NCES 2011–033)*. U.S. Department of Education, National Center for Education Statistics. Washington, DC: U.S. Government Printing Office.

Buehl, D. (2005). Scaffolding. Retrieved November, 27, 2014, from http://weac.org/articles/readingroom_scaffolding/

Burke, K., & Greene, S. (2015). Participatory action research, youth voices, and civic engagement. *Language Arts, 92*(2), 387–400.

Cahill, C. (2004). Defying gravity: Raising on scrounges through collective research. *Children's Geographies, 2*(2), 273–286.

Camangian, P. (2008). Real talk: Transformative English teaching and urban youth. In W. Ayers, T. Quinn, & D. Stovall (Eds.), *Handbook of social justice in education*. Mahwah, NJ: Lawrence Erlbaum, Inc.

Camangian, P. (2010). Starting with self: Teaching autoethnography to foster critical caring literacies. *Research in the Teaching of English, 45*(2), 179–204.

Camangian, P. (2015). Teach like lives depend on it: Agitate, arouse, and inspire. *Urban Education, 50*(4), 424–453.

Cammarota, J., & Fine, M. (Eds.). (2008). *Revolutionizing education: Youth participatory action research in motion*. New York, NY: Routledge.

Cammarota, J., & Romero, A. (2011). Participatory action research for high school students: Transforming policy, practice, and the personal with social justice education. *Educational Policy, 25*(3), 488–506.

Carey-Webb, A. (2001). *Literature and lives: A response-based, cultural studies approach to teaching English*. Urbana, IL: National Council of Teachers of English.

Delpit, L. D., & White-Bradley, P. (2003). Educating or imprisoning the spirit: Lessons from ancient Egypt. *Theory into Practice, 42*(4), 283–288.

Dewey, J. (1916). *Democracy and education: An introduction to the philosophy of education*. New York, NY: Macmillan.

Duncan-Andrade, J. M. R., & Morrell, E. (2008). *The art of critical pedagogy: Possibilities for moving theory to practice in urban schools*. New York, NY: Peter Lang.

Finn, J., & Voelkl, K. (1993). School characteristics related to student engagement. *Journal of Negro Education, 62*, 249–268.

Fisher, D., & Frey, N. (2007). Implementing a schoolwide literacy framework: Improving achievement in an urban elementary school. *The Reading Teacher, 61*, 32–45.

Freire, P. (1970). *Pedagogy of the oppressed*. New York, NY: Continuum.

Freire, P., & Macedo, D. (1987). *Literacy: Reading the word & the world*. South Hadley, MA: Bergin & Garvey.

García, A., Mirra, N., Morrell, E., Martínez, A., & Scorza, D. A. (2015). The council of youth research: Critical literacy and civic agency in the digital age. *Reading & Writing Quarterly, 31*(2), 151–167.

Gutiérrez, K. D. (2008). Developing a sociocritical literacy in the third space. *Reading Research Quarterly, 43*, 148–164.

Hansberry, L. (1959). *A raisin in the sun*. New York, NY: Random House.

Kahne, J., & Middaugh, E. (2008). *Democracy for some: The civic opportunity gap in high school* (Working Paper 59). College Park, MD: The Center for Information and Research on Civic learning and Engagement (CIRCLE).

Kempa, D. (2013, March 14). Hustle and Florin. *Sacramento News & Review*.

Macdonald, C. (2016, June 24). Florin high students call for restored bus service. *Elk Grove Citizen.*

McIntyre, A. (2000). Constructing meaning about violence, school, and community: Participatory action research with youth. *Urban Review, 32*(2), 123–154.

Mintrop, H., & Sunderman, G. L. (2009). Predictable failure of federal sanctions-driven accountability for school improvement—And why we may restrain it anyway. *Educational Researcher, 38*(5), 353–364.

Mirra, N., García, A., & Morrell, E. (2015). *Doing youth participatory action research: Transforming inquiry with researchers, educators, and students.* New York, NY: Routledge.

Mirra, N., Morrell, E., Cain, E., Scorza, D., & Ford, A. (2013). Educating for a critical democracy: Civic participation re-imagined in the council of youth research. *Democracy and Education, 21*(1), Article 3.

Miwok Unified School District. (2017). *School accountability report card.* Retrieved October 8, 2017, from http://www.egusd.net/wp-content/uploads/sarcs/short/FlorinHS.PDF

Morrell, E. (2004). *Becoming critical researchers: Literacy and empowerment for urban youth.* New York, NY: Peter Lang.

Morrell, E. (2006a). Youth-initiated research as a tool for advocacy and change in urban schools. In S. Ginwright, P. Noguera, & J. Cammarota, J. (Eds.), *Beyond resistance! Youth activism and community change: New democratic possibilities for practice and policy for America's youth* (pp. 111–128). New York, NY: Routledge.

Morrell, E. (2006b). Critical participatory action research and the literacy achievement of ethnic minority groups. In *National Reading Conference Yearbook, 55*, 1–18.

Morrell, E. (2007). Critical literacy and popular culture in urban education: Toward a pedagogy of access and dissent. In C. Clark & M. Blackburn (Eds.). *Literacy research for political action and social change* (pp. 235–255). New York, NY: Peter Lang.

Morrell, E. (2008). *Critical literacy and urban youth: Pedagogies of access, dissent, and liberation.* New York, NY: Routledge.

Newmann, F., Wehlage, G., & Lamborn, S. (1992). The significance and sources of student engagement. In F. Newmann (Ed.), *Student engagement and achievement in American secondary schools* (pp. 11–39). New York, NY: Teachers College, Columbia University.

Paris, D., & Alim, S. H. (2017). *Culturally sustaining pedagogies: Teaching and learning for justice in a changing world.* New York, NY: Teachers College.

Pearson, P. D., & Gallagher, M. C. (1983). The instruction of reading comprehension. *Contemporary Educational Psychology, 8*, 317–344.

Ravitch, D. (2010). *The death and life of the great American school system: How testing and choice are undermining education.* New York, NY: Basic.

Rogers, J., Morrell, E., & Enyedy, N. (2007). Studying the struggle: Contexts for learning and identify. *American Behavioral Scientists, 51*(3), 419–443.

Sleeter, C. E., & Grant, G. A. (2009). *Making choices for multicultural education* (6th ed.). New York, NY: Wiley.

Snyder, T.D., & Dillow, S.A. (2015). *Digest of Education Statistics 2013 (NCES 2015–011).* Washington, DC: National Center for Education Statistics, Institute of Education Sciences, U.S. Department of Education.

Steinberg, L. (1996). *Beyond the classroom: Why school reform has failed and what parents need to do.* New York, NY: Touchstone.

Torre, M. E., & Ayala, J. (2009). Envisioning participatory action research. *Entremundos Feminism & Psychology, 19*(3), 387–393.

Torre, M. E., & Fine, M. (2006) Participatory action research (PAR) by youth. In L Sherrod (Ed.), *Youth activism: An international encyclopedia* (pp. 456–462). Westport, CT: Greenwood Publishing Group.

Wright, D. E. (2015). *Active learning: Social justice education and participatory action research.* New York, NY: Routledge.

Valenzuela, A. (1999). *Subtractive schooling: U.S.-Mexican youth and the politics of caring.* Albany, NY: State University of New York Press.

CONCLUSION

We began this book with a story about Zach who was penalized by school authorities for his Spanish-language use. From that single incident, to the wider range of oppressions and opportunities about which we collectively write, we find ourselves amidst a rich mass of complexity and contradiction. In recent days, the country has witnessed an increase in incidents similar to Zach's in 2005, with 867 reported acts of "hateful harassment" ten days after the 2016 presidential election (Southern Poverty Law Center, 2016). We are in a time where social movements can begin with a hashtag; where protectors resist corporate-state violence against sacred indigenous lands, water and people; where the Black Lives Matter movement demands recognition of and actions against systemic anti-black racism; where the Supreme Court ruled in favor of marriage equality; where DACA, deportations, and building walls describe the state of immigration in the U.S.; where mass shootings of LGTBQ-identified Latinxs occur in presumed safe spaces; where a president was elected despite or because of a platform based on a celebration of white-supremacist, Islamophobic, xenophobic, and heteropatriarchal ideologies. It is in this socio-political context that we offer a discussion of PAR EntreMundos as a pedagogy of the Americas, where we envision an education that matters in our daily lives and communities.

The journey of this book has taken us across varied disciplinary terrains. Beginning with theoretical and intellectual legacies, we moved to a set of foundational principles, pivoting to a series of examples in the field, and ending with implementation of this framework in the context of a grow-your-own teacher education initiative. In addition to communicating our theorizing in the introductory section, we include practical materials such as sample readings, assignments, activities, and products from past projects in the PAR examples. In doing so, we attempt to articulate a PAR EntreMundos that operates, though at times with tension, within an education context.

Common Threads and Cross-Stitches

Across the projects, there are similarities and differences of note in terms of the context, type of collaborative, and issues addressed. Cammarota, Cushing-Leubner & Eik, Gonzalez, Irizarry and Rodríguez all describe PAR projects that are classroom based, taking place over the course of a semester or academic year. Several of these projects were the result of ongoing University-High School partnerships, where students received high school credit as part of the existing school curriculum or elective and were taught, at least in part, by university researchers. In Gonzalez's chapter, it is a first year high school teacher who is incorporating PAR in his classroom. In Irizarry's Project FUERTE, one additional aim was to attract high school students of color to the teaching profession. Deeply rooted in Freirean praxis and critical race theories, Gonzalez, Cammarota and Rodríguez's projects started with local issues identified by the classroom community of students, with topics ranging from late-room policies to issues of language discrimination. Ayala & Zaal's project was short term, occurred in an out-of-school context, included partnerships between Universities and youth-serving community-based organizations, involved three cities, and offered high school youth members college credit. The project began with an issue, the changing graduation requirements in high school, and developed a collective around it in order to affect policy change. Similarly, Mayorga's D+CPAR project occurred in an out-of-school context, built a collective around an issue and engaged with local community organizations. Distinctively, Mayorga's youth co-researchers came from a higher education context and their work used the tools of technology and social media. This evolved into a design that the author labeled digital historical ethnography, that facilitated a richer socio-political analysis. Like Ayala & Zaal, Rivera and

Pedraza's PAR collective at El Puente included a partnership with a community based organization, educators (teacher-artists), and university researchers. Rivera and colleague's project had in common with some of the other studies presented here, a place-based focus that was long-term. In contrast to these projects, however, at El Puente, the collective consisted largely of adults—educators, and was more of a layered PAR experience that deeply integrated the arts in its process and expression of action. Baker & Berta-Ávila's paper also focused on adult populations—specifically, their project occurred within the context of a teacher education program with newly-developed PAR infused curricula. PAR was layered in both instances: with the program Baker & Berta-Ávila described, teacher candidates learned about PAR in their classes and in turn engaged their own students in PAR projects as part of their student teaching experience. In El Puente, the collective of educators and researchers developed a creative action approach to PAR which they in turn implemented in their high school classrooms. In the spirit of an EntreMundos approach, where multiplicity and complexity are prominent features, these examples we call layered involved PAR happening across levels of interaction, engaged in one setting in order to spread to several others. This was the case with Irizarry's Project Fuerte as well. Youth's involvement in PAR was related to both individual academic outcomes, and larger goals of improving the teaching profession by creating critically-conscious, community-based, home-grown educators starting in high school.

Whereas school-based PAR projects involving youth typically focus on outcomes related to the youth themselves, in particular, with regard to their individual development, Baker & Berta-Ávila, like Rivera, found that personal transformation occurred with the adults (student-teachers/teaching artists) who engaged in this approach as well. For example, in Baker & Berta-Ávila's work, it became clear from the close exchange of ideas, questions, and responses with the student-teachers that PAR would not only foster a pedagogical/paradigm shift but also a personal transformation. PAR facilitated a liberating experience in which the challenges facing student-teachers of color were confronted and alleviated. Thus, the PAR journey became a political awakening for the adults. Student teachers felt affirmed to be in the NLERAP cohort supporting a liberatory pedagogy like PAR, but also knew that they were not alone. The feeling of reassurance (we have their back) and learning how to navigate inequitable school structures became part of the transformational process and fostered an environment of trust.

Across these chapters, the areas of inquiry explored had deep personal resonance to the collectives studying them and addressed issues of social justice from a critical perspective. For example, Cushing-Leubner & Eik and Cammarotta's chapters both discussed language discrimination, with the former framing the issue within a language rights framework. Education policies and the racialized neoliberal ideologies (see Mayorga this volume) that are shaping them, underlie many of the issues identified by the PAR collectives as in need of changing, from the inequalities built into high stakes testing to push-out practices in school. However, there were not only discussions of the multiple and interlocking forms of oppression youth and adults confront every day, but also woven into these projects were stories of agency and hope through connection, re-membering, and creative praxes.

Tensions and Choques in the Work

Gloria Anzaldúa (1987) eloquently describes the choques, clashes or conflicts that are experienced within the multiplicities we carry. In a PAR EntreMundos approach, we take seriously these tensions and use them as a space from which to theorize, ask questions, create knowledge and act, even through the pain and struggle. Here we consider some of the choques we encountered across these projects, and offer them as shared moments of vulnerability and complexity within concientizacion, alongside its power and hopeful praxis. One choque involves the issue of power, as a participatory stance interrupts hierarchies and empowers groups who are marginalized. However, equalizing power necessitates challenging existing structures, which can be seen as a threat in need of countermeasure, as we have seen in Arizona and may see escalate across the country.

Ultimately, PAR EntreMundos develops students' critical consciousness and agency with bringing about change, in these cases, within the education system. However, state policymakers sometimes feel threatened when key stakeholders, such as students, in the education system become critical of its education policies. For instance, Arizona youth from the SJEP (see this volume) were consistently pushing for the expansion of PAR and cultural relevance in the curriculum. The Arizona Department of Education was opposed to having curriculum engage youth in a critical perspective and activism for social justice. Arizona state lawmakers decided to put an end to the SJEP and the ethnic studies department in which the program was housed. In 2010, they passed HB 2281, which banned the SJEP and the ethnic studies program in Tucson Unified School District. Our belief is that the Arizona policymakers and lawmakers were operating with a very narrow and traditional perspective of youth development in which young people are supposed to be spoken to and not speak up for rights and justice. PAR EntreMundos works against or is in tension with this traditional perspective of youth development by encouraging young people to have voice, particularly with matters that affect them personally as with schooling. It is unfortunate that policymakers sometimes fail to see the value in PAR EntreMundos despite the positive youth outcomes of higher levels of community and school engagement.

A related choque involves the question of legitimacy and expertise. A tenet of PAR is that knowledge is co-constructed, often between those who are viewed in the larger society as experts (based on university credentials for example) and those who are most impacted by the issue under study. However, the inclusivity of this stance, where multiple dimensions of expertise are recognized, is often the basis of challenging its legitimacy and rigor. One of the tensions we have observed with PAR is the extent to which it has infiltrated the K–12 and higher education context. All of us in this volume, and many of our associates engaged in PAR across the U.S., have closely followed PAR over the last couple of decades. While we have all individually engaged in this work in our respective higher education institutions, schools, and communities, we wonder about the ways in which PAR may actually "hit a wall" within the context of the academy. For instance, many of us have individually and collectively delivered presentations nationally (and internationally) on our PAR work. There are always motivated and politically conscious graduate students who approach us stating, "I would love to do a PAR dissertation but my institution or committee won't allow it". This tension within the academy speaks to epistemological issues (and other power/political issues) that have a stronghold on "legitimate" research, not to mention the role that foundations may play in determining whether this work is funded, the extent to which it flourishes, or is accepted as a sound research approach within the university context. On the other hand, and in support of funders and foundations, are those examples who are supporting visionary PAR work, albeit outside of the university context. We have observed that PAR work is thriving within the non-profit/community-based context. We suggest that we look to some solid models where PAR projects have thrived and continue to advocate for this work within the university context.

A third choque occurs in employing a liberatory, EntreMundos PAR framework within an education reform context couched in neoliberalism. In many ways, PAR EntreMundos runs counter to the assumptions underlying some of the existing measures of accountability. Standardization presumes a set way knowing, assessed using static measures with a single response deemed legitimate. A PAR EntreMundos works from a position of fluidity, multiplicity, and messiness. Given this, how can the competing framework of schools and the principles of PAR live in the same space? How do such outcomes as conscientizacion, inquiry and organizing towards social justice, fit with school demands for increased academic achievement as measured by standardized assessments? We take seriously the R in PAR—the research and collective inquiry form the basis of deep critique and concientization. In the projects described in this book, youth and adults read literature, collected data through interviews, surveys, personal narratives, and artistic forms, analyzed data together, conducted presentations in front of groups of youth and adults, and developed plans of action to be implemented in real world contexts. We see that in developing concientization and organizing with community, there is a foundation of skills that are acquired along the way. In taking local actions towards community improvement, accompanied by the appropriate supports, skills in critical thinking and engagement are addressed. These are questions that social-justice oriented teacher education programs also contend with, as they prepare their candidates with the tools they need to navigate these choques.

Research has noted the limiting impact a social justice orientation has on student teachers in credential programs; the solution cannot be the elimination of such efforts but rather a strategic shift in the approach. An observable aspect that can influence a long-term social justice commitment in the field is the intentional choice of our prospective teacher candidates. As teacher candidates of color, their lived experiences and political awareness of being "other" based on race, language, class, gender, etc., can resonate with their students (Bower-Phipps, Homa, Albaladejo, Johnson, & Cruz, 2013; Freire, 1970). Thus, the questions credential programs ought to pose are the following: How do we develop opportunities to (1) challenge student teacher paradigms and pedagogical frames that become sustainable? And (2) encourage students of color to enter the field? What we have found to be successful is the development of an intentional recruitment pipeline coupled with the instruction of sustainable social justice pedagogy via PAR EntreMundos.

An intentional recruitment pipeline coupled with the instruction of sustainable social justice pedagogy via PAR EntreMundos is critical because nationwide there are programs that desire to prepare future teachers with the knowledge and skills to develop rigorous relevant curriculum with a social justice paradigm. However, to foster and prepare future teachers to view themselves as social justice educators is not an easy task. The harsh reality is that the field of education still confronts quite a variance in who enters the profession—not only ethnically but also in the context of their own social political consciousness. For example, the teaching profession has made little change over the past 50 years (Faltis, 2013) specifically in two areas: (1) the teaching force still does not reflect the student population found in classrooms today. Over 70% of the traditional teaching force is still White middle-class females, and (2) student teachers ultimately do not view teaching as a political act (Freire, 1970). Thus, student teachers do not find the need (often due to White/class privilege) to reflect on their own positionality/conscientization (Freire, 1970) and the impact it can have in perpetuating inequities. As a result, credential programs espousing a social justice paradigm in the hopes of changing student's beliefs about diversity and social justice are short lived (Cooper, 2013). The long term change hoped for is minimal because it is difficult for novice teachers to sustain a Multicultural/Social justice paradigm and pedagogy when they truly lack the skill level to see and do not have to see the overlay/integration of content/pedagogy within a social justice framework.

Futuros in PAR EntreMundos

We see PAR having a greater presence in Education, Psychology, and Community Health literatures. At academic conferences in the U.S., we recall struggling to find panels that featured any PAR projects, or digging deep to search for articles that named PAR as an important feature in the work. Some curricula and texts that focus on the "how-to" of using PAR as a method are being published. Texts that critique this approach, in particular, the ways in which it can be co-opted, are also available. While we take heart in this, we too often see PAR in Education framed as a youth development strategy, where it originally was an approach centering around youth as producers of creative inquiry and organizing work with communities. PAR is now a phenomenon of its own in U.S. education literature. So where do we go from here? What does an EntreMundos approach to PAR contribute? In looking to the future of a PAR EntreMundos, we express our hopes and intentions with a set of statements listed below.

We Believe PAR Extends the Conversation on Educational Outcomes

In thinking about the future of PAR, it is important to remain critical of the "outcomes" of this work. Within the conventional paradigm of academic "achievement", existing approaches will have us focus largely on test scores, especially after spending nearly 15 years in the No Child Left Behind era. Yet, even within this context, PAR work was able to thrive, both in response to the conditions created by a Test Prep Pedagogy environment (Rodríguez, 2011) and as a cultural and historical necessity within the U.S. schooling context. In other words, PAR has and will likely always be necessary as long as education reform and policy approaches are inequitable and subtract and punish students, schools, and communities for their so-called underperformance. We believe that PAR not only serves as a methodological and pedagogical approach (Rodríguez & Brown, 2009) to engage communities, but it serves as a tool to transform communities and push the envelope in challenging us to consider other so-called achievement indicators. For instance, high school students' participation in PAR work not only offers a space to learn about the research process, but provides opportunities to present their research, engage peers and communities in critical dialogues, envision and create practical and policy solutions with local (and national) implications and become public intellectuals. These are outcome-based opportunities and experiences that may not otherwise exist within the conventional classroom/school context. Moreover, "outcomes" of PAR need not be solely situated within the bodies of youth, but can extend to those of adults and communities.

We Believe PAR Is Creating Tomorrow's Latinx Leaders

The knowledge, experiences, and skills that tomorrow's Latinx leaders need will likely come from opportunities that are facilitated by PAR-related experiences. Tomorrow's leaders need a critical consciousness that allows them to "read the word and the world" as stated by Paulo Freire. Tomorrow's Latinx leaders will need to be able to engage in cross-cultural, cross-generational, and cross-community efforts. This work necessitates individuals who are not just outcome-oriented but process-oriented as well. Tomorrow's Latinx leaders also need to be bridge-builders, relationship-sustainers, and community actors. They will need to work with people, not over them, be conscious of power dynamics driven by race, gender, immigration status, class, language, nationality, sexuality, and be politically savvy for collective action and results. Tomorrow's leaders will need to be able to create when opportunities are absent, build when opportunities arise, and collectively thrive for the purposes of equity, love, and justice for and with our communities across Las Américas. PAR EntreMundos is one attempt to help us get there.

We Believe that PAR EntreMundos Ideally Consists of Multigenerational Collectives Engaged With Intergenerational Learning and Organizing Work

We use the terms multigenerational and intergenerational in ways consistent with Sánchez and Kaplan (2014), who make the following distinction:

> ...the term multigenerational is primarily being used to refer to the simultaneous presence of more than one generation whereby intergenerational alludes to what actually takes place between the generations—for instance, interaction/separation, cooperation/competition, or convivial learning/independent learning.... (p. 475)

PAR collectives in education can be youth-centered in terms of context or issue, but often have some degree of age multiplicity, with typically, at least one adult. Just as there can be differences within groups based on class, gender, sexuality, race/ethnicity, and immigration status, generation is a dimension of difference and commonality at work. We suggest that this is a dimension to attend to more explicitly within collectives, as young people, adults, and elders each bring a set of knowledges that are situated within generational or temporal contexts. As contact zone theory suggests (Pratt, 1991; Torre, 2005), having people of different ages in the same room is not sufficient, but intergenerational exchanges and negotiations within the collective are critical to the process. In advocating for multigenerational classrooms in higher education, for example, Sánchez and Kaplan (2014) find that intergenerational learning, through moments of cooperation, conflict, or ambivalence, can foster social and personal change. Similarly, as multigenerational PAR collectives are spaces of learning and change work, it is an important part of the process to reflect on the relationships between members, on their roles and power within the group, and on their generational positionality and nature of intergenerational exchange.

We Believe That PAR Helps Our Communities Thrive, Flourish, and Build

Because PAR directly engages with many of the challenges facing local schools, communities, and other education "spaces", we believe it is important to use PAR as a tool to transform our communities. The historical, cultural, and educational inequalities that continue to impact our communities need to be met with deliberate action, and we believe PAR is one such strategy to help our communities engage and thrive.

This is particularly the case in our current national climate, where on the ground and in policy contexts we see discussions of mass deportations, Muslim registry, repealing of DACA, further divestment of public education, and a normalizing of white supremacy. In the days after the election, we have witnessed in our classrooms and communities students and colleagues expressing deep anxiety, sadness and fear. This was followed by actions of protest, in the form of walkouts, marches, letters and petitions against hate and exclusion, transforming the worries and outrage into a reaffirmation of active stances to protect our rights, dignity, and humanity. PAR EntreMundos can help bring us together crtically and deepen our responses in challenging oppressive policies and discourses. It provides a concrete and intentional approach that names, identifies, critically analyzes and creates a transformational resistance (Solórzano & Delgado-Bernal, 2001) to counter the normalizing of white supremacy. Enacting the PAR EntreMundos principle of *concientization de la colectiva*, is evermore urgent, as we strategize and organize together in a broader collective of classrooms, with communities, to impact local, social, and policy change. Forging these colectivas will help buffer against the increased scrutiny and push back on the types of liberating inquiry, critique and action we have and continue to work towards.

PAR engages community stakeholders, creates practical and policy solutions for and with our communities, and allows us to envision new approaches to education in our communities. We focus on the lived experiences of Latinxs in discussing PAR EntreMundo's potential, but these strategies, informed by histories in conversation with current realities, can be used across communities to collectively engage the challenges and opportunities faced in our times. Perhaps we can imagine this as a praxis of hope (Haran, 2010; McInerney, 2007) with elements addressing the realities of current and historical material inequities, past and present traditions and knowledges from the ground up, and a view to a future of transformative education as a collective making.

These beliefs are offered not as mere intellectual exercise, but rather, as embodied praxis, where philosophies and practices are mapped onto bodies, relationships, systems and local and global communities. We have tried to live our beliefs. We have struggled and transformed personally and collectively, and continue to do so. We have used our whole hearts and minds to tell stories, heal wounds, access our lineages, imagine new realities, create possibilities and offer our togetherness as sacred medicine. We invite you to explore these embodied beliefs as a potential pathway to connection, creativity and change in learning and leadership.

We Believe That PAR Must Be Deeply Self-Reflective

Although PAR has the potential to transform and empower communities, non-reflective approaches can have the opposite effect. We have witnessed self-described PAR presentations, particularly work claiming to be YPAR, that reinforces generational, racial and gender hierarchies by highlighting certain voices or representing youth inauthentically without their physical presence. To avoid reproducing inequities, PAR EntreMundos should start at the point of self-reflection and address internal power dynamics within the collective. Social change will not happen unless we challenge our own conscious and dysconscious (King, 1991) tendencies to dominate or silence partners within our own communities. The ways in which PAR has been co-opted to reproduce hegemonic practices, relegating its central tenet of participation to a buzzword, empty of its radical origins, have been rightly critiqued (Alejandro Leal, 2010). This is a phenomenon we need to pay particular attention to as we engage in our own PAR work with youth and communities.

Parting Thoughts

To describe a PAR EntreMundos as a pedagogy of las Americas, we draw from the past, present and future, across the intimate geographies of our *bodymindspirits*, and the multiplicity and complexity of our knowledge and experiences.

From the stories of our ancestors, the scholarship in our fields, the inquiry we collaboratively engage, the lived experiences we claim, the material, social and political structures that border our lives, and shared acts of hope for the future. In a PAR EntreMundos, we can hold all these in both harmony and contradiction, within a mestizaje, within a "complex personhood" (Guishard, 2009; Tuck, 2009). As reflected in our principles, we frame this work collectively as movement-making, as well as transformative personally and academically, which Ayala captures below in her poem.

Past present future
Future present past
We press our palms through undulations of time
Fingers touching the skin of collective memories
Lips speaking our reclaimed ancestries.
A Past future present,
present future past that
we see, we feel, we taste,
we live, we shape, we make.
Through the salt shapes of tears
the red dawns of hope
the scent of fears,
we swim in liquid dreams of possibility
across and EntreMundos,
amidst the ripples of becoming.
With fistfuls we act, change, create
holding the swirling silhouette of
pastpresentfuture.

References

Alejandro Leal, P. (2010). Participation: The ascendency of a buzzword in a neo-liberal era. In Andrea Cornwall & Deborah Eade (Eds.), *Deconstructing development discourse: Buzzwords and fuzzwords*. GB: Practical Action Publishing/Oxfam. Retrieved from http://www.guystanding.com/files/documents/Deconstructing-development-buzzwords.pdf

Anzaldúa, G. (1987). *Borderlands/La frontera: The new Mestiza*. San Francisco, CA: Aunt Lute Books.

Bower-Phipps, L., Homa, T. D., Albaladejo, C., Mello Johnson, A., & Cruz, M. C. (2013). Connecting with the "Other" side of us: A cooperative inquiry by self-identified minorities in a teacher preparation program. *Teacher Education Quarterly, 40*(2), 29–51.

Cooper, P. M. (2013) Preparing multicultural educators in an age of teacher evaluation systems: Necessary stories from field supervision. *Teacher Education Quarterly, 40*(2), 7–28.

Faltis, C. J. (2013). Engaging "the other" in teacher education. *Teacher Education Quarterly*, 40(2), 3–7.

Freire, P. (1970). *Pedagogy of the oppressed*. New York: Seabury Press.

Guishard, M. (2009). The false paths, the endless labors, the turns now this way and now that: Participatory action research, mutual vulnerability, and the politics of inquiry. *Urban Review*, 41(1), 85–105.

Haran, J. (2010). Redefining hope as praxis. *Journal for Cultural Research: Special Issue: Hope and Feminist Theory*, 14(4), 393–408.

King, J. (1991). Dysconscious racism: Ideology, identity, and the miseducation of teachers. *The Journal of Negro Education*, 60(2), 133–146.

McInerney, P. (2007). From naïve optimism to robust hope: Sustaining a commitment to social justice in schools and teacher education in neoliberal times. *Asia-Pacific Journal of Teacher Education*, 35(3), 257–272.

Pratt, M. L. (1991). *Arts of the contact zone Profession 1991* (pp. 33–40). New York, NY: Modern Language Association.

Rodríguez, L. F. (2011). Over-coming test prep pedagogy: Getting urban high school students to educate pre-service teachers using liberatory pedagogy. In B. Schultz (Ed.), *Listening to and learning from students: Possibilities for teaching, learning, and curriculum*. Charlotte, NC: Information Age Publishing.

Rodríguez, L. F., & Brown, T. M. (2009). Engaging youth in participatory action research for education and social transformation. *New Directions for Youth Development, 123*, 19–34.

Sánchez, M., & Kaplan, M. (2014). Intergenerational learning in higher education: Making the case for multigenerational classrooms. *Educational Gerontology*, 40(7), 473–485. doi:10.1080/03601277.2013.844039

Solórzano, D. G., & Bernal, D. D. (2001). Examining transformational resistance through a critical race and LatCrit theory framework Chicana and Chicano students in an urban context. *Urban Education*, 36(3), 308–342.

Southern Poverty Law Center. (November 29, 2016). Ten days after: Harassment and intimidation in the aftermath of the election. Retrieved from https://www.splcenter.org/20161129/ten-days-after-harassment-and-intimidation-aftermath-election

Torre, M. (2005). The alchemy of integrated spaces: Youth participation in research collectives of difference. In L. Weis & M. Fine (Eds.), *Beyond silenced voices*. Albany, NY: State University of New York Press.

Tuck, E. (2009). Re-visioning action: Participatory action research and Indigenous theories of change. *Urban Review*, 41(1), 47–65.

APPENDICES

Appendix A: Chapter 2

Table A.1: Selected Student-Driven Research Projects—The PRAXIS Project

Topic	Research question(s)	Methods	Findings	Implications
School environment	How does the school's image affect students?	–Surveys (N=100)	• Students ranked restroom sanitation as most important environmental factor • Restrooms and paint scheme require the most improvement	• Creating and sustaining a tidy school environment requires commitment • Lack of pride in school environment leads to lack of pride in City
Tardy policy	Does the tardy policy work?	–Surveys	• 70% of students believe tardy policy doesn't work • Most students are late to period 1 • Transportation is the #1 reason they are late • 53% of students believe the policy decreases attendance • 47% of students believe people who are sent to in-house detention usually don't go at all	• Mark students tardy instead of following the tardy policy procedure • Create longer passing periods • When late, allow students to go to another teacher's classroom instead of in-house detention because they will miss less class
Quality of education	What is the overall quality of education teachers are giving their students?	–Surveys (N=116)	• Most students rated English teachers above Math and History in listening, interactive activities, and approachability • History teachers most helpful/math teachers ranked lowest	• Math classes need to be provide a more comfortable learning environment in order to succeed (like English & history classes)

Dropouts	Why do students drop out?	–Surveys (N=100) –Interviews with 3 administrators	• The most popular belief is that students drop out because of laziness • No students remained in school because of motivating teachers • Future goals is the main reason students stayed in school	• More communication to students about issues • More opportunities to participate in school activities • More teacher motivation in the classroom • Student-led support group
Teacher pedagogy	Does the way someone teaches affect the education of the students?	–Surveys (N=100)	• Only 13% of teachers spend more than 15 minutes a week outside of class to help students • 80%+ students said they receive some, little or no individual attention from teachers	• Counselors should frequently check students grades to help them stay on track • Teachers should realize that they make a difference in students' lives • Student council to communicate school issues to administration • Students' voices needs to be heard
Teacher effectiveness	How do teachers instruct and how does it affect students?	–Surveys (N=132)	• 78% of students rated their teachers as good • Top three qualities for a teacher: energy, patience, and knowledge of the material • 75% of students said their teachers spend 10 minutes teaching • Only 40% of students believe their teachers care about them • Biggest motivation for students is their parents • 54% of students said their teachers follow the standards as it establishes order • Students believe AP teachers are more motivating	• Teachers need to go beyond the "call of duty"

Source: Rodríguez, L. F. (2014). *The time is now: Understanding and responding to the Black and Latino dropout crisis.* New York, NY: Peter Lang Publishing.

Appendix B: Supporting Materials for NJUYRI

Note: Materials were developed
with input from members of the NJUYRI

Excerpts from the course syllabus, some of the data collection forms, facilitator guides and analysis forms are included here.

Appendix B.1: NJUYRI Course Syllabus Excerpts

Excerpts from Syllabus outline

Course title: Current Social Problems

Requirements:
Students will be required to attend Saturday research camps at Saint Peter's College, local meetings at their high school or community organization, writings online and in research journals, and a portfolio of products including the work of the research. The work of the project including collective decision making on the research methods, possible interviews, focus groups, field notes, quantitative and qualitative data analysis, photography, creation and presentation of products. This work will be organized into a portfolio.

30% Attendance
15% Youth research camps at Saint Peter's College.
15% Local meetings
20% BlackBoard Posts
20% Research Journals
This is a collection of reflections during and after the research camps.
20% Binders/Portfolios

The portfolios are made up of your research journals, field notes, and all the work you complete as part of the research. Include all the individual and group products, presentations (outline, powerpoint, photographs), data collected, reports, etc.

10% Reflection Paper

Write a 5–7 page paper that reflects on the project as a whole, the process, skills developed, skills contributed, struggles, accomplishments, hopes and disappointments. This should be the final piece of your portfolio.

Overview

Date	*Day*	*Activity*	*Topic*
January		Local meeting 1	Overview and introductory activities
		Local meeting 2	Prepare presentations
	31	Youth research camp At Saint Peter's College 1	Study the issue, analyze data, finalize research questions
February		Local meetings	Preliminary Data collection: taking field-notes **BlackBoard post due**
March		Local meetings	Support for and feedback on data collection **BlackBoard post due**
	28	Youth research camp At Saint Peter's College 2	Methods training: interviews, focus groups, etc.
April		Local meetings	Data collection: interviews, etc. **BlackBoard post due**
May		Local meetings	Support for and feedback on data collection **BlackBoard post due**
June	6–7	Overnight youth research camp	Data analysis; findings; creating products
		Local meetings	Continue work on findings, products **BlackBoard post due**
August	22	Final youth research camp	Finalize products, rehearse actions/presentations **Portfolio and final reflection due**

Source: Jennifer Ayala and Mayida Zaal

Appendix B.2: NJUYRI Sample Agenda for Research Camp

9:00–9:30	Continental Breakfast
9:30–10:00	Opening activity
10:00–10:15	Policy Updates: Stan Karp, Education Law Center
10:15–11:15	Overview of the weekend and video *Echoes of Brown*
11:15–12:45	Data analysis: Quantitative
	Closed-ended survey questions
	Computer Lab, Loyola Hall.
	Individual and pair work
12:45–1:30	Pizza lunch
1:30–2:30	Data analysis: Qualitative
	Interviews and open-ended survey questions
	Small group work
2:30–4:30	Creating products based on findings
	Small group work
4:30–5:30	Salsa lesson
5:30–7:30	Cookout @ the Social Justice House
7:30–8:30	Break
8:30–10:00	Pool Party

Appendix B.3: NJUYRI Sample Assignment #1 (Source: Mayida Zaal)

Name _____   Date_____

Reviewing and Analyzing Data

In preparation for the first Research Camp held on January 31, 2009 at Saint Pe-ter's College, please review the charts and information provided to you from the New Jersey School Report Cards and respond to the questions listed below. You may contact Mayida Zaal mzaal@gc.cuny.edu or Dr. Jennifer Ayala at jayala@spc.edu if you have any questions before Saturday.

Review the NJ School Report Card for _____
    (Name of school)

    1. What does the data tell you?
    2. What stands out?

3. What does the data say about:
    a. About the school's performance on the Math HSPA?
    b. About the school's performance on the Science HSPA?
    c. How do the school's results compare to the district's results? To the state's results?
4. Based on the chart, what percentage of students in the school graduated "via the SRA process"?
    a. How does that percentage compare to the percent of "all who graduated by passing HSPA"?
5. Notice the chart that reports drop out rates. According to this chart, what is the percentage of students "who dropped out during the school year"? Who does this percentage leave out?
6. Now examine the chart that reports enrollment by grade. Notice the number of students enrolled in 9th grade during the 2003–2004 academic year. Now notice the number of students enrolled in 12 grade four years later in 2006–2007. What is the difference? How can you explain the difference?

Appendix B.4: NJUYRI Sample Assignment #2 (Source: Mayida Zaal)

Conducting Interviews

Directions: *Interview at least 1–2 peers, teachers, parents, graduates or administrators using the questions we developed as a group. You can find these on BlackBoard.*

Note: To get fuller responses from interviewees, remember to use probes like, "Can you give me an example?" or "Could you tell me what you mean by…?" Feel free to add questions that may come to you while you are doing the interview.
    Before you begin each interview, be sure you have a copy of:

1. the consent form for the interviewee to sign
2. the digital recorder to record the interview
3. the interview protocol
4. the interview reflection
5. copy of the survey (to be completed at the end of the interview if time allows)

Teacher Interview Protocol

1. In what school district do you teach?
2. What grade(s) and subject(s) do you teach?

Knowledge/opinions about the proposed changes

3. What have you heard about the High School Redesign proposal/plan by the Department of Education? [Show them or read them description]
4. How do you feel about the ability of all students to succeed with new graduation requirements?
5. In your opinion, do you have the tools and resources to implement these new requirements? Can you give me examples of what you have or what you would need?

Impact on teaching

6. How would the end-of-course (EOC) exams affect your teaching practices?
   a. What do you think would happen if this plan failed?
7. How would you help students who are not succeeding to improve?
8. How can instruction change to reach all students?
9. What is the role of technology in your teaching practice?

Alternatives

10. If you were in charge of the redesign plan, how would you go about preparing students for their future?
11. As alternatives to end-of-course exams, how can students demonstrate understanding of subjects taught?

Interview protocol for State Department of Education Officials [developed by the NJUYRI]

1. Some of us recently took the HSPA, and based on our observations many students found the exam difficult and felt nervous taking it; our concern is that we would have to do this every year for a number of tests. In your opinion what do you think about the change from HSPA to the end of the year exams?

a. How effective do you believe this system will be, considering the already low passing figures for the HSPA?
2. Many of us work very hard to prepare for the HSPA attending early morning tutoring sessions or staying after school. What is the state's plan to prepare students for the end of the year course exams?
   a. What other programs will be developed for students to help assist them in meeting these new graduation requirements?
3. How do you think schools have to change to be ready for the changes that will be part of the high school redesign plan, so no child would be left behind?
4. Why do you think there's an achievement gap between urban and suburban schools?
   a. How will the high school redesign plan increase or decrease the gap?
5. What will happen to the students who don't pass?
6. What was considered in developing these graduation requirements?
   a. Was student input taken into account?
7. As alternatives to end-of-course exams, how can students demonstrate understanding of subjects taught?

Appendix C: PAR EntreMundos: A Practitioners Guide

Reprinted with permission from Valenzuela, A. (Ed.), *Growing critically conscious teachers: A social justice curriculum for educators of Latino/a youth*. New York, NY: Teachers College Press.

PAR *EntreMundos*: A Practitioner Guide was created by the NLERAP PAR committee as a companion piece applying more directly the theoretical work presented in the book A Pedagogy of the Américas. The Guide operates from the PAR EntreMundos principles to channel the work through a critical consciousness lens while establishing democratic, equitable relationships among participants. These principles are explained through theoretical lineages that delineate PAR's ontology and epistemology. Based on the latter foundation, A *Practitioners Guide* provides a developmental progression of key questions and activities to prepare those interested in applying a PAR approach to action-based inquiries. The Guide is divided into four subsections, as follows:

1. Overview of PAR: This explains what Participatory Action Research entails and describes some of its theoretical lineages.
2. Guiding Principles: This subsection identifies eight general principles that guide the collective inquiry in which PAR is grounded.
3. Guiding Questions and Practices: This subsection provides questions, examples, and activities tied to the PAR guiding principles. These practices and questions can be used to inform and shape curriculum and pedagogy.
4. Research Process: This subsection lists potential methods for data collection, analysis, and dissemination, along with an example of one research process.

Overview of Participatory Action Research (PAR)

Research in communities has traditionally provided a way for "outsiders" to study the particulars of a community in the name of objective science. In this tradition, a researcher picks a topic, comes into a space, studies it, leaves, and then draws conclusions, with little input from those who were being studied and little interest in making a contribution to the community itself.

Participatory Action Research (PAR) turns this view upside down by making the researchers and those being researched partners in the inquiry process. This means that the group as a whole—the researchers and the researched—make decisions collectively. For example, decisions are collectively made on what to study and how to study it, as well as what kind of knowledge will be the goal of the study and what kind of action(s) will be taken in response to the knowledge gained. The research collective is usually made up of people who are interested in a particular equity- or justice-related issue and/or who are in some way deeply affected by the issue to be studied. The thinking behind this approach is that those who are most affected by inequities or injustices have important insights and knowledge about how to apply remedies. Therefore, this group should play an important part in the research process and outcome(s). In research that focuses on schooling and educational contexts, the "most affected" groups often include students, which is why Participatory Action Research includes a subfield called YPAR (where Y stands for "Youth").

PAR is not new. We can trace its ancestries across many years and multiple disciplines. NLERAP's approach to PAR, building on what Torre and Ayala (2009) have termed PAR *EntreMundos*, is steeped in Freirian praxis, critical race and borderland theories, creative processes and wisdom traditions,

South American liberation psychologies, and social movement histories. The four theoretical and conceptual lineages are described as follows:

Southern Tradition. Our PAR work is rooted in what some have termed the Southern (Hemisphere) tradition of PAR, which incorporates Freire's (1970) notion of praxis. Praxis is the process by which *critical reflection* and *creative, conscious action* are combined to formulate an approach to gaining knowledge that is then utilized for initiating change. Praxis involves critically examining a situation and then taking action to bring about changes that lead to equitable social and economic outcomes. The experience of initiating change produces knowledge that in turn improves critical thinking about the situation and creates possibilities for facilitating change (Fals-Borda & Rahman, 1991).

Critical Race Theory. PAR *EntreMundos* is vigorously committed to engaging in practical and policy changes that are driven by a systems-of-domination analysis, including race and racism, sexism, classism, heterosexism, and others (plus their intersectionalities). PAR *EntreMundos* challenges dominant ideologies as it aims to provide a counter-narrative to historical and contemporary struggles facing Latinos/as and other marginalized groups in the U.S. (Delgado & Stefancic, 1999; Solórzano & Yosso, 2002), privileging the voices, experiences, and knowledge bases of our communities and focusing efforts on social justice in our classrooms, schools, and communities (Berta-Ávila, Tijerina-Revilla, & Figueroa, 2011; Cammarota & Fine, 2008; Irizarry, 2011; Rivera, Medellin-Paz, & Pedraza, 2010).

Feminist Theorizing. Our feminist lineages underscore the ideas related to standpoint, intersectionalities, and embodiment. The positions we hold within our social, cultural, and political contexts situate the knowledge we create, influence the angles we see, and impact the connections we make. Therefore, it is important to acknowledge who we are in relation to the work we do (Collins, 1991; hooks, 1984; Hurtado, 1996). A feminist perspective also encourages us to *theorize from the flesh*, as Moraga and Anzaldúa (1981) viscerally write, to build understandings, theories, and knowledge from the pain, exploitation, resistance, and joy we have lived through body and spirit (Lara, 2002). It reminds us that there are multiple, interacting perspectives that inform our truths, a living dialectic.

Indigenous Cosmologies. PAR EntreMundos also seeks to reclaim and re-shape (for the modern era) wisdom from ancient traditions. The aim is to awaken spiritual activism by integrating body/mind/spirit (Lara, 2002), us-ing healing arts and the medicine of song, dance, story, and silence (Arrien, 1993), and asking timeless questions, such as Who am I/we? What is life? What do I/we seek from life? What is our relationship to the natural world? (Paiva, 1992). PAR *EntreMundos* also seeks to reclaim and reshape (for the modern era) *wisdom from ancient traditions.*

PAR Guiding Principles

In the context of schooling, part of the goal of the PAR *EntreMundos* ap-proach is to co-create transformative spaces of education through collec-tives of research and social action. These collectives include youth, edu-cators, and community members as partners in inquiry and action-based processes focused on addressing educational disparities. We expect this ap-proach to produce more meaningful research and community activism as a whole. In addition, the power of the process itself can have a deep impact on the individuals undertaking it. Those who participate in PAR are of-ten transformed when they recognize their potential to produce knowledge that can foster change. Thus, PAR is ultimately a systematic and collective approach to inquiry (using PAR Guiding Principles) that leads to the pro-duction of knowledge applied for the purpose of facilitating greater equity and justice. Highlighted below are some general principles which, building on the work of NLERAP's PAR committee, guide our view of PAR as *En-treMundos.*

Participation. Practitioners and stakeholders should be involved in all steps of research (design, data collection, analysis, dissemination), as full participants in the process (versus as subjects).

Critical Inquiry. The work needs to be grounded in critical-race and decolo-nizing theories, which examine the sociohistorical, sociopolitical, and materi-al contexts and conditions of our lives.

Knowledge Co-construction. Knowledge that informs action is produced in collaboration with communities, where researchers and researched become a collective of knowledge-producers/actors.

Power With(in). The collective critically reflects its own process, fosters trusting relationships of mutuality between members, examines power within the group, and engages in deep self-inquiry.

Indigenous Cosmologies. In the spirit of an approach to PAR that is *EntreMundos* and that grows from the Southern Tradition, we see it as a way to reclaim and reimagine indigenous ways of knowing and engaging in this work as a healing process for the individual and community.

Creative Praxes. The methods for collecting and presenting data are embedded in the cultural and creative productions of the local community. These may include poetry, music, dance, theatre, and other forms of cultural and artistic expression.

Transformational Action. Participants are committed to conscious action and social change using creative praxes and an engaged approach to policy that Lopez and Valenzuela simply term, "engaged policy" (Lopez, 2012; Valenzuela & Lopez, 2015).

Concientización para la colectiva. This work is part of a movement, not simply separate sets of isolated actions, whose goals include critical consciousness, social justice, and mutual liberation/emancipation from oppression.

Guiding Questions and Practices

We offer the PAR principles as a developmental guide for consideration, rather than as a formula that presupposes a "standard" way of conducting PAR. However, we have come to understand that the principles do not stand alone. They are also built upon with guiding questions and various learning experiences that enrich the engagement that students, practitioners, and community members have with PAR. What follows are questions, examples, and activities tied to the PAR principles that inform and shape curriculum, pedagogy, and the research interests of those involved.

Principle: Participation

QUESTIONS

- Who is most impacted by the issue proposed for investigation? Why and how?
  o Who should be at the table?
  o What ways can the collective build community as the group initially comes together?
  o What process is the group using to make decisions?

There are two possible starting points for entering a participatory process:

a) where the issue is already established and a community needs to be created;
b) where the community is already established and defined and the issue has to be collectively determined.

EXAMPLE A: Graduation Standards

In *a Pedagogy of the Américas*, one of the PAR examples describes a project focused on a state proposal to change graduation standards by adding a set of new requirements, including adding several standardized end-of-course exams. Although students (and teachers) are the ones likely to bear most of the impact of this kind of change, typically, they are not consulted about policy decisions. In this case, students were invited to participate in research on graduation standards, and also to engage in action that responded to the proposed change in standards.

ACTIVITY A: Peer Invitations

Participation is an essential element for creating sustainable transformative action. If, as in the example above, young people are critical stakeholders, one way of encouraging engagement is to ask one or two students to gather a group of their peers to join with educators and community members in circles of conversation about the issue(s) of concern to them.

EXAMPLE B: Social Justice Education Project (SJEP)

Students who enroll in the Social Justice Education Project form a community of participants engaged in developing PAR projects. The students then form smaller groups (five to eight students per group) that use particular generative themes to guide project work.

ACTIVITY B: I AM Poetry

This activity begins with a process to develop themes connected to students' social and political realities. For instance, poetry with strong emotional content and language could be used to generate these themes. Facilitators provide a poetry template (I AM) and model the process. Then, participants in groups of no more than eight persons are invited to collectively produce their own words and prose related to their lived experiences.

Principle: Critical Inquiry

QUESTION: What literature/readings, media, and/or people can the collective identify that offer a critical perspective on historical and current social and political issues?

EXAMPLE: Educational Dialogues

Educational Dialogues can be used to engage students, providing opportunities to use theories of liberation and oppression and to think with a critical consciousness. For instance, one educational dialogue involved young people gathering to generate themes based on their personal schooling experiences (both empowering and disempowering ones). One student described his third-grade experience of language discrimination. Through dialogue, the group uncovered some underlying, disempowering policies and practices. Another student shared her empowering experience with a sixth-grade teacher who supported and nurtured her vision of pursing a college education. Her experience became the catalyst for discussions about social beliefs, behaviors, and common experiences across the collective.

ACTIVITY: Suggested Readings

Anzaldúa, G. (1987). Borderlands. La Frontera: The new Mestiza. San Francisco, CA: Spinsters/ Aunt Lute.

Cammarota, J., & Fine, M. (Eds.). (2008). Revolutionizing education: Youth participatory action research in motion. New York, NY: Routledge.

Delgado, R., & Stefancic, J. (Eds.). (1999). Critical race theory: The cutting edge. Philadelphia, PA: Temple University Press.

Fals-Borda, O., & Rahman, M. A. (1991). Action and knowledge: Breaking the monopoly with participatory action research. New York, NY: Apex Press.

Freire, P. (1970). Pedagogy of the oppressed. New York, NY: Continuum.

Irizarry, J. G. (2011a). *The Latinization of U.S. schools: Successful teaching and learning in shifting cultural contexts*. Boulder, CO: Paradigm Publishing.

López, P.D. (2012). *The Process of Becoming: The Political Construction of Texas' Lone STAAR System of Accountability and College Readiness*. University of Texas at Austin: Dissertation.

Park, P. (1999). People, knowledge, and change in participatory research. *Management Learning*, 30(2), 141–157.

Shor, I. (1993). Education is politics: Paulo Freire's critical pedagogy. In P. MacLaren & P. Leonard (Eds.), *Paulo Freire: A critical encounter*. New York, NY: Routledge, pp. 24–35.

Solórzano, D., & Yosso, T. J. (2002). Critical race methodology: Counter-storytelling as an analytical framework for education research. *Qualitative Inquiry*, 8, 23–44.

Torre, M. E. (2009). Participatory action research and critical race theory: Fueling spaces for *nos-otras* to research. *Urban Review*, 41(1), 106–120.

Torre, M. E., & Ayala, J. (2009). Envisioning participatory action research *EntreMundos*. *Feminism & Psychology*, 19(3), 387–393.

Valenzuela, A. & López, P.D. (2015). The National Latino/a Education Research and Policy Project: Origins. In M. Lavadenz & A.C. Muniz, *Latino Civil Rights in Education: La Lucha Sigue*. New York, NY: Routledge Press.

Principle: Knowledge Co-construction

QUESTIONS

- What are some important issues to address in the community? Why?
- How is this principle prioritized when we collect, analyze, interpret, and share data?
- How does knowledge co-construction emerge and cycle throughout the PAR process?

EXAMPLE: Root Causes

In Cammarota's SJEP, symptoms and root causes of collectively defined issues were identified, and a PAR project was developed to address them. Specifically, dropping out of school, not attending classes, and performing poorly academically were identified as symptoms. Later, students named colonization as a root cause of discrimination, and then English-only policies were highlighted as practices sustaining the other symptoms of discrimination.

ACTIVITY 1: Dialogical Pedagogy—Why Do Students Drop Out of School?

In Rodríguez's PRAXIS Project, participants used dialogical pedagogy to help them identify root causes of the dropout issue, moving from the personal to the collective and social. The same process can be applied to other issues. One way to make effective use of dialogical pedagogy is to start with a free-flowing session of brainstorming, recording participants' ideas on flipchart paper or a whiteboard. Then, participants should form small groups where they can reflect on the generated list and begin to narrow down themes. Following this, they discuss and decide what emerge as the most significant issues across all the small groups. Narrowing that list to approximately five issues will give the group as a whole a manageable entry point for exploring key issues of collective concern. These dialogues can also become data.

ACTIVITY 2: Problem Tree

Once themes have been identified, they must be problematized. For instance, if justice is named as a theme, then the question is, "What is the problem form of justice?" The answer provides the starting point for inquiry. A problem tree is then co-developed, taking the initial problem and identifying symptoms and root causes. A PAR project is designed to address the issue at its root cause. For instance, using English-only policies as the example, the tree might include the following:

- *branches/leaves*: discrimination, dropping out of school, not attending classes, performing poorly academically
- *trunk*: English-only policies
- *roots*: colonization, systems of domination (racism, sexism, and others)

Principle: Power With(in)

QUESTIONS
- Where is each group member in the process?
- What steps is the collective taking to reflect on what is happening with the group throughout the project?
- How are group members' feelings and needs being taken into account as the collective tackles the difficult issues?

EXAMPLE 1: Political Autobiography

As Lilia Bartolomé (2004) has argued, to develop a foundation for critical engagement in and with communities it is necessary to develop a sense of political and ideological clarity. This exercise provides a space for participants to connect their current social and political awareness with formative moments or events that helped to shape their political identity. Participants are also encouraged to connect their political and ideological development with key ideas presented in the suggested readings (e. g., Freire's *Pedagogy of the Oppressed*, listed in the suggested readings above, for the Critical Inquiry Principle).

ACTIVITY 1: Political Autobiography

In this exercise, facilitators begin by sharing their personal and political narratives (these might include stories about schooling, family, or immigration, for example). Then, participants are invited to reflect on and write about personal relationships and experiences (struggles, insights) as a way of locating their individual stories (political, psychological, ideological, and intellectual narratives) within broader sociohistorical and political contexts and theories. This exercise provides all participants with an opportunity to dialogue and connect their *selves* with the concepts the group has read collectively.

ACTIVITY 2: Process Check

In any process, particularly when it is associated with a group (e.g., a high school or university class) or organization (PAR collective), it is imperative to engage in a series of process checks with the participants in order to assess individual participation and overall group development. These checks should be frequent (every 2–3 weeks) and may be done verbally and within a group format. However, some participants may not be comfortable sharing verbally or in front of the group. Another option is to have participants write answers to questions such as, "Where Am I in the Process?" and "What are my questions/concerns/fears/hopes?" Participants can then brainstorm about how best to share and process this information with the collective in order to better understand the group and its individual participants. This exercise can also be liberating for individuals who have not had the opportunity to share their inner feelings and perspectives about their experiences.

EXAMPLE 2: Emotions Workshop

During part of the process at El Puente Academy for Peace and Justice, young people were guided through an emotions workshop where readings on the science of emotions were assigned, neuroscience and psychology research was shared, and personal experiences were explored. The workshop also included practice with exercises designed to illuminate the physiological power of emotions, especially as related to our belief systems and behaviors (Damasio, 1999; LeDoux, 1998; Pert, 1997; Zull, 2002).

ACTIVITY 3: State Shifting

One of the exercises introduced during the emotions workshop was state shifting (Day, 2007), which involves participants first thinking about an emotionally charged situation, then writing down the story, listing the emotions experienced, and naming how the emotions felt in their bodies. Then, participants deliberately pause, engaging in deep breathing and heart-centered visualization. Finally, the emotionally charged situation is revisited from this relaxed, centered state of being and new insights are chronicled.

ACTIVITY 4: Graffiti Walls

In the process of doing critical research work, information or situations arise that stir up strong feelings that need an outlet. Sometimes, young people do not feel comfortable verbalizing these emotions, may have trouble articulating them, or may express them in ways that are not productive to the group. Rather than ignore or suppress strong feelings, one strategy utilized by the Public Science Project (Fine, Roberts & Torre, 2004) is to offer "graffiti walls", places where people can write or draw their feelings about a particular issue in an uninhibited, safe way. Taping blank paper to the walls of a room and providing containers of crayons or markers is a simple way to create graffiti walls. Facilitators can structure the use of the walls by offering prompts and a specific time in the day to do this: "take a few minutes now to write or draw something that stood out to you today" [...or] "something that you really disagreed with/made you mad, etc". After the initial structured activity in which everyone participates, the graffiti wall is left up for the remainder of the group's time together. Then, at various points (typically during break times, but sometimes during an intense activity), members of the collective can return to the graffiti wall on their own to add other words or images. The group might also close the day's (or week's) activities with an informal debriefing, using the graffiti wall to set the agenda: group members walk alongside the wall, reading and processing the words and images there, and then they have an opportunity to discuss, as a group, the activities and issues recorded on the wall. This gives each collective member an opportunity to process the feelings involved in doing critical research.

Principle: Indigenous Cosmologies

QUESTIONS

- How can individuals' physical, emotional, and spiritual ways of knowing—especially wisdom traditions—be incorporated into PAR work?
- How can healing rituals support activist efforts?
- In what ways has the Southern Tradition influenced current understandings of PAR in the U.S.?

EXAMPLE: Recognizing Transhistorical Consciousness: The Role of Students

José Carlos Mariategui, a Peruvian political philosopher of the early 20th century, wrote about the significance of indigenous identities across the Américas. One of Mariategui's core essays on education appeared in his book, *Seven Interpretive Essays of the Peruvian Reality* (1928/1971). This text references the International Congress of Students held in Mexico City in 1921. Two core demands were identified by students from across the Américas: Students should have a direct role/say in educational governance, and they should play a role in determining what and how content is taught. In today's educational context, students often have these same expectations, yet the U.S. school system seems to be constantly moving in a dramatically different direction. In what ways do students have a voice? How are they silenced? Keep in mind that voice can be vocal, physical, spiritual, intellectual, etc.

ACTIVITY 1: Mask-making

One integrated arts activity that a senior facilitator at El Puente Academy for Peace and Justice uses is mask-making. The facilitator guides young people through a process of combining wisdom from their indigenous (often *Taíno*) cultures (gleaned through reading, storytelling, and discussion) with the creation of art (such as paper *maché*, painting, and design). Mask-making could be used in a PAR process to craft physical symbols of oppressive policies and practices, personal histories of trauma, and/or representations of desired and imagined identities. The masks also could be used in rituals and simple ceremonies created to burn away destructive patterns/systems, for example; or to celebrate new personal, collective ways of being.

ACTIVITY 2: Theatre of the Oppressed

Theatre activities can be used to encourage PAR groups to embody different identities through role-play and sociodramas. For instance, Theatre of the Oppressed and Forum Theatre techniques (Boal, 1993) invite participants to use situations from their daily lives, animating them and allowing audience members to become actors in the scene. That is, "spectators become spect-actors", stopping the scene, becoming participants in the action and, ultimately, informing the development of the personal, collective, and sociopolitical drama. As PAR group members try on different roles (e.g., of the oppressor, of an ancestor), new opportunities for healing, compassion (for self and others), and transformation emerge.

ACTIVITY 3: Movement Meditation

The art of movement provides another way for PAR participants to integrate embodied experiences. As biologists and neuroscientists affirm, the human brain works best when the body is in motion (Medina, 2008). PAR project concepts are often profoundly complex and emotional. Movement can help release the biopsychosocial tension and trauma that inevitably arise during PAR sessions, and may also nurture personal and collective healing. In addition, movement can open the possibility for authentic, creative vision work, where new ways of being in the world are imagined. Some examples of movement from wisdom traditions include deep breathing, shaking, tapping, yoga, and free-form dance.

Principle: Creative Praxes

QUESTIONS

- How do (or could) the community's cultural arts inform the PAR process?
- Research is often seen as strictly logical and deductive. How can creative, imaginative, synthesizing activities be integrated into PAR work?
- How can creativity be incorporated into data collection and analysis?
- What are different ways the group can artfully express/communicate its message and findings to various audiences?
- How can opportunities for play as well as for work be incorporated into the PAR process?

EXAMPLE 1: Informal Conversations and Play

To promote a common understanding of the research process for the New Jersey Urban Youth Research Initiative (NJUYRI) what Maria Torre and Michelle Fine term "research camps" (Public Science Project, 2012) were developed. These are day-long or overnight events that may involve undertaking intensive critical work, learning different ways of collecting data, analyzing information, constructing interview questions, coming up with action plans, etc. Because such work is often very intense, it makes sense to incorporate opportunities for "down time" and informal play. Often, informal processing opportunities occur spontaneously in trains or buses "on the way home" from a session or presentation. In the NJUYRI example, two popular down-time activities were volleyball (the high school and adult researchers played together in games facilitated by members of the college volleyball team) and music and salsa dancing. Opportunities like these provide participants with other ways of seeing and interacting with each other. Play offers respite from the work, and it also can be another way to process the day's work and build community (Brown, 2010).

EXAMPLE 2: Community Performance Theatre

The Creative Justice Approach (CJA) is a conceptual framework for learning, rooted in creativity and social justice (Rivera et al., 2010). One way that El Puente Academy for Peace and Justice implemented the CJA is through integrated arts projects. In these projects, facilitators (or teachers) and young people engage in a critical and creative process to address current community issues through inquiry and action. In their academic classes, students learn about an issue (or issues) from multiple disciplinary perspectives (those of the humanities, physical, and social sciences, for example). Then, they engage these complex concepts through visual (painting, sculpting, mask making, collaging, photography), performing (theatre, dance, music, spoken word/storytelling), and media arts (video/documentary making). Finally, a multi-arts community production is created and performed in neighborhood venues (local schools, gardens, community organizations, arts galleries) as an educational offering, sharing both what was learned and what action can be taken. Residents, activists, artists, and political representatives are invited to attend the performance and engage in dialogue about next steps.

ACTIVITY 1: Maps

Maps are integrated into PAR processes to elicit thoughts and emotion about an issue or area of inquiry using a creative medium. Given that human beings think in pictures which the brain then translates into words, encouraging El Puente and El Puente Academy for Peace and Justice research participants to share their dynamic and embodied insights, experiences, and feelings through art before engaging in the verbal dialogue of an interview enabled them to map whole concepts and journeys, creating a portal into rich conversation. Participants were given a prompt (for example, "map your learning experience at this school") and provided with paper, markers, crayons, scissors, and other materials to craft their maps. We then discussed their maps together, beginning a dialogue about the issue.

ACTIVITY 2: PhotoVoice

An alternative strategy that can be integrated into a PAR project is PhotoVoice. PhotoVoice offers an opportunity to utilize documentary photography to engage in a creative reflection process of naming the problem for inquiry, interpreting the problem from a personal standpoint, analyzing the problem using a macro lens, and, finally, engaging in creative transformative action that leads to community enhancement (Ada & Beutel, 1993). In this activity, the PAR facilitator/team invites participants to respond to guided questions by taking photos of images they feel represent experiences, realities, and understandings related to a specific guided question. The following three-part process has proven useful: (1) begin by conducting two or three rounds of photo taking. After each round, ask participants to identify photos (possibly 4 or 5) that most closely correlate with the research question(s); (2) develop a narrative (in either written or oral form) that embodies the photos chosen; and (3) engage in a group dialogue with the PAR facilitator/team to determine the generative themes that emerge at an individual level and within a whole-group context (Wang, Wu, Tao, & Carovano, 1998).

Principle: Transformational Action

QUESTIONS

- What can be done about what was learned through the research?
- When should action(s) happen?
- Who needs to hear/know about what was learned?

- What is the best way to convey the message that needs to be heard?
- In what ways does a public presentation of the findings to key stakeholders serve as a transformative act? For whom and why?
- What are the broader policy implications of this work?

EXAMPLE 1: Social Justice Education Project: Actions Taken by Students

The SJEP students created a video revealing the substandard conditions at their high school. The students distributed copies of the video to school board members, administrators, teachers, and other students. Two months after the release of the video, the principal began to invest money in the school to improve conditions, including repairing bathrooms, ceilings, and water fountains, and updating library materials and technology.

ACTIVITY 1: Demonstrating Expertise: Reflections on Past Experiences

Every day, students and teachers engage in transformative acts in the classroom. However, it is rare to find situations where these same students and teachers are given the opportunity to be public about their work. In this activity, PAR participants are encouraged to think of a moment when they were given the opportunity to demonstrate expertise, either as a student or teacher. What personal impact did this experience have? What impact did it have on others? Why?

EXAMPLE 2: Community Report-Backs

The NJUYRI collective formed around a shared desire to take action on a changing educational policy. Thus, transformational action was part of the process during and after the research project. Multiple products and venues were used for dissemination, and as a multisite collective, local actions were taken independent of the collective's efforts. One group, for instance, created their own video and staged a viewing in their local environment. Another group developed a workshop on the issue for middle school students in their community, and a third group made a presentation to their local board of education. The PAR team produced a policy report, based on survey and interview findings, and distributed it at the culminating collective presentation—a community report-back session. With an audience of 75 community organizers, state department of education officials (including the President of the State Board of Education), parents, educators, college students and faculty, young and adult members of the collective jointly reported on the findings of the study. The presentation included a discussion of the research methods and analysis in addition to spoken-word performances, clips from the video documentary one group produced, and an invitation to the audience to participate in devising solutions. Reports were distributed alongside youth-created postcards emblazoned with slogans about the issue. Because the collective members, with their various community and political connections, were actively involved in creating the audience, the policy discussion following the presentation was a constructive one, where community members and school board officials engaged in sometimes tense, but productive, dialogue.

ACTIVITY 2: Demonstrating Expertise: Presenting Research to a District School Board

Once data have been collected and findings are developed, the PAR collective can present their work to relevant stakeholders. Participants should use the findings to identify the most relevant audiences (school boards, city officials, teachers, parents, youth, etc.). Participants can also determine if and when media and other public outlets for information distribution are useful and necessary. Finally, it is vital that participants identify allies to support their work, especially if the findings are controversial or critical.

Principle: *Concientizacion para la colectiva*

QUESTIONS

- What do social justice and freedom mean to the individual participant? To the group as a whole?
- In what ways does a recognition of liberating/oppressing experiences serve to engage critical consciousness and encourage movement towards social justice goals?
- How have the actions of each individual informed the group's consciousness about particular issues? In what ways is the collective reflecting on the knowledge gained from engaging in specific actions?
- How can the collective's work be connected to and shared with others engaged in similar political projects (*intercambios*)?

EXAMPLE: *Caring Is a Constant*

A PAR committee member offered these reflections on PAR work: "It is beautiful for me because I contribute to my community in a way that helps young people live healthy and productive lives. It is like gardening. It is wonderful for me because I can go into the community and witness beauty being cultivated, young lives blossoming. Even when the soil erodes or weeds and parasites threaten the garden, you continue to work because you feel responsible for the plant. Caring is not something you do intermittently; it is a constant. Thus, you work to revitalize the space. PAR is part of a movement".

ACTIVITY 1: Principles

Experiences that emerge from such activities as political autobiographies and educational dialogues become generative principles that guide the work and analysis of the PAR group. A facilitator would guide a reflective process inviting participants to synthesize individual and collective experiences and explore principles of transformation (both personal and social). Since PAR is a social movement, this process of reflection allows participants to see how local projects are connected to other regional, national, and global PAR initiatives.

ACTIVITY 2: PAR Gatherings

PAR gatherings of young people, community organizations, educators, and policy makers could be organized, virtually and/or in-person, with different PAR collectives, possibly through the NLERAP regions (as well as nationally/ globally). Such gatherings could become a space to share crosscutting efforts and to engage in movement building.

RESEARCH PROCESS

There is no "standard" approach or specific, step-by-step formula for conducting PAR. Yet, because the issue(s) and research question(s) are collectively identified, and because the PAR group collects and analyzes data to address the research question, it is imperative to use an iterative process that counters hegemonic modes of traditional research and aligns with the ontology and epistemology of PAR. Below, we divide the research process into three categories: 1) potential data collection methods; 2) types of data analysis strategies; and 3) ways of sharing research findings. A list of associated strategies accompanies each category. This subsection closes with a brief description of the research process of one project, as an example.

Data Collection Methods

- Surveys
- Interviews (structured, semi-structured)
- Focus groups
- Meeting notes, archival documents
- Newspaper articles
- Artwork
- Visual art: maps, paintings, sketches, masks, photography (photovoice)
- Performing arts: spoken word, songs, theatre scripts, dance choreography
- Videos, documentaries
- Journals, blogs, social network posts, tweets
- Free-form writing
- Student-generated artifacts
- Participant observation (field notes)
- *Testimonios* and oral histories
- Policy analysis (e.g., comparing zero-tolerance policies across schools/districts)

Data Analyses and Interpretation

- Coding analysis for generative themes
- Voice-centered analysis
- Interpretive poetics
- Survey analysis
- Statistics
- Grounded theory

Findings Dissemination

- Reports, essays, newspaper/journal articles, books
- Poetry and spoken-word performances
- Theatre productions
- Gallery exhibitions
- Videos and documentaries
- Website development
- Policy briefs
- Public presentations
- Court testimony

Research Process Example

The NJUYRI chapter describes how developing a common framework for PAR took place in research camps addressing proposed changes by the state on students' graduation requirements. Once the research questions were identified, the intergenerational collective of high school youth researchers, community partners/educators, and university professors brainstormed in small groups about potential data collection methods that could be used to respond to the guiding research question. The group decided on surveys, interviews, and equipment inventories (this meant inspecting their schools to identify, count, and examine the quality of lab equipment, classrooms, etc.). The data analysis was generally conducted in small intergenerational groups, though the university partners did some preparation beforehand. Numerical data, as well as text from open-ended sources, were included in the analysis. Tables with percentages and transcripts from open-ended survey data were prepared beforehand, along with some probing questions for each small group to discuss in their analysis and interpretation of findings. Also, there was a workshop on how to use Microsoft Excel and a brief introduction to SPSS statistical analysis software. For the qualitative data, a sample set of analytic codes was created to provide starting points prior to the small group work; the small groups then revised these codes (creating, deleting, recasting) and applied them to the transcripts. (Had more time been available, it would have been preferable to create each code "from scratch" in these intergenerational groups, as well as to create the numeric tables with percentages, mean scores, and other descriptive statistics grouped together.) Each small group documented their insights on flipchart paper and presented their analyses to the larger group. A large-group discussion of general findings and interpretations of what the smaller groups shared ended the analysis portion of the research camp.

References

Ada, A. F., & Beutel, C. M. (1993). Participatory research as a dialogue for social action. Unpublished manuscript, University of San Francisco at San Francisco.

Anzaldúa, G. (1987). *Borderlands. La Frontera: The New Mestiza.* San Francisco, CA: Spinsters/Aunt Lute.

Arrien, A. (1993). *The four-fold way: Walking the paths of the warrior, teacher, healer and visionary.* New York, NY: HarperOne.

Bartolome, L.I. (2004). Critical pedagogy and teacher education: Radicalizing prospective teachers. Teacher Education Quarterly, 31 (1), 97–122.

Berta-Ávila, M., Tijerina-Revilla, A., & Figueroa, J. (Eds.). (2011). Marching students: Chicana and Chicano activism in education, 1968 to the present. Reno, NV: University of Nevada Press.

Boal, A. (1993). Theatre of the oppressed. New York, NY: Theatre Communications Group.

Brown, S. (2010). Play: How it shapes the brain, opens the imagination, and invigorates the soul. New York, NY: Avery Trade.

Cammarota, J., & Fine, M. (Eds.). (2008). Revolutionizing education: Youth Participatory Action Research in motion. New York, NY: Routledge.

Collins, P. H. (1991). Black feminist thought: Knowledge, consciousness, and the politics of empowerment. New York, NY: Routledge.

Damasio, A. (1999). The feeling of what happens: Body and emotion in the making of consciousness. New York, NY: Harcourt.

Day, J. (2007). Being what you want to see: Bringing emotional mastery into everyday life. San Bruno, CA: Shinnyo-en Foundation.

Delgado, R., & Stefancic, J. (Eds.). (1999). Critical race theory: The cutting edge. Philadelphia, PA: Temple University Press.

Fals-Borda, O., & Rahman, M. A. (1991). Action and knowledge: Breaking the monopoly with participatory action research. New York, NY: Apex Press.

Fine, M., Roberts, R., & Torre, M. (2004). Echoes of Brown: Youth documenting and performing the legacy of Brown v. Board of Education. New York, NY: Teachers College Press.

Freire, P. (1970). Pedagogy of the oppressed. New York, NY: Continuum.

hooks, b. (1984). Feminist theory: From margin to center. Cambridge, MA: South End Press.

Hurtado, A. (1996). The color of privilege: Three blasphemies on race and feminism. Ann Arbor, MI: The University of Michigan Press.

Irizarry, J. G. (2011a). The Latinization of U.S. schools: Successful teaching and learning in shifting cultural contexts. Boulder, CO: Paradigm Publishing.

Lara, I. (2002). Healing Sueños for academia in G. Anzaldúa and A. Keating (editors) this bridge we call home: Radical visions for transformation. New York, NY: Routledge.

LeDoux, J. (1998). The emotional brain: The mysterious underpinnings of emotional life. New York, NY: Simon and Schuster.

Lopez, P. D., Valenzuela, A., & García, E. (2011). The critical ethnography of public policy for social justice. A Companion to the Anthropology of Education, 547–562.

Mariategui, J. C. (1971). Seven interpretative essays on Peruvian reality. Austin, TX: University of Texas Press.

Medina, J. (2008). Brain rules. 12 Principles for surviving and thriving at work, home and school. Edmonds, WA: Pear Press.

Moraga, C., & Anzaldúa, G. (1981). This bridge called my back: Writings by radical women of color. Watertown, MA: Persephone Press.

Paiva, A. P. (1992). Y...El anciano hablo [And...The elder spoke]. Cusco, Peru: J.C. Editors.

Pert, C. (1997). Molecules of emotion: The science behind mind-body medicine. New York, NY: Scribner.

Public Science Project. (2012). Retrieved from http://publicscienceproject.org/

Rivera, M., Medellin-Paz, C., & Pedraza, P. (2010). *Imagination for the imagined nation. A creative justice approach to learning.* New York, NY: Center for Puerto Rican Studies, Hunter College, CUNY.

Solórzano, D., & Yosso, T. J. (2002). Critical race methodology: Counter-storytelling as an analytical framework for education research. *Qualitative Inquiry, 8,* 23–44.

Torre, M. E., & Ayala, J. (2009). Envisioning participatory action research EntreMundos. *Feminism & Psychology, 19,* 387.

Wang, C. C., Wu, K. Y., Tao, Z. W., & Carovano, K. (1998). Photovoice as a participatory health promotion strategy. *Health Promotion International, 13*(1), 75–86.

Zull, J. (2002). The art of changing the brain. Enriching the practice of teaching by exploring the biology of learning. Herndon, VA: Stylus.

EDITOR BIOS

Jennifer Ayala, Ph.D., is a professor in the School of Education at Saint Peter's University in Jersey City, New Jersey and director of the college's center for undocumented students. She has worked on participatory action research projects with high school and college age youth in after-school settings and with teachers integrating PAR in high school curricula. Past work has focused on Latina mother-daughter relationships, youth voice in education policy, PAR processes in and outside the classroom, erasure and high school closures, Latinxs experiences in higher education. Recent journal publications include: Ayala, J. & Galletta, A. (2012). Documenting disappearing spaces: Erasure and remembrance in two high school closures and Fine, M., Ayala, J., Zaal, M. (2012). Public science and participatory policy development: Reclaiming policy as a democratic project.

Margarita Ines Berta-Ávila, Ed.D., is a professor in the College of Education at Sacramento State University. She received her doctorate in International and Multicultural Education in the School of Education at the University of San Francisco. She majored as an undergraduate in Chicana/o Studies from the University of California, Davis and pursued a M.A. in Education and a teaching credential from Claremont Graduate University. Dr. Berta-Ávila taught for seven years in the public school system, third—twelfth grades. Currently, Dr. Berta-Ávila teaches courses on English language learners, curriculum development, and social political foundations in education. Dr. Berta-Ávila is active in testifying at the Capitol and/or other venues with respect to access and equity in education for English Language Learners, students of color, and/or other marginalized communities. In addition, Dr. Berta-Ávila pursues her scholarly work within the areas of Participatory Action Research (PAR), bilingual education/English Language learners, critical pedagogy/multicultural/social justice education, and Chicana/o educators in the field. In collaboration with Dr. Julie Figueroa and Dr. Anita Tijerina-Revilla an edited volume titled "Marching Students: Chicana/o Activism in Education, 1968 to the Present" was released in the spring of 2011.

Julio Cammarota, Ph.D., is an associate professor in Multicultural Education at Iowa State University. His research focuses on participatory action research with Latinx youth, institutional factors in academic achievement, and liberatory pedagogy. He has published articles on family, work, and education among Latinxs and on the relationship between culture and academic achievement. He is the co-editor of two volumes in the Critical Youth Studies series published by Routledge/Falmer Press: Beyond Resistance! Youth Activism and Community Change: New Democratic Possibilities for Practice and Policy for America's Youth (2006) and Revolutionizing Education: Youth Participatory Action Research in Motion (2008). Dr. Cammarota has published an ethnography of Latina/o youth entitled, Sueños Americanos: Barrio Youth Negotiate Social and Cultural Identities (University of Arizona Press, 2008). His work has been instrumental with advancing social justice in education and youth development.

Melissa Rivera, Ed.D., is a scholar, who conducts, teaches and writes about participatory action research (PAR). She has dedicated the last 20 years to PAR with public schools and universities, community arts and entrepreneurial organizations and a women's maximum-security prison, using an approach to learning and human development rooted in developmental, women's and humanistic psychology, ancient spiritual traditions, creativity and expressive arts, critical theory and conscious activism. Her passion for personal transformation, community development and social justice has inspired the co-development of arts and educational programs and co-authorship of scholarly and popular publications with young people, educators and entrepreneurs, artists and activists (such as *Latino Education: An Agenda for Community Action Research. A Volume of the National Latino/a Education Research and Policy Project* with Pedro Pedraza). She received her undergraduate education from Brown University and her doctorate from the Harvard Graduate School of Education.

Louie F. Rodríguez, Ed.D., is an associate professor of Educational Policy Analysis and Leadership and Education, Society, and Culture in the Graduate School of Education at the University of California Riverside. Prior to this position he was on the faculty for seven years at CSU, San Bernardino. Dr. Rodriguez is the author of three books, *Intentional Excellence: The Pedagogy, Power, and Politics of Excellence in Latina/o Schools and Communities* (2015), *The Time is Now: Understanding and Responding to the Black and Latina/o Dropout Crisis in the U.S.* (2014), and *Small Schools and Urban Youth* (with Gilberto Conchas, 2007) and several articles and book chapters. He attended San Bernardino Valley College and CSU, San Bernardino where he majored in psychology and became a McNair Scholar. After serving as a middle-school counselor/intervention specialist and later as a high school math teacher, Dr. Rodriguez completed two master's degrees and a doctorate in Administration, Planning and Social Policy from Harvard University. His research focuses on issues of educational equity by studying the experiences of Latinx and Black high school students. At CSUSB, Dr. Rodriguez was the principal investigator of the *PRAXIS Project, Participatory Research Advocating for Excellence in Schools.* This school/community-based project aimed to study and advocate for educational excellence by directly engaging youth, educators, and community-stakeholders in the process of empirical research to positively impact educational policy and practice at the local and regional levels. He is a frequently invited speaker to address school culture, Latinx excellence, and student engagement issues for schools, districts, and communities.

María Elena Torre, Ph.D., is the founding Director of The Public Science Project and faculty member in Critical Psychology and Urban Education at the Graduate Center of the City University of New York. She has been engaged in critical participatory action research nationally and internationally for nearly 20 years with communities in neighborhoods, schools, prisons, and community-based organizations seeking structural justice. Her work introduced the concept of "participatory contact zones" to collaborative research, and she continues to be interested in how democratic methodologies, radical inclusion, and a praxis of solidarity can inform a public science for the public good. She is a co-author of *Echoes of Brown: Youth Documenting and Performing the Legacy of Brown v. Board of Education* and *Changing Minds: The Impact of College on a Maximum Security Prison*, and her writing can be found in volumes such as the *Handbook of Qualitative Research in Psychology*, *Participatory Action Research Approaches and Methods: Connecting People, Participation, and Place*, the *Handbook of Action Research*, and in journals such as *Feminism and Psychology*, the *Journal of Social Issues*, *Qualitative Inquiry*, and the *Journal of Critical Psychology*. A recipient of the Michele Alexander Award from the Society for the Psychological Study of Social Issues of the American Psychological Association for Early Career Excellence in Scholarship, Teaching, and Service, she is presently serving on the New York City Mayoral Taskforce on School Climate, and co-leading "What's Your Issue?" a participatory study with LGBT and gender non-conforming youth of the priorities, dreams, and desires of LGBT and GNC youth.

CONTRIBUTOR BIOS

Susan Baker has taught in public schools at the kindergarten through high school levels in Soledad, Watsonville, and Los Angeles, California, and Arlington, Virginia. She has worked primarily in bilingual settings with students who are English learners, and has taught literacy in English and Spanish. Baker earned her doctorate from Stanford University and is currently a professor in the Department of Teacher Credentialing at California State University in Sacramento. Her principal areas of focus in her teaching include supporting teacher candidates in developing literacy and academic language skills for students who are acquiring English as an additional language. Professor Baker's research interests include the development of biliteracy, the use of culturally sustaining pedagogy in teacher education, and the fostering of teacher/parent relationships across social class, cultural, racial, and linguistic boundaries. She is currently the Principal Investigator for the CSU Sacramento branch of the California Reading and Literature Project.

Jenna Cushing-Leubner is a Ph.D. candidate in second languages education at the University of Minnesota. She is multilingual and of European origin. Her research revolves around enactments of culturally sustaining and revitalizing pedagogies in U.S. schools, particularly toward multilingual youth of color's education for self-determination. Her research incorporates critical participatory action research and participatory design research with language educators and multilingual youth in K-12 schools and focuses on Spanish as a heritage language and English as an additional language teachers doing this work despite the constraints of monolingual and Eurocentric schooling.

Francisco De Jesus joined the Urban Youth Research Initiative as a high school junior. He has since graduated from Saint Peter's University, with a major in Communications and minors in Graphic Arts and Journalism. Francisco is now working as a Client Service Technician at Saint Peter's University.

Jennifer Eik is a Spanish as a heritage language teacher in Minnesota, where she has developed and taught high school Spanish courses for multilingual Latinx youth for four years. She anchors her language teaching in intra-ethnic studies and social justice issues, exploration and expansion of community cultural wealth, and critical race approaches to language use. Together with youth, they navigate the use of YPAR in public school spaces. Her focus is on growing critically conscious intellectuals with strong hearts for one another and clear understandings of their beautiful, multiple, and intertwined ethnic and linguistic identities.

Rubén A. González has been a teacher at Florin High School, in Sacramento, California for three years, where he teaches English and AVID. Prior to this, Rubén worked with migrant and immigrant youth, grades third through twelfth, in central and northern California for three years as he completed his undergraduate studies at Sacramento State University. Rubén is also a teacher-activist/organizer with the Association of Raza Educators (ARE) and Ethnic Studies Now (ESN)-Sacramento. His research interests include critical pedagogy, participatory action research, and social justice education.

Dr. **Jason G. Irizarry** is an Associate Professor in the Department of Teacher Education & Curriculum Studies at University of Massachusetts-Amherst. He received his doctorate from the University of Massachusetts Amherst and has taught undergraduate and graduate courses in multicultural education, culturally responsive curriculum development, urban education, and participatory action research. A former middle school teacher in New York City, his research focuses on urban teacher recruitment, preparation, and retention with an emphasis on increasing the number of teachers of color, culturally responsive pedagogy, youth participatory action research, and Latinx students in U.S. schools. A central focus of his work involves promoting the academic achievement of youth in urban schools by addressing issues associated with teacher education. Manuscripts documenting the findings of his research have been published or accepted for publication in a variety of peer-reviewed journals in the field including the American Educational Research Journal, Teachers College Record, Education and Urban Society, Multicultural Perspectives, the Journal of Latinos and Education, Teaching and Teacher Education, and the Centro Journal of Puerto Rican Studies and others appearing as chapters in various books. His book, The Latinization of U.S. Schools: Successful Teaching and Learning in Shifting Cultural Contexts (Paradigm Publishers, 2011), was recently awarded the Phillip C. Chin Book Award from the National Association for Multicultural Education.

Stan Karp is Director of the Secondary Reform Project for New Jersey's Education Law Center. Previously, he taught English and journalism to high school students for 30 years in Paterson, NJ. He is an editor of Rethinking Schools magazine and co-editor of several books, including Rethinking Our Classrooms: Teaching for Equity and Justice, and Rethinking School Reform: Views from the Classroom.

Edwin Mayorga is an Assistant Professor of Educational Studies and Latin American and Latino Studies at Swarthmore College (PA). He directs the Education in our Barrios project (#BarrioEdProj), a participatory action research project that examines educational policy and community development in Latinx core communities in Philadelphia and New York City, the Critical Education Policy Studies (#CritEdPol) blog and online journal, and the Philadelphia Community, School, College Partnership (CSCP) research project. He is co-editor of *What's Race Got to Do with It? How Current School Reform Maintains Racial and Economic Inequality*. (Peter Lang; 2015; co-edited with B. Picower). He is a national board member of the National Latino/a Education Research and Policy Project (NLERAP).

Cristina Medellin-Paz, Ph.D., is currently an Assistant Research Scientist at playLabNYU at NYU Steinhardt. Her work focuses on exploring opportunities for play-based experiences in urban early childhood classrooms using the Early Childhood Time-Use in Schools-Profile. Her research interests center on identifying effective strategies for incorporating playful opportunities in early childhood classrooms that serve diverse low-income children through research and professional development. She has a specific interest in understanding the role of play in meeting the needs of Latino communities. Rather than focusing on the gaps in school readiness and opportunities for play, her work takes a strengths-based approach to examine the role of culture and context in understanding how development unfolds within different settings. Cristina received her B.A. in psychology from Hunter College, City University of New York, and her Ph.D. in developmental psychology from the Graduate Center, City University of New York.

Pedro Pedraza is a founding staff member of the Centro de Estudios Puertorriqueños at Hunter College, City University of New York. As a research director in the area of Language Policy, he directed various research projects on the nature of bilingualism in the city's Puerto Rican community. These consisted of ethnographic, sociolinguistic and survey investigations that culminated in an interdisciplinary analysis and overview of language use patterns combined with a variety of individual linguistic abilities co-occurring and being created in the daily social interactions of community members embedded in their natural social networks. These efforts were followed by action/intervention studies in the intergenerational acquisition of literacy by school children and adults participating in a bilingual adult education program. This led to a participatory action research study of a community-founded alternative high school with a social justice curriculum attentive to the sociocultural and historical context of students backgrounds and community utilizing the arts across the curriculum. In his advocacy work Pedro founded the Puerto Rican Latino Education Roundtable composed of activists, practitioners, and academics dedicated to influencing the formation of education policies in New York City, especially those policies affecting bilingual students and programs and Puerto Rican/Latinx students in general. At the national level the same was attempted with the formation of the National Latinx Education Research and Policy Project (NLERAP) that focused on research and policy advocacy as well as a program addressing the dire need for community native/indigenous teachers to serve Latinx students. As the director of the Centro's CUNY-Caribbean Exchange Program, he co-organized and initiated with Martha Rodriguez the first two conferences on Woman Writers of the Hispanic Caribbean and their diasporic communities on the U.S. mainland. In addition, he initiated, organized and founded the first two conferences on the visual arts from artists originating from the Hispanic Caribbean and all Latinx artists within the U.S. now maintained by the Latinx program of the Smith-sonian institution. He has served on numerous boards, and presently in his retirement is active on the board of NLERAP, the East Harlem Block Nursery Schools, and Los Pleneros de la 21, an AfroBoricua dance and musical group dedicated to maintaining folkloric traditions of the Puerto Rican nation.

Mayida Zaal, Ph.D., is an Associate Professor in the Department of Second-ary and Special Education at Montclair State University. Her scholarship fo-cuses on understanding the experiences of marginalized youth in national and international contexts. She works collaboratively with educators to develop and study participatory action research as pedagogy.

INDEX

Yolanda Medina and Margarita Machado-Casas
GENERAL EDITORS

Critical Studies of Latinos/as in the Americas is a provocative interdisciplinary series that offers a critical space for reflection and questioning what it
means to be Latino/a living in the Americas in twenty-first century social,
cultural, economic, and political arenas. The series looks forward to extending the dialogue to include the North and South Western hemispheric relations that are prevalent in the field of global studies.

Topics that explore and advance research and scholarship on contemporary topics and issues related with processes of racialization, economic exploitation, health, education, transnationalism, immigration, gendered and
sexual identities, and disabilities that are not commonly highlighted in the
current Latino/a Studies literature as well as the multitude of socio, cultural,
economic, and political progress among the Latinos/as in the Americas are
welcome.

To receive more information about CSLA, please contact:

Yolanda Medina (ymedina@bmcc.cuny.edu) &
Margarita Machado-Casas (Margarita.MachadoCasas@utsa.edu)

To order other books in this series, please contact our Customer
Service Department at:

(800) 770-LANG (within the U.S.)
(212) 647-7706 (outside the U.S.)
(212) 647-7707 FAX

Or browse online by series at:

WWW.PETERLANG.COM